# THE
# HOT BREAD KITCHEN
## COOKBOOK

ARTISANAL BAKING

THE

# HOT BREAD KITCHEN

*Cookbook*

🌾🌾🌾

FROM AROUND THE WORLD

JESSAMYN WALDMAN RODRIGUEZ
and the bakers of Hot Bread Kitchen
with Julia Turshen

CLARKSON POTTER/PUBLISHERS
*New York*

Copyright © 2015 by Jessamyn
Waldman Rodriguez
Principal photographs by Jennifer May
© 2015 by Jennifer May
Additional photographs by Evan Sung
© 2015 by Evan Sung

Published in the United States by
Clarkson Potter/Publishers, an imprint
of the Crown Publishing Group, a
division of Penguin Random House LLC,
New York.
www.crownpublishing.com
www.clarksonpotter.com

CLARKSON POTTER is a trademark
and POTTER with colophon is a
registered trademark of Penguin
Random House LLC.

Library of Congress Cataloging-in-
Publication Data
Rodriguez, Jessamyn Waldman.
    The Hot Bread Kitchen cookbook:
artisanal baking from around the world /
Jessamyn Waldman Rodriguez and the
Bakers of Hot Bread Kitchen with Julia
Turshen. —First edition.
        pages cm
    Includes bibliographical references
and index.
    1. Bread.  2. International cooking.
I. Turshen, Julia. II. Title.
    TX769.R66 2015
    641.59—dc23          2014048697

ISBN 978-0-8041-8617-9
Ebook ISBN 978-0-8041-8618-6

Printed in China

Design by Marysarah Quinn
Cover photographs by Jennifer May
Back cover portrait by Evan Sung
Food styling by Erin McDowell
Prop styling by Barbara Fritz

Photographs by Evan Sung appear
on the following pages: 17, 21, 57, 67, 94,
130, 144, 185, 191, 198, 220, 235, 263, 273,
293, 294
Photograph on page 59 copyright
© Matthew Cylinder
Photograph on page 145 courtesy
of the author

10  9  8  7  6  5  4  3  2  1

First Edition

To Eli, Dahlia, and Emile
I couldn't (and wouldn't) do this without you.

To all the bakers and staff of Hot Bread Kitchen,
from then until now.

# CONTENTS

# Introduction

At five o'clock every morning, while most people in New York City are still dreaming, industrial mixers are spinning inside Hot Bread Kitchen in East Harlem. Lutfunnessa, one of our bakers, boils a pot of water and measures local whole wheat flour for a batch of chapati. While she rolls the dough into perfect rounds, Nancy drains dried corn kernels she has soaked overnight. As head of tortilla production, she will make thousands of delicious, toothsome tortillas in three varieties, each from a different heritage corn. At 6 a.m., Ela comes in to start mixing yeasted doughs for the day, starting with *nan-e qandi*, a cakey Persian bread. Twenty other doughs will follow, which will be shaped and baked into more than seventy different breads. Throughout the day the mixers combine whole-grain levains, pungent spices, local flours, and New York City water to bake traditional versions of a global array of breads—sourdoughs, a German rye, flatbreads galore, and sweet Mexican *conchas*. There is no off switch; every hour of every day, something is rising at Hot Bread Kitchen.

At first glance, Hot Bread Kitchen looks like other bakeries. But, behind the braided challahs and loaves of multigrain, a powerful mission prevails. Hot Bread Kitchen is a social enterprise that provides a life-changing education and opens doors for low-income minority women. The social part of the equation means that bakery trainees learn the skills they need to get management-track positions in the food industry or to start their own food businesses. The enterprise part means that we use the money earned from each loaf of bread to pay for training. Our business pays for our mission.

The secret sauce at Hot Bread Kitchen is that the very women we train inspire the artisan breads we bake every day. Our product line is diverse and authentic because we use recipes that have been passed down by generations of women.

The flash of inspiration for Hot Bread Kitchen came from a fortuitous misunderstanding. In 2000, I applied for a job at a micro-finance organization called Women's World Banking. I didn't get the job, and some time afterward a family friend asked about my interview at Women's World *Baking*. The missing letter sparked something in me. Never mind *banking*. Women's world *baking* conjured up an image of an international female baking collective—a concept that resonated with me because it married my passion for food with my commitment to social justice.

Every culture has a staple bread, and in most countries women keep alive that baking tradition. You would expect that in the United States, especially here in New York, a city rich in immigrant populations, women would parlay those skills into baking jobs. But visit any professional bakery in North America and you will see how few women there are—less than ten percent of all bread bakers.

My dream was that Hot Bread Kitchen could right that imbalance, and, of course, bake great bread with an emphasis on regional specialties you can't find everywhere. And in helping women professionalize their homegrown skills and passion for food, Hot Bread Kitchen would create a pipeline of new bakers to change the face of the baking industry.

But at age twenty-one, with no money, no baking experience, a freshly minted BA, and a lot of idealism under my belt, I was in no position to launch a social enterprise bakery. As you do with dough, I let the idea rest—proof, as we say in the industry—and began my career in a completely different area.

I grew up in Toronto in a family fascinated by food. My great-grandfather, who had immigrated to Canada from Russia, ran a Jewish bakery there for years, Perlmutter's Bakery. They made beautiful ryes. My mother also likes to take a bit of credit for Hot Bread Kitchen because she and I baked challah together on Friday afternoons for Shabbat dinner. I have vivid memories of mixing dough with her, feeling it on my hands as I helped roll it out, the smell of the loaf as it rose and then emerged, browned and sweet from the oven. Bread is in my blood.

After college—and after that fateful failed job interview—I pursued a career in public policy and international affairs. I was the Youth Ambassador for the Canadian Landmine Foundation, trying to help free war-ravaged areas of landmines. At the same time, I became interested in immigration policy. I went to work for the United Nations Development Program in Costa Rica. After completing a master's in public administration at Columbia University, I worked at NGOs and for the United Nations focusing on human rights, education, and immigration issues. Then I worked as part of the leadership team at a high school in Brooklyn. Along the way I kept returning to the idea of *women's world baking*. I told many people about it, secretly hoping that someone else would make it happen. When no one did, I decided to pull together the pieces to launch Hot Bread Kitchen.

First things first, I needed to learn how to bake professionally. I took bread-baking classes at the New School and did a *stage* (apprenticeship) in the bakery at Daniel Boulud's eponymous Michelin three-star restaurant under the head baker, Mark Fiorentino. My then-boyfriend, now-husband, Eli Rodriguez, had worked at Daniel, and he introduced me to Mark, who gently corrected my pathetic baguette-rolling skills and taught me most of what I know about baking. And despite my crazy days of working early mornings in a bakery and then running a high school, the experience confirmed that I *loved* baking and fueled my desire to pursue the immigrant women's baking collective.

With the requisite amount of baking knowledge under my belt, we baked the first official Hot Bread Kitchen bread in 2007 in my own very hot home kitchen in a walk-up apartment on Pacific Avenue in Brooklyn. It was actually a tortilla from nixtamalized corn—the traditional, healthful way to make whole-grain tortillas—made by my first employee and friend, Elidia Ramos, with a recipe straight from her native Puebla, Mexico. I began selling corn tortillas (page 92) and multigrain loaves (page 153) in the summer of 2007 at a farmers' market in Harlem. People liked our breads, and I was happy to chat with everyone about my vision for the bakery. That summer, I was a baker, retailer, buyer, janitor, and chief grant writer (though my mom assisted with that last one). We started to grow, and Elidia soon brought her niece, sister, and eventually her daughter to our late-night baking shifts (we even used the ovens at Daniel a couple of times to bake our breads). Our bread community was expanding.

Eager to grow beyond my apartment's kitchen counters, I rented overnight shifts of commercial kitchen space in Queens. Our distribution channels grew to include specialty shops—Saxelby Cheese in Essex Street Market was our first wholesale client for lavash. In 2008, I hired my first non-baking staff person, Katrina Schwartz—a talented jack-of-all-trades—and we worked really hard to get things off the ground. In June 2009, we took office space in Gowanus, Brooklyn, still baking bread overnight in Queens.

Hot Bread Kitchen grew quickly, and in December 2010 we moved to our current and permanent home in East Harlem (also known as El Barrio). Our full-scale commercial bakery is located in La Marqueta, an old indoor market space under the elevated trains built by Mayor Fiorello La Guardia in 1936. The market's original purpose was to "clean up" the neighborhood by bringing street vendors under one roof. While it was something of an anti-immigrant "get-them-off-the-streets" policy decision, the market thrived for decades. In its heyday, the market stretched along Park Avenue from

111th to 116th Streets, and it's said that ten thousand people a day stopped there. Unfortunately for La Marqueta, when grocery stores started carrying plantains and other tropical fruits, and the demographics and eating habits changed in El Barrio, shoppers visited less frequently. All of the market buildings closed except the one that we are housed in—Building 4.

When I first visited the dramatic space in 2009, I fell in love. There were a handful of vendors like Mama Grace, who sells West African provisions, has been there for decades, and has a steady following; while other stalls were occupied by vendors engaged in various forms of illicit commerce— but the ghost of vibrant enterprise was there. The forward-looking City of New York supported Hot Bread Kitchen's move into La Marqueta as a way to bring entrepreneurs back to the space. It was a long process after that first visit. But one of the happiest days of my professional life was when we moved our baking operations, offices, corn grinder, and small staff into our new 5,000-square-foot bakery alongside vendors selling fresh groceries, dried fish, and African specialties. It was a new home, but it felt as if we had been there forever.

When we moved into the space, I launched a companion program to the bakery, HBK Incubates, an incubator kitchen that allows small food start-ups, just as mine had been, to transition from idea to reality. We select ambitious food entrepreneurs who are ready to formalize their businesses, and help

bring their products to market by providing certified commercial kitchen space and business resources. Many people obsessed with good food share the Hot Bread Kitchen space!

We've gone from a far-fetched idea to a thriving bakery and training program in a few years. That workforce of two—Elidia and me in my apartment—has burgeoned to sixty-one. And as our trainee staff grows, so does what we make. Our breads are sold in New York City's farmers' markets and GrowNYC Greenmarkets and at retail stores from Dean & DeLuca to Whole Foods—we even ship internationally. We also supply bread to more than eighty restaurants across the city.

This brings me to the book you hold now. This eclectic collection of recipes includes specialties we bake and sell at Hot Bread Kitchen, such as apple and cheddar focaccia (page 81), *m'smen* filled with kale (page 31), and luscious chocolate cherry rolls (page 257). In addition to breads, the book includes recipes for the dishes we cook at home for our families, like *byrek*, an Albanian savory cheese pastry (page 212), Vietnamese bahn mi sandwiches (page 195), Bangladeshi beef curry (page 38), and *torta*, Dominican corn bread (page 237). You'll find recipes from at least twenty different countries and, of course, from our shared home—New York City. These recipes reflect the foods that emerge when you live in the diaspora. We've even included the recipe for Hot Bread Kitchen's legendary bialy, the one that world bialy maven Mimi Sheraton—who literally wrote the book on them—believes is the best one ever.

Alongside the recipes you will meet some of the people who are part of our baking family, and you'll learn their kitchen secrets. Fanny, a bakery graduate and member of our culinary incubator, teaches you how to make *morocho* (page 226) and *tortillas de tiesto* (page 225)—the Ecuadoran answer to coffee and a doughnut. Margaret, a graduate who now bakes at Amy's Bread, shares her recipe for coconut buns from fresh coconut (page 238). And Nancy shares her recipe for the tastiest guacamole (page 113).

Another feature of the book is business tips, or recipes for entrepreneurship. I have learned a lot about running a social enterprise, management, politics, bread, and myself (both of my kids are "bakery babies," arriving *after* the birth of the bakery) by growing this organization. I share some of this knowledge for entrepreneurs of all stripes. While our breads taste fantastic and are second-to-none, knowing the story behind a recipe and the people who bring it to you makes it that much better.

In the end, this cookbook is like Hot Bread Kitchen itself—more than the sum of its parts, *way* more than just baking. It's about the human spirit and what makes us rise—the food we share, of course.

# Bread-Baking Tips

The tips that follow, which include many tricks of the trade, are useful to review before you begin baking at home. Whether you're an experienced bread baker or not, these tips will help you dive into any recipe in the book with confidence.

- Dough recipes are written to be made using a stand mixer. I did this because lots of people have them now and, truly, if you invest in a stand mixer you will be more likely to bake bread on a regular basis. Of the many conveniences and benefits a stand mixer offers, one is that you can combine all of the ingredients together at once and let the machine and dough hook attachment do the mixing and kneading for you.

- That said, making bread without a mixer is a wonderfully Zen pursuit (and a good biceps workout). If you don't have a mixer, follow these tips to mix by hand:
  - In a large bowl, dissolve the yeast in whatever amount of water is called for in the recipe. The water should be warm (about body temperature).
  - Add the flour a cup at a time, stirring to incorporate it each time before you add more. Once you have added half of the flour called for in the recipe, stir in the same direction with a wooden spoon for 5 minutes for gluten to form. Let that mixture sit for 15 minutes.
  - Add the remaining ingredients (i.e., salt, sugar, milk, and oil) and then add the remaining flour, ½ cup at a time, stirring with a spoon. Once it's too hard to stir, turn the dough out onto a floured surface and knead to make a smooth dough.
  - There are some simple steps to effectively knead by hand. First, remove any rings or other jewelry. Second, give yourself enough space to work. If you have a wooden countertop or a large cutting board, now is the time to use it. Lightly dust your surface with flour. Shape the dough into a ball and then press it with the heel of your hand and push it forward slightly, then fold the dough back on itself. Repeat this push and pull over and over again; the kneading should be rhythmic and almost meditative. Think about maintaining a smooth skin around the outside of the dough. Don't push down so hard that you break the skin, ending up with a shaggy mess. You are looking for a shiny surface, which will take about 10 minutes of vigorous kneading (depending on how strong your hands are).

- Something that we teach trainees on their first day in the bakery is what to do if dough starts to stick to their hands. Nothing says "novice" like a pair of dough-covered hands trying to shape a loaf! If you are kneading or shaping dough and your hands start to get covered with dough, stop! Rub your hands together over the sink or garbage can until all of the old dough is off. Add a bit more flour to the work surface and start again. A light touch and a light coating of flour will help ensure that you don't get gummed up again.

- Similarly, if your dough starts to stick to the table, stop! Use a bench knife or a large knife to scrape the dough off the table. Your goal is to keep the mass of dough together.

- Throughout the book, you are instructed to "turn out dough onto a lightly floured work surface" or something similar. Pay particular attention to these instructions. If you use too much flour, you won't get the required folds to stick and you'll change the hydration of the bread, which will affect flavor and texture. If you use too little flour, your hands will get doughy (see above), the dough will stick to the table, and you won't be able to create the smooth shapes

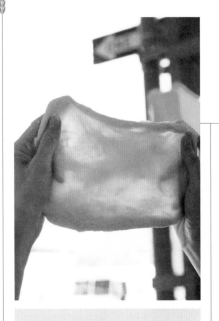

*Whether you mix your dough in a mixer or by hand, the final check to make sure the gluten in your dough is properly developed is called the **windowpane test**. Tear off a small piece of dough about the size of a golf ball. If it is sticky, dredge it through a little extra flour to make it easy to handle. Use your hands to gently stretch the dough from all sides until it forms a thin, nearly transparent layer that you can see the light through if you hold it up to an actual window or light. If you can stretch the dough to that state, it means the gluten is developed and your bread is ready to rise. Simply press the small dough ball back into the large one and proceed. If, on the other hand, your dough tears before you can stretch it thin enough to see the light through it, keep kneading it until it passes the test. The windowpane test does not work with doughs that have whole grains, nuts, or seeds in them, nor is it necessary with ryes.*

desired. Use your hands to sprinkle or almost spray your work surface with no more than 2 tablespoons of flour—the motion we use in the bakery is like tossing a Frisbee. The "how" isn't essential, but your goal is to get a consistently flour-covered table—think of the thickness and opaqueness of a heavy frost on your windshield (see the photographs on page 123 of a well-floured surface).

- There is a common pattern in working with yeasted dough: work, rest, work, rest, bake. Be patient and let the resting stages have their fair share of time. The fermentation that happens during rest helps develop the flavor and structure of the bread.
  - o **WORK 1:** Combine the ingredients and either knead the dough by hand or let your mixer do it for you. This is when the yeast is distributed and the gluten, the protein in the wheat, starts to develop.
  - o **REST 1:** Set the dough aside to rest. In home bakery terms, this is letting the dough rise; in professional terms, it's referred to as the bulk fermentation, or proofing. Sometimes you might fold the dough before or during

this step to regulate the temperature, distribute the sugars, and develop gluten.
  - o **WORK 2:** Divide the dough and shape into rolls, loaves, boules, baguettes, and more.
  - o **REST 2:** Give the yeast more time to metabolize (gorge itself on the glucose in the flour). Carbon dioxide is created by the yeast and it gives bread air pockets.
  - o **BAKE:** And eat! It's best to let breads cool for at least 1 hour before cutting into them and serving, if you can wait that long.

- Time has an immense impact on the fermentation process. All the recipes suggest how long to let a dough or a loaf rise. This is only a suggestion! In addition to time, all recipes will provide a visual cue like "until the dough is puffy and soft." Yeast doesn't wear a watch, so pay attention to these cues—they are more important than the time suggested. Another way to check that your dough is ready for the next step (i.e., the fermentation has taken hold) is to lightly touch the dough with your finger. It should have less resistance than a filled balloon and, when you take your finger away, there should be a dimple.

- For some dough, we recommend at minimum a 20-minute rest period once the flour and water have been quickly integrated in the mixer. The fancy name for this is an autolyse, but you can just think of it as a moment for the flour and water to "get to know" each other. This enables the flour to hydrate, or absorb the water. This rest period allows gluten to be developed with a shorter mix time (4 to 6 minutes) and is another way to coax more flavor out of flour.

- Temperature also impacts fermentation. Yeast thrives in warm environments. We recommend letting breads rise at room temperature. The ideal temperature for proofing your breads is 70 to 73°F/21 to 23°C. Most kitchens and homes, however, are warmer than that. So, if need be, find a cool place in your home to let your breads rise.

- It is possible—and in many cases preferable—to mix some doughs and refrigerate them to slow down fermentation, which gives the dough more time to develop. It also makes bread baking something that can happen on your schedule. To do this, mix the dough as instructed, put in a covered container, and let rest at room temperature for 45 minutes. Then refrigerate for a few hours, up to overnight. Remove the dough from the fridge and let it return to room temperature before shaping and, of course, resting again, then finally baking.

- I recommend baking yeasted breads on parchment paper. This is the easiest way to move fragile, fully risen, puffy loaves into the oven and onto a pizza stone. (This means a bread's final rise must be done on parchment paper.) The parchment, which may start to brown during baking, should be discarded after one use.

- Steam is an important ingredient for creating a crisp, shiny crust on a loaf of bread. You add it to the oven so that the crust remains soft and expands easily. Then, as the steam begins to evaporate, the sugars in the dough will begin to caramelize, leaving the bread with a browned crust. There are several methods for creating steam in a home oven. My personal favorite also happens to be the easiest: Put a baking dish on the oven floor while it heats up and then, when you open the oven to put the bread in, carefully add 10 ice cubes to the dish. Close the door as quickly as you can and you're all set. I want to reiterate the need to be careful. Putting your hands in a 500°F/260°C oven and then creating steam can be treacherous. Proceed with caution.

## Storing Bread

I am frequently asked about the best ways to store artisan breads. Here are a few tips.

- Never keep bread in the fridge. It just sucks moisture right out of it.

- Crusty bread to be consumed within 24 hours: Store it in a paper or cloth bag at room temperature. Or keep it naked, cut side down, on a cutting board to protect the crumb from the air.

- Crusty bread that won't be consumed within 24 hours: As soon as you get it, slice it and freeze it in a sealed, airtight bag. Thaw slices as you need them and heat them lightly in a toaster, skillet, or 300°F/150°C oven.

- Soft breads to be consumed within 3 days: Store in a breadbox or a sealed plastic bag. For any longer than that, slice the bread, freeze it, then thaw and reheat as above.

- Tortillas, *m'smen*, and other flatbreads can be frozen or refrigerated as directed.

- Buy or bake smaller loaves more frequently. Nothing beats fresh bread.

# Notes on Equipment and Ingredients

The act of baking bread predates modern gadgets and the availability of dozens of flours; truthfully, you need nothing but a bowl, your hands, and heat to turn flour and water into bread. That said, what follows are recommendations for useful equipment and the best ingredients to stock your pantry.

## EQUIPMENT

A **kitchen scale** is very helpful. We never use cup measurements in the bakery—everything is measured by weight to guarantee accuracy. I've provided cup measurements in the book along with weights, but I strongly encourage you to weigh the ingredients so that your results are as reliable as possible. Digital scales are easy to use and there are plenty of good models out there for less than twenty-five dollars. Using a scale makes for better results and easier cleanup. If you don't use a scale, take note of the method on page 22 for measuring flour.

If you plan on baking a lot, a **stand mixer** with a **dough hook** is a worthwhile investment that will last you a lifetime. At the bakery, we have huge spiral mixers where both the bowl and the attachment spin in opposing directions. At home, you can mimic this by stopping your mixer every so often and scraping the contents of the bowl with a rubber spatula to ensure that your ingredients are mixing evenly. Home mixers can jump around a bit when mixing

stiff doughs, so use them on a stable work surface and make sure the top of the machine is locked into place when mixing by flipping the lock/unlock lever into place. Depending on the dough that you're mixing, you might also have to put a hand on top to keep it from rocking off the counter. That said, bread is older than gadgets—and all of the recipes can be mixed by hand using lots of good old elbow grease (see page 15 for more on mixing doughs by hand).

**Baking sheets** are essential for baking. A baking sheet in this book refers to one that measures 13 × 18 inches/33 × 46 cm and has a 1-inch/2.5 cm rim. In industry speak, these are referred to as half-sheet pans. Stainless steel is the best option and happens to be the most affordable one.

The recipes in this book call for a **loaf pan** that measures 9 × 5 × 3 inches/23 × 13 × 7.5 cm (8-cup capacity). I prefer stainless steel.

**Parchment paper** is called for in many recipes. If you plan to do a lot of baking, it's worth seeking

out parchment paper sheets that are precut to fit into your baking sheets.

A **bench knife** or **dough scraper** (below) is useful for cutting dough, portioning it, and cleaning up your work surface. It's also great for transferring chopped vegetables and other ingredients from your cutting board to a pot or pan.

A **bread lame** (see page 125), which is simply a razor-like blade with a handle, makes slashing your breads before they go into the oven a precise task. You can also use

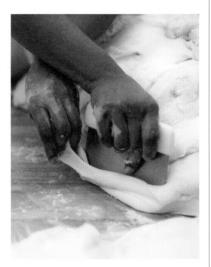

## INGREDIENTS

There is a lot of flour in this book! Regardless of brand, I strongly recommend using unbleached, unbromated flours, which have fewer chemical residues and more vitamins. I use organic flours and local flours whenever possible. It isn't called out in the recipes, but always use the highest-quality flours available. Make sure you're buying flour from a grocery store with high turnover so that the flour is fresh—check the date if it has one.

While we use dozens of **flours** at Hot Bread Kitchen, this book features eight different types:

- o **ALL-PURPOSE:** I recommend King Arthur all-purpose, which is widely available, but these recipes will work just as well with other readily available all-purpose flours.
- o **BREAD:** Bread flour contains more protein than all-purpose, which makes it a good choice for batards and boules.
- o **WHOLE WHEAT:** I use locally grown and milled whole wheat because it adds depth of flavor to grain-centric breads. As you become a more experienced baker, try the same recipe using whole wheat flours from a variety of micro-mills. If you can't find a local source, King Arthur and Bob's Red Mill both make versions that are easy to find.
- o **RYE:** You can buy it in specialty baking stores, some

a very sharp paring knife, but it doesn't allow for the same control and you will be more likely to tear the bread.

A **pizza stone** turns any home oven into a bread oven. It holds heat and will help your breads bake from the bottom and keep crusts crisp. You can also use unglazed tiles from home goods stores. Purchase as many as you can to maximize the surface area of your oven rack.

A clean **spray bottle** filled with water is great to have on hand for bread baking. I call for one in some of the recipes in this book.

Use a **wire rack** that you would use to cool cookies to cool bread for a full hour.

grocery stores, or online from Bob's Red Mill (go for the dark rye flour, since it's their most flavorful variety) or King Arthur. This is another place where you can play with locally grown flours with good results.

o **SEMOLINA:** Available from Bob's Red Mill.

o **TEFF:** Available from Bob's Red Mill.

o **RICE:** Available from Bob's Red Mill.

o **MASA HARINA:** This is a nixtamalized corn flour. Maseca is a common brand, but Bob's Red Mill makes one that I prefer.

Note that if you're not weighing your flour (which I highly recommend), use the "stir-spoon-sweep" method: Transfer the flour from the bag to a roomy storage container and stir your flour with a large spoon to break up any clumps and aerate it. To measure, spoon the flour into a dry-ingredient cup measure until the cup overflows on all sides, then sweep the top level with a flat tool such as a dinner knife. Do not attempt to "eyeball measure" flour using a partially filled cup; if a recipe calls for 1½ cups flour, you must use a 1-cup measure and a ½-cup measure. And be careful not to tap the cup on your counter, or spoon flour from one part of the cup to another, or press the flour with the back of the spoon. These will pack the flour in the cup—and you will end up with more flour than the recipe should have.

**Yeast** is always active dry yeast, commonly purchased in ¼-ounce/6.75 g packets that each contain 2¼ teaspoons yeast. Check to see that your yeast is not past its expiration date before using it. Active dry yeast can be added directly to dry ingredients if you are using a stand mixer and you use water at 100 to 110°F/37 to 43°C. For hand mixing, I recommend dissolving first (see page 15).

**Salt** is always kosher salt and I use Diamond Crystal brand. If you use another brand of kosher salt, such as Morton's, the same volume or weight measure of salt will be twice as salty, so use half as much.

**Olive oil** is always extra virgin, since it has the most flavor. You don't need to spend a lot of money to get a good-quality olive oil.

**Canola oil** is called for throughout the book. Feel free to substitute any other neutral-tasting oil such as vegetable oil anywhere canola is called for. For frying, you can substitute peanut oil or safflower oil.

**Milk** is always whole and preferably organic. Purchase locally produced milk if possible.

**Butter** is always unsalted unless otherwise noted. When used in doughs, butter should be at room temperature before being incorporated (except for Empanada Dough, page 220).

**Ghee,** clarified butter that is used often in Indian baking and cooking, is used in some breads such as Paratha (page 40) and Naan (page 70). If you can't find ghee, you can make your own by following the directions on page 40. Or you can, quite simply, substitute an equal amount of unsalted butter for ghee.

**Eggs** are always large eggs, preferably organic. Purchase locally produced eggs if possible.

**Yogurt** is always plain, full-fat yogurt, preferably local and without stabilizers. I always buy yogurt at the farmers' market.

**Sugar** is regular old white granulated sugar unless otherwise noted (e.g., confectioners' sugar or dark or light brown sugar).

**Honey** is always light, such as clover, because it is commonly available and mild.

**Maple syrup** is always real, not imitation, and can be any grade depending on whatever strength and flavor you prefer.

# PRIMORDIAL BREAD

## UNLEAVENED FLATBREADS

In most parts of the world, women do the baking, and in many homes you'll find them making flatbreads, the staple of family meals. Flatbreads are some of the most popular breads we make at Hot Bread Kitchen. They are also some of the easiest to make on the open hearth or stovetop, especially the unleavened ones, as there's no worrying about how quickly your dough is rising. With a few tricks and techniques, you can do amazing things with the combination of flour, water, salt, and perhaps a bit of fat.

Koutar, one of our graduates, makes *m'smen*, a flaky flatbread eaten with honey, for her husband as often as she can. They are in New York without family, and it is the only thing that makes him less homesick for Morocco, his home country. In fact, many of the women who work at Hot Bread Kitchen start and end their days making flatbreads for their families, even though they spend eight hours baking bread professionally.

There are no better breads than the ones in this chapter to commence a book about the world's breads and the women who make them. Preparing these recipes doesn't take much forethought (you can have breads on the table in as little as an hour), but they, like all of the bread recipes in this cookbook, communicate home and love.

# Baking Tips for Unleavened Flatbreads

Full disclosure: This chapter's title is a bit of a misnomer. There is actually no such thing as an unleavened bread. While these breads have no yeast or baking soda, steam is the under-recognized leavening agent at work. Created when water mixed into flour hits 212°F/100°C in the oven, steam introduces pockets of lightness in flatbreads.

The tips below apply to the recipes throughout the chapter and are useful to know as you enter the world of bread making.

- Let flatbread doughs rest as specified in the recipes. While there is no yeast in these doughs, mixing activates the gluten, which gives them structure and makes them resistant to shaping. Letting the doughs rest for at least 15 minutes will mean that you will be able to shape them with ease.

- The majority of flatbreads in this chapter, and many in the next one, are baked on a griddle, as opposed to in the oven. This is a much more fuel-efficient, economical way to make fresh bread on a daily basis, and it will not heat up your house (important if you live near the equator). Different cultures have different types of pans to cook the bread over an open flame. The common denominator is a heavy, flat cooking surface that maintains a constant temperature. In Mexico, a *comal,* a smooth, flat griddle made of clay or metal, is used for tortillas, whereas in Ecuador tortillas are cooked on large clay griddles called *tiestos.* In India, a *tava,* or *tawa,* is used for roti and paratha; it is virtually identical to a comal. In Ethiopia, injera is cooked on a *mitad.* My recommendation is to invest in a plancha—a large griddle made out of cast iron that can straddle two burners. While you can get the same effect by using a cast iron skillet, a larger surface area will allow you to make many breads at once, which is great because, let's face it, one *m'smen* is never enough! Season your plancha well according to the manufacturer's instructions.

- When you bake any of the lavash crackers (pages 49 to 51), be sure to sandwich the dough between two baking sheets as instructed. This will guarantee that your crackers come out flat, even, and crisp.

- The lavash crackers (pages 49 to 51) and the matzos (page 42) will crisp as they cool, so don't worry if they aren't as brittle as you expect them to be when you take them out of the oven.

# M'SMEN

MAKES 12 (7-INCH/18 CM) SQUARES; SERVES 12

4 cups/500 g **ALL-PURPOSE FLOUR**, plus more for shaping

½ cup plus 2 tablespoons/100 g **SEMOLINA**, plus more for shaping

1½ teaspoons **KOSHER SALT**

1¾ cups/400 g **WATER**

2 teaspoons, plus 6 tablespoons/ 95 g **CANOLA OIL**, plus more for shaping

6 tablespoons/85 g **SALTED BUTTER**, melted

I first tasted *m'smen* traveling in Morocco. I bought a piece of the tender, buttery, flaky bread drizzled with honey from a street vendor. It was an exquisite culinary experience. So years later, in 2009, when the Arab American Family Support Center referred three strong candidates from Morocco to our training program, my first question was, "Do you know how to make *m'smen*?" One of the three, Bouchra, taught us how to make the bread and, much to her surprise, it quickly became one of our best sellers. *M'smen*, also called *rghaif* or *melloui*, is often served with Fresh Mint Tea (page 33), but we hear from our customers that they use it for all sorts of things, including making tuna sandwiches. You can mix and divide the dough up to 8 hours before shaping, allowing ample time for the gluten to relax.

1. Put the flour, semolina, and salt in the bowl of a stand mixer fitted with a dough hook. Add the water and 2 teaspoons/10 g of the oil and, with the mixer on low, mix until everything is well combined, about 2 minutes. Increase the speed to medium and mix until the dough is smooth, shiny, elastic, and pulls away from the sides of the bowl, about 6 minutes.

2. Generously coat a rimmed baking sheet with oil. Coat a large, smooth work surface with oil (a granite, stainless steel, or Formica countertop is ideal). Transfer the dough to the oiled surface. Using oiled hands, form a ring with your thumb and index finger and use it to squeeze off pieces of the dough into 12 equal balls (each should weigh about 3 ounces/85 g). Put the balls on the oiled baking sheet and roll them around so that they're coated with oil, but keep the balls separate from one another. Put the entire baking sheet in a large plastic bag or cover loosely with plastic wrap

and let the dough rest at room temperature for 30 minutes.

3. Meanwhile, put the remaining 6 tablespoons/85 g oil in a small bowl, add the melted butter, and stir to combine.

4. Re-oil the work surface. Working with one piece of dough at a time, use the palm of your hand to flatten the ball and then continue to apply downward pressure with your palm to stretch it out into a rough circle about 10 inches/25 cm across that's so thin it's nearly translucent. Using your hand, cover the surface of the dough with 1 tablespoon of the butter mixture and then sprinkle with a dusting (about 1 teaspoon) of semolina. Use a rubber spatula to lightly mark the midline. Fold the top of the dough circle down so that the edge extends about ½ inch/1.5 cm beyond the line. Repeat that fold from the bottom so that the two edges overlap the center. Then fold in

*recipe continues*

each of the other sides in the same way to form a 3-inch/7.5 cm square. Transfer the *m'smen* squares to the oiled baking sheet seam side down and let rest for at least 15 minutes. Form the remaining breads in the same manner, warming the butter mixture if it begins to solidify.

**5.** Proceeding in the same order in which you formed the breads, put each square on a lightly oiled piece of parchment paper and stretch it with your palm until it has slightly more than doubled in size. If they resist stretching, let them rest a bit more before proceeding. Each finished *m'smen* should be a 7-inch/ 18 cm square. Cut the parchment so that it extends just slightly beyond the square. Do not stack the breads as you stretch them—they will stick together.

**6.** Heat a large griddle over medium-high heat until a drop of water sizzles away almost immediately.

**7.** You can cook as many *m'smen* at a time as your skillet or griddle will hold. Lay the breads paper side up in the skillet and then peel off the paper as soon as the breads begin to firm; it will come away easily. Cook the *m'smen* until they turn first translucent and then brown in spots, 2 to 3 minutes per side. Transfer to a wire rack while you continue cooking the rest.

**8.** *M'smen* are most delicious eaten warm, but once cooled, they can be stored for up to 5 days in an airtight container in the refrigerator. They freeze well for up to 3 months. Reheat *m'smen* for 1 minute on each side in a hot dry skillet before serving.

# KALE, ONION, AND CHEDDAR M'SMEN

MAKES 12 (7½-INCH/19 CM) SQUARES; SERVES 12

1 tablespoon **EXTRA-VIRGIN OLIVE OIL**

7 tablespoons/100 g **UNSALTED BUTTER**

1 medium **WHITE ONION**, finely chopped

1 bunch **CURLY KALE**, stemmed and finely chopped (about 6 cups/400 g)

2 cups/190 g coarsely grated **SHARP CHEDDAR CHEESE**

6 tablespoons/85 g **CANOLA OIL**, plus more for shaping

**M'SMEN DOUGH** (page 28), formed into 12 balls and rested

*M'smen* is great alone, but it's also great with such savory fillings as spicy ground lamb. We developed this kale and cheese version to highlight some of the delicious produce grown by our neighboring vendors at the farmers' market. Feel free to substitute other seasonal vegetables for the kale: Greens such as spinach and Swiss chard are delicious, but so are chopped ramps, asparagus, leeks, mushrooms, and even grated squash.

**1.** Heat the olive oil and 1 tablespoon/15 g of the butter in a skillet over medium heat. Add the onion and cook, stirring now and then, until the onion is translucent, about 10 minutes. Transfer to a medium bowl and set aside to cool.

**2.** Meanwhile, bring a large pot of water to a boil. Add the kale, return to a boil, and cook until bright green, about 2 minutes. Drain the kale, rinse with cold water, and drain again. Squeeze the kale with your hands to extract as much liquid as possible.

**3.** Add the kale to the onion along with the cheddar. Stir to combine all of the ingredients.

**4.** Melt the remaining 6 tablespoons/85 g butter in a small saucepan. Pour into a small bowl and stir in the canola oil.

**5.** Generously coat a rimmed baking sheet with canola oil. Coat a large, smooth work surface with canola oil (a granite, stainless steel, or Formica countertop is ideal). Working with one ball of dough at

a time, use the palm of your hand to flatten the ball and then continue to apply downward pressure to stretch it out into a rough circle about 10 inches/25 cm across that's so thin it's nearly translucent. Using your hand, cover the surface of the dough with 1 tablespoon of the butter mixture and then scatter the surface with about ⅓ cup/50 g of the kale mixture. Fold the top of the dough circle down so that the edge extends about ½ inch/1.5 cm beyond the center of the circle. Repeat that fold from the bottom so that the two edges overlap the center. Then fold in each of the other sides in the same way to form a 4-inch/10 cm square. Transfer the *m'smen* squares to the oiled baking sheet seam side down and let rest for at least 15 minutes. Form the remaining breads in the same manner, warming the butter/oil mixture if it begins to solidify.

**6.** Proceeding in the same order in which you formed the breads, put each square on a lightly oiled piece of parchment paper and stretch it

*recipe continues*

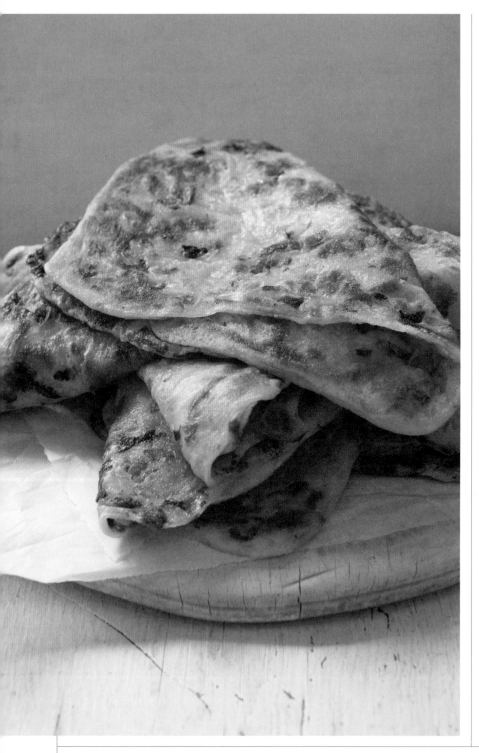

with your palm until it has slightly more than doubled in size. If they resist stretching, let them rest a bit more before proceeding. As you stretch, the filling will start to spread and may peek through in places. That is okay, just work gently to minimize tearing of the dough. The finished *m'smen* should be a 7½-inch/19 cm square. Cut the parchment so that it extends just slightly beyond the square. Do not stack the breads as you stretch them—they will stick together.

**7.** Heat a large griddle over medium-high heat until a drop of water sizzles away almost immediately.

**8.** You can cook as many *m'smen* at a time as your skillet or griddle will hold. Lay the breads paper side up in the skillet and then peel off the paper as soon as the breads begin to firm; it will come away easily. Cook the *m'smen* until the dough turns first translucent and then golden brown and the cheese chars slightly in spots, 3 to 4 minutes per side. Transfer the cooked *m'smen* to a wire rack while you cook the rest.

**9.** Serve warm. Store leftovers in an airtight container at room temperature for up to 4 days. Filled *m'smen* freeze well for up to 3 months. Reheat for about 2 minutes on each side in a hot dry skillet.

# FRESH MINT TEA

**SERVES 4**

5¼ cups/1.25 liters **BOILING WATER**

1 tablespoon **CHINESE GUNPOWDER GREEN TEA**

¼ cup/50 g **SUGAR**, or to taste

1 large bunch **FRESH MINT**, including stems

For a traditional Moroccan breakfast, *m'smen* (page 28) is drizzled with honey and served alongside a glass of mint tea. To do this right, you'll need a metal teapot and gunpowder tea. Gunpowder tea is a green tea; its leaves are rolled into small pellets, which are said to resemble gunpowder (they aren't lethal). This treatment of the leaves, also applied to oolong, helps to preserve the flavor of the tea. In Morocco, mint tea is consumed all day and served sweet—try it like that at least once before adjusting to your taste.

**1.** Rinse a metal teapot with ¼ cup/60 ml of the boiling water and discard—this will heat your pot. Add the tea leaves to the pot. Pour the remaining 5 cups/1.2 liters boiling water over the tea and let steep for 2 minutes. Stir in the sugar and mint sprigs and let steep for 3 minutes more.

**2.** Stir one last time to make sure the sugar is dissolved. Pour through a strainer into 4 small glasses, holding the teapot at least 12 inches/30 cm above the glasses as you pour so that you aerate the tea and bubbles collect on the surface.

# WHOLE WHEAT CHAPATIS

**MAKES 12 (6-INCH/15 CM) ROUNDS; SERVES 12**

1¾ cups plus 1 tablespoon/
415 g **WATER**

1 teaspoon **KOSHER SALT**

2¼ cups/290 g **WHOLE WHEAT
FLOUR**, plus more for shaping

**NOTE:** Lutfunnessa uses a traditional chapati rolling pin to form these—it's small and has ridges that impart texture to the chapati. You can find them in Indian grocery stores or online (see sources, page 291); or you can simply use a standard rolling pin.

Lutfunnessa (see page 36), who learned how to make chapatis with her mother in Bangladesh, taught me how to make these whole wheat flatbreads when she started at the bakery. Because the flour is cooked in boiling water, these chapatis stay soft and pliable for several days (rare for a flatbread) and can be served at room temperature or heated up quickly in a dry skillet.

**1.** Put the water and salt in a medium saucepan, bring to a rolling boil, and remove from the heat. Add the flour all at once and stir vigorously with a wooden spoon to integrate; the dough will be dry and coarse. Cover the pot with a lid and let the mixture sit for 2 minutes to let the flour fully hydrate.

**2.** Transfer the flour mixture to the bowl of a stand mixer fitted with a dough hook. Mix on low until the dough is smooth, looks like thick cookie dough, and doesn't stick to your hands when you touch it, about 4 minutes.

**3.** Transfer the dough to a lightly floured work surface and knead lightly until the dough is smooth, about a minute. Roll the dough into a thick rope and use a bench scraper to cut the dough into 12 equal pieces (each should weigh about 2 ounces/57 g). Roll each piece into a ball on the work surface. Press each ball into a 2-inch/5 cm disk. With a floured rolling pin, roll each disk into a 6-inch/5 cm thin round.

**4.** Meanwhile, heat a large griddle or cast iron skillet over medium-high heat.

**5.** Line a basket with a clean kitchen towel. Working with one chapati at a time (or more if your griddle is large enough), cook the chapati on the first side for just 15 seconds. Turn the chapati and cook on the second side until the underside is barely browned and the edges are dry, about 45 seconds. Turn the chapati again and cook until the first side is lightly browned, about 30 seconds to 1 minute depending on the heat. The chapati will likely puff up as it cooks—this is a good thing! It means the water in the dough is steaming and making the chapati tender. The chapati will deflate as it cools. Transfer the cooked chapati to the basket and cover with the ends of the towel to keep it warm while you continue cooking the remaining chapatis.

**6.** Serve warm. Store leftovers in an airtight plastic bag at room temperature for up to 3 days. Reheat on a griddle or in a 300°F/150°C oven for a few minutes until they're nice and warm. Don't cook them too crisp, though, or they will lose their pliability.

## LUTFUNNESSA ISLAM, PRODUCT COORDINATOR FOR LAVASH AND GRANOLA

As she was growing up in Bangladesh, Lutfunnessa was taught by her mother how to make chapatis from scratch. Her mom made them daily for just about every meal, drizzling them with honey in the morning and serving them alongside spiced curries in the evening (see Beef and Potato Curry, page 38). The chapati recipe came with Lutfunnessa to America and, lucky for us, to Hot Bread Kitchen when she became part of our team.

A former political science teacher in Bangladesh, Lutfunnessa joined her husband in New York in 1996. They had a son and a daughter whom Lutfunnessa cared for at home. When the kids were both in school, she looked for work outside the home. Lutfunnessa saw a flyer for Hot Bread Kitchen when we were still in Queens in 2010. The training program appealed to her because it was paid, it was with a team of women, and it didn't require her to interact with the public too much (which intimidated her because of her limited English and experience). For us, she was a good fit because, like the rest of us, she loves food and thinks about it all the time, she works with resolve and determination, and her chapatis (page 35) are exceptional! Lutfunnessa excelled in the training program, taking intensive English, math, and baking theory. When we moved to Harlem and she graduated, we promptly hired her back to manage the production of our lavash and granola.

The first bread that Lutfunnessa mixes in the morning is chapati. Next she prepares the dough for lavash, stretching piece after piece on the backs of baking sheets. She then mixes huge tubs of oats and nuts and more for granola. Near the end of her shift she'll jump out of production for Managers Lunch—a chance for first-time managers to share strategies and woes of managing an ever-changing team of trainees.

On Sundays, Lutfunnessa trades her baking skills for her sales skills as the manager of our stand at the Greenmarket in Jackson Heights, Queens. Lutfunnessa speaks Bengali, English, and after five years at Hot Bread Kitchen, proficient Spanish, which all serve her well in the ethnically diverse neighborhood. She has a loyal following among farmers' market shoppers and does her shopping with the other vendors (see Greenmarket Vegetables, Bangladeshi-Style, opposite). When Lutfunnessa trains new staff, she tells them, "to be a good sales person, you have to be good at talking to your customers." While this seems self-evident, it indicates a notable transformation for someone who originally sought a behind-the-scenes job. Lutfunnessa's newfound outgoing nature inspires new trainees—and sells a lot of bread.

Lutfunnessa's experience at Hot Bread has brought her full circle; she is once again a teacher. Part of her job as a manager is helping new trainees learn how to make our breads. She still loves working with so many women from different backgrounds. In fact, when someone asks Lutfunnessa what her next chapter in life might be, she laughs, "This is my last job. I don't plan on ever leaving!" *Inshallah.*

# GREENMARKET VEGETABLES, BANGLADESHI-STYLE

SERVES 6 TO 8

KOSHER SALT

¾ pound/340 g **FRESH BEANS** (such as green beans, wax beans, or Romano beans), topped and tailed and cut into 1-inch/2.5 cm pieces (about 3 cups)

½ small **GREEN CABBAGE**, cored and roughly chopped (about 4 cups/453 g)

1 medium **CARROT**, peeled and cut into ½-inch/1 cm dice

¼ cup/55 g **EXTRA-VIRGIN OLIVE OIL**

1 small **HOT YELLOW ONION**, halved and thinly sliced into half-moons

12 **GARLIC CLOVES**, thinly sliced

1 (1-inch/2.5 cm) piece **FRESH GINGER**, peeled and minced

3 small **HOT FRESH GREEN CHILE PEPPERS**, left whole (seeded if you want less heat)

1½ teaspoons **PANCH PURAN** (see Note)

½ small head **CAULIFLOWER**, broken into small florets (about 4 cups/400 g)

3 **BELL PEPPERS** (preferably 3 different colors), cut into ½-inch/1 cm dice

1½ cups/190 g shelled **ENGLISH PEAS**, (frozen can be used)

1 packed cup/40 g **FRESH CILANTRO LEAVES**, roughly chopped

Here is how Lutfunnessa cooks the seasonal vegetables she buys on Sundays at the farmers' market. This recipe can be made with a single vegetable (all cauliflower or all cabbage, for example) or a combination, such as the ingredients listed here. The constants are garlic, fresh ginger, chile peppers, cilantro, and *panch puran,* a mixture of whole spices including fenugreek, nigella, cumin, black mustard, and fennel seeds. Serve with a pile of warm Whole Wheat Chapatis (page 35).

**1.** Bring a large pot of water to a boil and salt it generously. Add the beans, cabbage, and carrot and cook until they become just a bit tender, about 2 minutes. Drain the vegetables.

**2.** Meanwhile, heat the olive oil in a large pot over medium-high heat. Add the onion, garlic, ginger, chile peppers, and *panch puran* and cook, stirring, until the mixture is very fragrant and the onion is just beginning to soften, about 5 minutes. Stir in the blanched vegetables, the cauliflower, and bell peppers and season with a few large pinches of salt. Cover the pot and cook, stirring every so often, until the vegetables are softened and fragrant, about 25 minutes.

**3.** Stir in the peas, cover, and cook just until the peas are bright green and tender, about 2 minutes. Season with salt to taste, remove and discard the whole chiles, and stir in the cilantro. Serve hot.

**NOTE:** To make *panch puran* at home, mix equal parts whole fenugreek, nigella, cumin, black mustard, and fennel seeds. Store in a sealed glass jar in a dark place (like a kitchen cupboard) for up to 6 months.

# BEEF AND POTATO CURRY

SERVES 6

6 tablespoons/85 g **CANOLA OIL**

2 pounds/900 g **CHUCK STEAK**, well trimmed and cut into 1-inch/2.5 cm cubes

**KOSHER SALT** and freshly ground **BLACK PEPPER**

1 large **YELLOW ONION**, cut into ¼-inch/6 mm dice

4 **GARLIC CLOVES**, minced

1 (2-inch/5 cm) piece **FRESH GINGER**, peeled and minced

½ teaspoon ground **DRIED RED CHILE PEPPER** or **CAYENNE**

2 teaspoons ground **CUMIN**

2 teaspoons ground **TURMERIC**

½ teaspoon ground **CARDAMOM**

½ teaspoon ground **CINNAMON**

3 cups/680 g **WATER**

4 large **RUSSET (BAKING) POTATOES**, peeled and cut into 1-inch/2.5 cm pieces

¾ cup/30 g **FRESH CILANTRO LEAVES**, roughly chopped

Another Lutfunnessa specialty, this curry, called *alu-maunsho torkerry* in Bangladeshi, is perfect on a cold night with, of course, plenty of warm Whole Wheat Chapatis (page 35) or a pot of basmati rice. Lutfunnessa also recommends making this recipe with a bone-in cut like a short rib, or cubes of boneless, skinless chicken thighs or lamb shoulder. As curries go, this is a relatively simple one to make with spices that you likely have at home. Let the beef brown well and use the caramelized bits to add depth of flavor to the dish. This cooks for almost 2 hours, so make sure to keep an eye on the liquid in the pot, adding more water if necessary.

1. Heat the oil in a large pot over medium-high heat. Pat the beef dry with paper towels, season with salt and pepper, and add to the pot. Cook the beef, turning the pieces a few times, until browned all over, about 10 minutes. Transfer the beef to a plate.

2. Reduce the heat to medium and add the onion, garlic, ginger, and chile to the pot. Stir in any brown bits of meat off the bottom of the pot. Season with salt and cook, stirring now and then, until the vegetables have softened and are beginning to brown, about 10 minutes. Add the cumin, turmeric, cardamom, and cinnamon and stir to combine. Cook until the spices are fragrant, about 1 minute.

3. Return the beef to the pot with the water and bring to a boil. Reduce the heat, cover, and simmer, stirring every now and then, until the beef is quite tender, about 1 hour.

4. Add the potatoes and continue to simmer, stirring now and then, until the potatoes are tender, another 30 minutes. Add water as needed to ensure the liquid nearly covers the meat. Season with salt and pepper to taste, scatter the cilantro leaves on top, and serve hot.

# PARATHA

1 cup/125 g **ALL-PURPOSE FLOUR**, plus more for shaping

1 cup/130 g **WHOLE WHEAT FLOUR**

¼ cup/40 g **RICE FLOUR**

1 teaspoon **KOSHER SALT**

⅔ cup/160 g **WATER**, plus more if needed

4 tablespoons/60 g **GHEE** (see Note) or **UNSALTED BUTTER**, melted but not hot, plus more for shaping and cooking

**NOTE:** If you cannot find ghee, you can use an equal amount of unsalted butter or you can make your own ghee. To make 12 tablespoons/170 g ghee, melt 16 tablespoons/225 g unsalted butter in a small saucepan over medium heat. Once the butter is melted, the white milk solids will separate from the clear, golden fat. Continue to cook the butter until the surface is foamy and the milk solids turn golden brown and fall to the bottom of the pan, about 10 minutes total. Remove the pan from the heat and strain the ghee through a cheesecloth-lined sieve into a bowl. Discard the contents of the cheesecloth. Store the ghee in a sealed jar in the refrigerator.

I was recently told that there used to be 365 types of Indian bread made from a wide variety of regional grains, most of which are now impossible to find. Paratha is one of the richest Indian breads and, depending on the region, shapes and fillings can vary greatly.

1. Put the all-purpose flour, whole wheat flour, rice flour, and salt in the bowl of a stand mixer fitted with a dough hook. On low speed, mix in the water and ghee until just combined, about 2 minutes. Increase the speed to high and mix until the dough is smooth and shiny, about 2 minutes. If the dough isn't smooth, add a little water.

2. Coat a rimmed baking sheet with some melted ghee. Transfer the dough to the baking sheet and lightly dust the dough with flour. Put the entire baking sheet in a large plastic bag or cover it loosely with plastic wrap and let the dough rest for 30 minutes.

3. Divide the dough into 2 equal pieces and, working on the baking sheet, roll each piece into a rope about 8 inches/20 cm long. Divide each rope into 8 equal pieces (each should weigh about 1 ounce/30 g). Roll each piece into a small ball. Put the dough balls on a floured work surface, lightly dust the dough with flour, and then cover with plastic wrap. Let them rest for 30 minutes.

4. Working with one dough ball at a time (keep the rest covered with plastic), flatten the dough into a disk and roll it on a floured surface into a 4-inch/10 cm round. Brush one side lightly with ghee and then fold the disk in half to form a semicircle. Fold it in half once more to form a triangle with a rounded edge (like a tiny slice of pizza). Roll the triangle into a 6-inch/15 cm round. Brush again with ghee, fold it into a triangle, and then reroll into a 6-inch/15 cm round. Repeat the folding and rolling with the remaining pieces of dough, being sure to keep everything except the piece you're working on covered with plastic wrap as you go.

5. Heat a griddle over medium-high heat. Brush the griddle with a little ghee. Working in batches, cook the paratha until the underside is browned, 1 to 2 minutes. Brush with ghee, flip over, and cook on the second side until browned, 1 to 2 minutes. Turn the paratha one final time and press down lightly with a spatula. Some of the paratha will puff up from the steam between the layers. Remove the paratha from the skillet and keep the stack covered with a clean kitchen towel as you continue cooking the rest.

6. Eat these warm or store them for up to 5 days in a sealed bag in the refrigerator. Reheat for 1 minute on each side in a hot dry skillet.

# PUSH AND PULL   MARKET VS. MISSION

There is nothing intuitive about balancing social mission and business acumen, because what is good for business doesn't always help the women we train. For example, every time we buy a new piece of production equipment, we increase efficiency, but we also reduce training opportunities. If a machine can divide a huge batch of dough into individual rolls, we save time and energy and, therefore, increase our profit margins. Sounds great, right? More money to pay for things like English classes and job placement. Yet we know that the process of dividing dough requires mathematical calculation and teamwork, both critical job skills. More important, when you have to hand-divide 250 *dozen* Parker House rolls, you learn to move with

a sense of urgency—something that every head baker in the world seeks in the employees they hire (and something really hard to teach!).

Good instinct and experience are essential to meet these challenges, but sometimes your gut alone doesn't give you the right answer. A decision about buying the dough-divider becomes more straightforward with a proper road map and savvy, committed staff who want to grapple with these challenges. (For the record, we have three dough-dividing machines—one loaf divider and two roll dividers—and learning to operate them, of course, has become a valuable skill for our bakers, who will invariably encounter these same machines in the span of their careers.)

Our road map is a set of organization-wide business objectives. Every Hot Bread Kitchen employee owns goals. The packers have three objectives they work toward; I have twelve. These goals are business oriented (e.g., we will increase our sales by 22.5 percent this year) and also target social outcomes (e.g., we will graduate twenty bakers into management-track jobs). This kind of road map is nothing new in the for-profit world—it is standard MBA management theory—but is less common for nonprofits. Bringing this clear, goal-oriented way of thinking into our mission has helped us not only stay on track with our business but also meet our social ambitions. The goals help us prioritize and figure out which side to favor at any given time between the push and pull of mission versus business.

We bake bread to create better opportunities for talented women. I never wanted to start a traditional nonprofit, nor did I want to start an artisan bakery. It is the marriage of market and mission that inspired Hot Bread Kitchen and inspires (and challenges) the talented staff every day. Our road map helps us to stay on course every step of the way.

# MATZO

MAKES 5 (12 × 8-INCH/30 × 20 CM) PIECES; SERVES 10

2 cups/250 g **ALL-PURPOSE FLOUR**, plus more for rolling

½ cup/65 g **WHOLE WHEAT FLOUR**

1 cup/225 g **WATER**

1½ teaspoons **KOSHER SALT**

1 tablespoon **EXTRA-VIRGIN OLIVE OIL**

**NOTE:** Since this recipe includes both salt and oil, tradition dictates that this matzo isn't appropriate for the Passover meal. However, if you'd like something that is closer to the more customary bread for the holiday, cut the salt in half and omit the oil.

I learned to bake bread when I apprenticed with Mark Fiorentino, the long-time boulanger at the Michelin-starred restaurant Daniel. One of my favorite memories from that time was making matzo to go into the restaurant's breadbaskets at Passover. Daniel is not even close to kosher, but much of the clientele is Jewish, so once a year the bakery turns into a matzo factory. Daniel Boulud would even come down and bless the ovens. Needless to say, it's the best matzo I've ever tasted. It has more salt than commercial matzo and a bit of oil, too. It is an easy flatbread that will knock the socks off friends and family at a Seder, or anytime as a stand-in for regular crackers.

1. Put a pizza stone on the middle rack of the oven and preheat to 500°F/260°C.

2. Put both flours, the water, salt, and olive oil in the bowl of a stand mixer fitted with a dough hook. On low speed, mix until all the ingredients are well combined, about 1 minute. Increase the speed to medium and mix just until the dough pulls away from the sides of the bowl, another 1 to 2 minutes, but no longer; you do not want to develop the gluten in this dough.

3. With wet hands, divide the dough into 5 equal pieces (each weighing about 3½ ounces/100 g). Cover the pieces with plastic wrap.

4. Working with one piece of dough at a time, dredge the dough in flour, shape it into a rough rectangle with your fingers, and then roll it on a sheet of parchment paper into a superthin rectangle about 12 inches/30 cm long and 8 inches/20 cm wide. (If you want traditionally shaped matzo, roll the dough into a 10-inch/25 cm square and use a pizza cutter or a knife to trim the edges.) As you roll, peri-odically loosen the matzo from the paper with an offset spatula or long knife and strew a little flour beneath it, which will allow you to roll it thinner. If the dough resists being rolled, let it rest for a few minutes.

5. Using a table fork, firmly prick the matzo through to the paper at ¼-inch intervals, making neat, even rows.

6. Put your matzo, with the parchment, onto the back of a baking sheet to transfer to the pizza stone. Slide the matzo off the pan and onto the stone. Bake until the surface has brown spots, 4 to 5 minutes. Now, if you desire some charred spots, put the matzo under a hot broiler on high for an additional minute to bring out some additional color. Transfer the matzo to a wire rack to cool (it will crisp as it cools). Discard the parchment paper.

7. Repeat the shaping and baking process until you have baked all of the dough.

8. Enjoy the matzo when cool. Store in an airtight container at room temperature for up to a week.

# GEFILTE FISH

**SERVES 12**

3 **CARROTS**, peeled

1 large **YELLOW ONION**, roughly chopped

1 pound/455 g coarsely ground **CARP**

1 pound/455 g coarsely ground **WHITEFISH**

1 pound/455 g coarsely ground **PIKE**

¼ pound/115 g coarsely ground **SALMON**

4 large **EGGS**, beaten

¼ cup/30 g **MATZO MEAL**

2 tablespoons **SUGAR**

1 tablespoon **KOSHER SALT**

2 teaspoons freshly ground **PEPPER** (use white pepper if you don't want any flecks in your gefilte fish)

½ cup/110 g **VEGETABLE OIL**

½ cup/115 g **COLD WATER**

**COOKING SPRAY**

Prepared **HORSERADISH**

**NOTE:** The hardest part of making this recipe is sourcing the fish, which you must order in advance from a fishmonger. I call for a combination of carp, pike, whitefish, and salmon in this recipe. You can grind your own boned fish using a meat grinder. Once you've got the fish, this is easy to prepare.

My great-grandmother Minnie Starkman was from Poland and made gefilte fish the old-fashioned way, starting with whole carp, which she would keep alive in the bathtub, and then clean and grind herself. She'd painstakingly form individual patties to poach in fish stock made from the carp's bones. It was a long, laborious process that left a pungent aroma in the house.

Her thoroughly modern daughter, my grandmother, found a recipe that involved chopped fish baked in a Bundt pan, her most beloved kitchen vessel (see opposite). Much simpler but definitely controversial, my grandmother's version has won over many who didn't grow up eating gefilte fish. Be sure to serve this with plenty of red horseradish with beets and Matzo (page 42) or Eier Kichel (page 46).

**1.** Preheat the oven to 325°F/165°C.

**2.** Roughly chop 2 of the carrots and put in a food processor with the onion. Pulse until pulverized, about a dozen 2-second pulses.

**3.** Transfer the vegetables to the bowl of a stand mixer fitted with the whisk attachment (or to a large bowl if you're using a handheld mixer). Add the carp, whitefish, pike, salmon, eggs, matzo meal, sugar, salt, pepper, and oil. Starting on low speed and increasing to medium, whisk the mixture, adding the water bit by bit as you go, until everything is evenly combined, smooth, and light, about 5 minutes (longer if you are using a hand mixer).

**4.** Coat a 12-cup/2.8 liter Bundt pan with cooking spray. Cut the remaining carrot into thin circles and put one slice of carrot in each large groove of the Bundt pan (snack on whatever carrot remains). Carefully fill the Bundt pan with half the fish mixture—try not to move the carrots. With wet hands, press down firmly to make sure that there are no air pockets. Fill the pan with the remaining fish and press it down again. Give the Bundt pan a few whacks on your work surface to settle the fish. Cover the top of the pan tightly with foil.

**5.** Put the Bundt pan on a rimmed baking sheet and transfer to the oven. Bake the gefilte fish until firm to the touch, about 1 hour and 20 minutes. Remove the foil and carefully drain off and discard the excess liquid. Return the pan to the oven, uncovered, to dry out the fish, an additional 15 minutes.

**6.** Remove from the oven and let sit for 10 minutes before carefully inverting onto a serving dish that fits it comfortably. Pat dry with paper towels and remove any white film from the outside. Let the gefilte fish cool completely. Cover with plastic wrap and refrigerate for at least 2 hours.

**7.** Slice and serve cold with plenty of horseradish.

# CHOPPED LIVER

**SERVES 8**

1 pound/455 g **CHICKEN LIVERS,** cleaned

3 tablespoons **EXTRA-VIRGIN OLIVE OIL**

**KOSHER SALT** and freshly ground **BLACK PEPPER**

5 medium **ONIONS,** each cut into 8 pieces

3 large **EGGS,** hard-boiled, peeled, and halved

3 tablespoons **CHICKEN STOCK**

**MATZO** (page 42) or **NEW YORKER RYE** (page 142)

This is my grandmother's recipe and I've always loved it. I should add that I love it as an accompaniment for matzo, but not as a dessert. This might seem like an unnecessary qualification, but for my eighth birthday, she made me a huge batch of chopped liver in a Bundt pan as a substitute for a birthday cake. Even though she covered it in candles, I cried. I eventually got over the birthday cake disappointment and now happily make and serve her recipe, albeit without candles.

**1.** Preheat the broiler to high and set the rack so it's about 6 inches/ 15 cm from the broiler. Line a rimmed baking sheet with foil.

**2.** Pat the livers dry with paper towels. Put the livers on the baking sheet, drizzle with 1 tablespoon of the olive oil and season generously on both sides with salt and pepper. Broil until browned and firm to the touch, about 3 minutes on each side depending on the strength of your broiler. Set the livers aside to cool while you prepare the onions.

**3.** Working in batches, pulse the onions in a food processor until roughly chopped.

**4.** Heat the remaining 2 tablespoons oil in a large skillet over medium-high heat. Add the onions and cook, stirring now and then, until all of their liquid has evaporated and they are deeply caramelized, about 40 minutes. Set aside to cool.

**5.** Pulse the livers in the food processor until minced. Add the eggs, chicken stock, and two-thirds of the onions. Pulse, scraping down the sides as necessary, until everything is minced and blended together but not completely smooth. Season with salt and pepper to taste.

**6.** Transfer the chopped liver to a serving dish and top with the remaining caramelized onions. Serve with plenty of matzo or rye bread.

# EIER KICHEL

3 large **EGGS**

1 tablespoon **CANOLA OIL**, plus
more for brushing

½ teaspoon **KOSHER SALT**

½ teaspoon plus 2 tablespoons
**SUGAR**

½ teaspoon **BAKING POWDER**

1 cup plus 3 tablespoons/150 g
**ALL-PURPOSE FLOUR**

This is like a Jewish answer to the delicious Spanish *torta de aceite*, a thin semisweet cracker that has become popular in the States in recent years. Depending on whom you ask, *eier kichel* is either a cookie or an accompaniment to gefilte fish—go figure. In my family, Minnie made these on the holidays and referred to them in English as "nothings." *Eier kichel* translates from Yiddish as a cookie made with egg, and this is one of the eggiest doughs in the book. It is meant to be sticky, and when the cookies are baked, they form domed, flying saucer–like shapes. Sprinkle lightly with sugar if you want to serve as a cracker with Gefilte Fish (page 44). Or add more sugar and some sesame seeds if you want to have them as a midafternoon snack with coffee—anytime you are in the mood for a little nothing.

**1.** Whisk the eggs in a large bowl until frothy. Whisk in the oil, salt, ½ teaspoon of the sugar, and the baking powder. Using a wooden spoon, integrate 1 cup/130 g of the flour in two additions, making sure the first addition of flour is fully mixed in before adding the second. The dough will be sticky but should pull away slightly from the bowl. If the dough is too sticky, add the remaining flour 1 tablespoon at a time until the dough is difficult to stir and pulls away from the sides of the bowl. Transfer the dough to a floured surface and knead it lightly. This will not be a smooth dough—it should be sticky. Cover the dough with plastic wrap or put the entire bowl in a large plastic bag and let it rest at room temperature for 20 minutes.

**2.** Preheat the oven to 500°F/260°C. Line 2 rimmed baking sheets with parchment paper.

**3.** Roll the dough into a log and pinch off into 12 equal pieces the size of golf balls (each weighing about 1 ounce/30 g). Working on a floured surface with one piece of dough at a time (keep the rest covered with plastic), flatten the dough lightly with your hands into a 2-inch/5 cm disk. Using your thumbs, stretch out one corner of the ball and then pull the stretched corner into the center of the ball and pinch in the middle. Repeat this process 3 more times, rotating your ball 45 degrees each time. Once you have a tight ball of dough, turn it over onto a well-floured surface and with a rolling pin roll it into a 4-inch/10 cm round that is no thicker than ⅛ inch/3 mm.

**4.** Put the round on one of the prepared baking sheets. Repeat with the remaining dough balls, lining up 6 rounds per pan. Brush the rounds with canola oil and sprinkle each one with ¼ teaspoon sugar (or more if you want to serve them as cookies).

**5.** Put the baking sheets in the oven, reduce the temperature to 400°F/205°C, and bake for 6 minutes.

**6.** Reduce the oven temperature to 300°F/150°C and bake until the *eier kichel* bubble and turn golden brown, 6 to 7 minutes longer.

**7.** Remove the pans from the oven, transfer the *eier kichel* to a rack, and let cool completely (they will crisp as they cool). Store any leftovers in an airtight container at room temperature for up to a week.

# WHOLE WHEAT LAVASH CRACKERS WITH SESAME SEEDS

MAKES 18 (6-INCH/15 CM) SQUARE CRACKERS

1¼ cups/295 g **LUKEWARM WATER**

2½ cups/315 g **BREAD FLOUR**, plus more for shaping

1½ cups/195 g **WHOLE WHEAT FLOUR**

¼ cup/55 g **EXTRA-VIRGIN OLIVE OIL**

2 tablespoons **HONEY**

2¾ teaspoons **KOSHER SALT**

**VEGETABLE OIL**

3 teaspoons **SESAME SEEDS**

**NOTE:** If you own 6 rimmed baking sheets and a very large oven, you can roll the dough and bake the crackers all at once. If not, work in batches, keeping in mind that the crackers need to bake sandwiched between 2 baking sheets at one point in the process.

These crackers, a crisp variation of Armenian flatbread, go well with cheese and dips. At the bakery, we cut off the rough edges so that the lavash crackers make neat rectangles—but we save the "imperfect" bits and sell them at farmers' markets. Now the imperfect ones are outselling the perfect ones! You can easily substitute other toppings for the sesame seeds, including poppy seeds, nigella seeds, or za'atar—a Middle Eastern spice mix that includes oregano, thyme, sesame seeds, sumac, and salt—or simply sprinkle them with kosher salt.

1. Combine the water, bread flour, whole wheat flour, olive oil, honey, and 2 teaspoons of the salt in the bowl of a stand mixer fitted with a dough hook. Mix on medium-low until a firm, supple dough forms and the sides of the bowl are clean, about 6 minutes.

2. Transfer the dough to a floured surface and divide it into 3 equal pieces (about 10½ ounces/300 g each). Cover the pieces loosely with plastic wrap or put them in a large plastic bag and let them rest at room temperature for 15 minutes.

3. Preheat the oven to 325°F/165°C.

4. Use a brush or your fingers to coat the underside of a 13 × 18-inch/ 33 × 46 cm rimmed baking sheet with vegetable oil. On a floured surface, roll out a piece of dough into a rectangle slightly larger than the surface of the baking sheet. If the dough springs back when you're rolling it, let it rest for a few minutes. Drape the rectangle over the underside of the baking sheet so it hangs over the edges a little.

5. Put the baking sheet in the oven and bake for 5 minutes. Remove the baking sheet from the oven and spray the surface of the lavash lightly with water from a spray bottle. Sprinkle the top with ¼ teaspoon of the salt and 1 teaspoon of the sesame seeds. Use a pizza wheel to cut the lavash into 6 squares, about 6 inches/15 cm. For flat crackers, cut along the edge of the pan (see photo).

6. Lower the temperature to 280°F/140°C. Cover the pan of lavash with a sheet of parchment paper and put a second baking sheet, inverted, on top, sandwiching the lavash between the pans. Bake the crackers until they're browned and crisp, about 35 minutes.

7. Repeat the process with the remaining pieces of dough.

8. Let the crackers cool completely before eating (they will continue to crisp as they cool). Store in an airtight container at room temperature for up to a week.

# SOFT LAVASH

**MAKES 4 LARGE (13 × 18-INCH/33 × 46 CM) RECTANGLES**

1¼ cups/295 g **LUKEWARM WATER**

2¼ teaspoons **ACTIVE DRY YEAST** (1 envelope)

4 cups/510 g **BREAD FLOUR**, plus more for shaping

¼ cup/55 g **EXTRA-VIRGIN OLIVE OIL**

2 tablespoons **HONEY**

3 teaspoons **KOSHER SALT**

**VEGETABLE OIL**

Lavash, a thin, pliable Armenian flatbread, is popular in Turkey, Iran, and, increasingly, North America. To make it in the traditional way, you need a clay oven. To accommodate home bakers, I have adjusted the recipe so that it is versatile and easy to make. With a little bit of yeast, this recipe could be the first of the next chapter (which includes other leavened flatbreads), but since it's in the same family as Whole Wheat Lavash Crackers with Sesame Seeds (page 49), I figured best to let it close this chapter. The yeast, and the fact that these crackers are baked just once, make this version soft and pliable, decidedly un-cracker-like, and good in place of pita. Serve it with Hummus (page 76), or with cheese.

**1.** Put the water, yeast, flour, olive oil, honey, and 2 teaspoons of the salt in a stand mixer fitted with the dough hook. Mix on low until the flour hydrates, about 2 minutes. Mix on medium-high for 5 minutes until a firm, supple dough forms. Do the windowpane test (page 16) to ensure that the gluten is fully developed.

**2.** Turn the dough out onto a floured surface and cut it into 4 equal pieces (about 7.5 ounces/215 g each). Put the pieces on a floured cutting board or baking sheet, cover the pieces loosely with plastic wrap or put them in a large plastic bag, and let them rise at room temperature for 30 minutes.

**3.** Preheat the oven to 325°F/165°C.

**4.** Remove one piece of dough from the plastic. Put the remaining pieces, still covered, in the refrigerator. Dust the piece of dough with flour and shape it into a rough rectangle with your fingers. Put the dough on a floured sheet of parchment paper and roll it into a rectangle that has the same dimensions as a rimmed baking sheet. While rolling, flip the dough to keep it even and periodically tug the paper from the sides to smooth the pleats. Be sure to roll *over* the edges so that the edges do not end up thicker than the middle. If the dough resists being rolled out, let it rest for a few minutes and then try again.

**5.** Transfer the dough, still on the parchment, to the *back* of the baking sheet (parchment side down) and again tug the paper from the sides to smooth the pleats. Lightly mist the dough with water from a spray bottle and sprinkle the dough with ¼ to ½ teaspoon kosher salt, to taste. Cover the dough with a second sheet of parchment and then top with a second inverted baking sheet to prevent the dough from shrinking and puffing up during baking.

**6.** Put the baking sheets in the oven and bake, rotating them halfway through baking, until the lavash is light golden brown, about 15 minutes. To test for doneness, remove the lavash from the oven and lift off the top pan and parchment to inspect it. The lavash should appear whitish in some spots, translucent yellow in others, and feel firm to the touch throughout. If it still looks or feels raw and doughy in places, replace the top sheet of parchment and the pan and return it to the oven for a few minutes more.

**7.** Repeat the entire process to shape and bake each of the remaining 3 pieces of dough, pulling them from the fridge as needed.

**8.** Enjoy the lavash warm. Store any leftovers loosely wrapped in an airtight plastic bag. Reheat in a low oven for a few minutes.

# SLIGHTLY ELEVATED

LEAVENED FLATBREADS

The first chapter of this book shares recipes for unleavened flatbreads—the fastest and most elemental breads in the world. This chapter takes things up a level, quite literally. Combining flour with not only water but also air and time, the breads in this chapter *raise* the bar. These recipes also offer many lessons about fermentation.

This chapter starts with injera (page 56), the staple of the Ethiopian diet. It's made of ground teff (a protein-rich grain similar to quinoa), mixed with water, and left to ferment for a day before cooking. Injera is one of the most amazing examples of how grain, water, air, and time can make something magical. At Hot Bread Kitchen, the story of injera can't be told without telling Hiyaw Gebreyohannes's story (page 59), one of Hot Bread Kitchen Incubates's greatest success tales. Talk about raising the bar!

This chapter travels. After injera there's Nan-e Barbari (page 64), a crispy Persian bread, Nan-e Qandi (page 69), a rich bread made with milk and butter, Naan (page 70), India's most renowned bread, and Olive Oil Focaccia (page 79), Italy's contribution to the world's great, versatile flatbreads.

*Shaping Nan-e Barbari*
*(page 64)*

# 100% TEFF INJERA

**MAKES 12 (12-INCH/30 CM) ROUNDS; SERVES 12**

4 cups/600 g **TEFF FLOUR**

5 cups/1135 g **WATER**, plus more as needed

**NOTES:** Hiyaw's recipe produces an injera that may have a stronger sour note and darker texture than what you might be familiar with if you've tried injera in restaurants. The reason for this is that he uses 100 percent teff. Its sour flavor may not be for everyone, so we've also included a recipe for a Hybrid Injera (page 58), which is a mellower cousin.

Injera requires a good non-stick, flat griddle pan with a blemish-free surface. It won't work if the nonstick coating is scratched. This dough has no gluten to bind it, so without the right cooking surface you will be frustrated by the bread tearing apart. We recommend a 12-inch/30 cm comal that has a lid. If you are going to make a lot of injera, consider investing in an electric *mitad* (see sources, page 291).

Hiyaw, an inspired entrepreneur and talented chef, was an early HBK Incubates member and started his Ethiopian catering company in our kitchens (see page 59). Injera, a spongy flatbread made with teff flour, an ancient gluten-free grain, is served underneath savory Ethiopian dishes. It's traditionally used as both food and utensil, so you tear injera into pieces and wrap up bites of food in it, eating the whole package with your hands. Injera's naturally fermented starter gives it a distinctive sour taste that cuts the richness of long-simmered soups and stews such as Doro Wat (page 62).

1. Whisk together the teff flour and water in a large bowl until a smooth batter forms. Cover the bowl tightly with plastic wrap, making sure there's space between the plastic wrap and the water (air is necessary for proper fermentation).

2. Let the batter sit at room temperature until it is foamy and quite fragrant, 24 hours. Keep the bowl covered the entire time. Do not stir the batter while it's fermenting.

3. After 24 hours, uncover the batter and if there is water on top, pour it off and discard (stop pouring once the water starts to get mixed with the batter). Whisk the batter until it's smooth. It should be the consistency of thick pancake batter; if it's too thick, add a bit more water.

4. Spread a clean kitchen towel over a large work surface. Put a 12-inch/30 cm nonstick skillet over high heat. Once it's hot (a drop of water will sizzle upon contact), using a fast hand, ladle ¾ cup/180 ml of the batter into the skillet starting in the middle and quickly moving around in a circle. Swirl the skillet to coat the bottom evenly with the batter—don't add more batter to fill the gaps. Adjust the heat as necessary so that the injera doesn't burn, and cook until the surface shows bubbles, about 30 seconds. Cover the skillet with a lid and let the injera cook until the surface loses its gloss, about 2 minutes more. You may need to remove the lid and wipe off the condensation once or twice. Invert the skillet onto a towel, letting the injera fall from the pan; you may have to gently tap the skillet on the work surface to release the bread.

5. Repeat with the remaining batter, stacking the injera between pieces of parchment paper as you go. Serve warm. Leftover injera, still separated by layers of parchment, can be stored in a plastic bag at room temperature for a day. Reheat in a skillet for a minute on each side.

# HYBRID INJERA

MAKES 12 (8-INCH/20 CM) ROUNDS; SERVES 12

2 cups/450 g **LUKEWARM WATER**

1 teaspoon **ACTIVE DRY YEAST**

½ cup/75 g **TEFF FLOUR**

1 cup/130 g **WHOLE WHEAT FLOUR**

½ teaspoon **KOSHER SALT**

**UNSALTED BUTTER**

Many Ethiopian restaurants serve injera that is made with a combination of wheat and teff flours. While this injera comes out quite dark and deliciously sour, it is more forgiving than one made with all teff flour (see page 56). In this recipe, I use whole wheat flour, add a bit of yeast and salt, and rub the pan with some butter, which isn't traditional but results in a delicious bread. These breads can be used as a plate for Ethiopian stews like Doro Wat (page 62) and Braised Cabbage and Carrots (page 63). Note that the distinct flavor in this bread develops during a long, 24-hour fermentation, which can be extended to 36 hours for even more sour flavor.

**1.** Put the water and yeast in a large bowl and whisk them together. Stir in the teff flour, whole wheat flour, and salt. Cover the bowl with plastic wrap and let the batter sit at room temperature for 24 hours (and up to 36 hours). It will begin to show bubbling activity within an hour, but needs 24 hours to fully sour and develop its strong flavor.

**2.** When you are ready to make the injera, whisk the batter until smooth. It should be runnier than pancake batter. Add additional water if necessary.

**3.** Spread a clean kitchen towel over a large work surface. Put an 8-inch/20 cm nonstick skillet over high heat. Once it's hot (a drop of water will sizzle upon contact), rub the pan with a thin layer of butter. Using a fast hand, ladle ¼ cup/60 ml of the batter into the skillet starting in the middle and quickly moving in a circle. Swirl the skillet to coat the bottom evenly with the batter—don't add more batter to fill the gaps. The injera should be no thicker than ¼ inch/0.5 cm. Adjust the heat as necessary so that the injera doesn't burn, and cook until bubbles appear on the surface, about 30 seconds. Cover the skillet with a lid and let the injera cook until the surface loses its glossy appearance, about 2 more minutes. You may need to remove the lid and wipe off the condensation once or twice. Invert the skillet onto the towel, letting the injera fall from the pan; you may have to gently tap the skillet on the work surface for the bread to release.

**4.** Repeat with the remaining batter, stacking the injera between pieces of parchment paper as you go. Serve warm. Leftover injera, still separated by layers of parchment, can be stored in a plastic bag at room temperature for a day. Reheat in a skillet for a minute on each side.

Hiyaw Gebreyohannes is a success story from HBK Incubates. His story begins in the Ethiopian desert, where he was born (his parents were on their way from their homeland to Djibouti). His family emigrated to Canada very soon after, settling in Toronto when Hiyaw was six. That far-from-the-desert, oft-frigid city was where he spent his childhood and teenage years.

For as long as Hiyaw can remember, the culture of food has played a prominent role in his life. "Family dinner was always an adventure in our house. Lots of people: uncles, aunties, cousins. The dinner table could be anywhere . . . all it needed was a big plate and all of us were ready to dig in." His parents ran three restaurants in Toronto, and his mother currently has two in Michigan. Early in the new millennium, Hiyaw made his way to New York City. His first experience as a partner in a New York restaurant was less than satisfying, so Hiyaw decided to forge a new career path in food, one that didn't involve restaurants.

To recover his bearings and roots, however, Hiyaw took a year to travel, mostly through Africa; he even contemplated moving back to Ethiopia to start a business. Luckily for food lovers in New York, Hiyaw ran out of money and had to come back to the States. His mother provided the food epiphany Hiyaw needed when she encouraged him to package the food he loved most. Just like that, a lightbulb flashed, and Taste of Ethiopia was born.

In early 2011, Hiyaw established the company in Michigan. Eager to return to New York, he started looking for a commercial kitchen space where he could prepare and package his food. He found his way to us in East Harlem, where, in addition to affordable kitchen space, he received classes on topics like branding, financial management, distribution, and employment law.

In the Incubator, Taste of Ethiopia grew quickly. A little more than a year later, the business had grown so impressively that Hiyaw needed more production space. The 800 pounds of food he was producing at Hot Bread Kitchen every week (which to us felt like a massive amount) is a small fraction of the 40,000 pounds Taste of Ethiopia now produces at a co-packing facility in upstate New York.

Hiyaw's packaged Ethiopian comfort food (think slowly cooked peanut chicken stew and collard greens prepared with spices like cardamom and caraway) is now served all over the continent. Currently, Hiyaw's daily life is less in the kitchen and more behind a computer as he continually expands his company's reach. Hiyaw—who speaks English, French, and Amharic—says that his motto has always been "Crawl, walk, run." Now, he says, he's ready to run. He wants to make healthy, delicious Ethiopian food as familiar across North America as pasta and sushi are. Proud to be the catalyst for such a change, Hiyaw is running a hugely successful food business. I am equally proud that its roots are at Hot Bread Kitchen.

*Doro Wat (page 62),*
*100% Teff Injera (page 56),*
*Braised Cabbage and Carrots (page 63)*

# DORO WAT

1 **LEMON**, halved

1½ pounds/675 g boneless, skinless **CHICKEN THIGHS**

¼ cup/55 g **VEGETABLE OIL**

1 large **RED ONION**, finely diced

3 **GARLIC CLOVES**, minced

1 (1-inch/2.5 cm) piece **FRESH GINGER**, peeled and grated

2 tablespoons **BERBERE SPICE**

1 teaspoon ground **CARDAMOM**

1 teaspoon ground **BLACK CUMIN SEEDS**

1 tablespoon **TOMATO PASTE**

1 large **TOMATO**, roughly chopped

**KOSHER SALT**

**NOTE:** To approximate berbere at home, toast 1 tablespoon coriander seeds and 1 table-spoon black peppercorns. Once cool, grind them with the seeds from 6 cardamom pods, 6 whole cloves, and 6 dried chiles de árbol. Mix in 1 tablespoon paprika, 1 tablespoon cayenne pepper, a pinch of ground ginger, and a pinch of ground cinnamon. Store in a sealed glass jar in a dark place (like a kitchen cupboard) for up to 6 months.

This traditional braised chicken is a popular Ethiopian dish always served with injera (pages 56 and 58). It's also a lesson in the richness of Ethiopian spices. Berbere—the word means "hot" in Amharic—is often considered the backbone of Ethiopian cooking, since it's found in so many dishes. A combination of many spices, it's become increasingly easy to find in large grocery stores and, of course, online. However, if you can't find it, you can make it at home (see Note). Black cumin seed, another spice that gets incorporated into the stew, is worth seeking out (available at Indian grocery stores), or you can substitute nigella seeds or regular cumin seeds.

**1.** Put the lemon halves in a large pot of water and bring it to a boil. Add the chicken (there should be enough water to cover it), reduce the heat, and let the chicken simmer until it is firm to the touch and completely cooked through, about 20 minutes. Transfer the chicken to a plate. Discard the lemons but reserve the cooking liquid.

**2.** Heat the oil in a large heavy pot over medium heat. Add the onion, garlic, and ginger and cook, stirring frequently, until the onion turns soft and translucent, about 10 minutes. Stir in the berbere spice, cardamom, and black cumin and continue to cook until the onion is golden brown and the spices become very fragrant, about 5 minutes.

**3.** Stir the tomato paste into the onion. Carefully arrange the chicken pieces on top in a single layer. Pour in just enough of the reserved cooking liquid to cover the chicken (reserve whatever's left for another use, such as making soup). Scatter the tomatoes over the chicken and season everything with salt. Bring the mixture to a boil over high heat, reduce the heat, and cover the pot. Let the chicken simmer until all of the flavors are nicely combined, about 20 minutes. Season to taste with salt before serving.

# BRAISED CABBAGE AND CARROTS

**SERVES 6**

2 tablespoons **EXTRA-VIRGIN OLIVE OIL**

1 large **RED ONION**, finely diced

**KOSHER SALT**

4 **GARLIC CLOVES**, minced

1 (1-inch/2.5 cm) piece **FRESH GINGER**, peeled and minced

1 tablespoon ground **TURMERIC**

4 large **CARROTS**, peeled and cut into ¾-inch/2 cm pieces

½ cup/115 g **WATER**

1 small **GREEN CABBAGE** (about 2 pounds/900 g), cored and cut into ¾-inch/2 cm pieces

This is classic Ethiopian comfort food. For a couple of glorious months, we hired Hiyaw to cater lunch for the Hot Bread Kitchen staff every Wednesday. I loved this soft, braised cabbage with carrots and still crave its enticing flavor from plenty of healthy turmeric. This stew is the perfect accompaniment for an Ethiopian feast of Doro Wat (page 62) and injera (pages 56 and 58). It's also so easy to prepare that it should be part of any family's regular weeknight repertoire; try serving it alongside a store-bought rotisserie chicken and a pot of rice and watch as everyone asks for seconds.

**1.** Heat the oil in a large pot over medium-high heat. Add the onion and a generous pinch of salt and cook, stirring now and then, until softened, about 8 minutes. Add the garlic, ginger, and turmeric and cook, stirring, until the vegetables are fragrant and just starting to brown, about 5 minutes.

**2.** Add the carrots, water, and a large pinch of salt and cook, stirring now and then, until the carrots are just starting to soften, about 7 minutes. Stir in the cab-bage in large handfuls, letting each batch wilt slightly before adding more. When all of the cabbage has been added, cover and cook over medium-low heat, stirring occasionally, until the cabbage is meltingly tender, about 35 minutes. The cabbage will release a lot of its own liquid as it cooks, but add a splash of water to the pot at any point if the vegetables threaten to stick to the bottom.

**3.** Season to taste with salt and serve warm.

# NAN-E BARBARI

MAKES 2 (14 × 5-INCH/35 × 13 CM) LOAVES; SERVES 6 TO 8

2 cups/450 g **LUKEWARM WATER**

2¼ teaspoons **ACTIVE DRY YEAST**
(1 envelope)

4 cups/510 g **BREAD FLOUR**, plus
more for shaping

2 teaspoons **KOSHER SALT**

**CANOLA OIL**

2 teaspoons **ALL-PURPOSE FLOUR**

½ teaspoon **SUGAR**

⅓ cup/80 g **COOL WATER**

1 teaspoon **NIGELLA SEEDS**
(aka black onion seeds)

1 teaspoon **SESAME SEEDS**

One of our most dramatic-looking breads is *nan-e barbari,* a 14-inch/35 cm oblong. A defining characteristic of the *barbari,* apart from its shape, is that its surface is spread with *roomal,* a flour and water paste, before baking, which puts a layer of moisture directly on the bread. This ancient bread-baking technique isn't seen much anymore, since steam ovens are common in bakeries. This recipe lets you create a bread with a great crust without having to introduce steam into the oven.

At the bakery, we make one long loaf, but unless you have a really big oven, you will likely make two lovely oblongs as directed here. *Nan-e barbari* makes a dramatic addition to any cheese plate. I especially like it served with feta, cucumbers, and olives.

**1.** Stir together the water and yeast in a stand mixer fitted with a dough hook.

**2.** Add the bread flour and salt and mix on low speed until the flour is integrated. Increase the speed to medium-high and mix until the dough is elastic, about 6 minutes. The dough should be cleaning the sides of the bowl. Coat the inside of a large bowl with canola oil and transfer the dough to it. Cover the bowl with plastic wrap or put the whole bowl in a large plastic bag and let rest at room temperature until the dough is softer than a firm balloon, is supple, and holds an indentation when pressed lightly, about 1 hour.

**3.** Turn the dough out onto a lightly floured work surface. Divide the dough in half (each piece should weigh about 490 g). Gently form each piece into a rectangle and perform a log roll (page 120). Loosely cover the pieces of dough with plastic wrap or a plastic bag and let rest at room temperature until

the dough has risen and is supple, about 30 minutes.

**4.** Meanwhile, combine the all-purpose flour, sugar, ½ teaspoon canola oil, and the water in a small saucepan. Cook the flour paste over medium heat, whisking, until bubbles form around the edges and it becomes thick and opaque, about 2 minutes. Set aside to cool.

**5.** Put a pizza stone on the lowest rack of the oven and preheat to 450°F/235°C. Let the stone heat up for at least 30 minutes.

**6.** Line the back of a baking sheet with parchment. Put one piece of dough on the parchment; leave the other covered and in a cool place. Gently pulling the ends and pressing down on the dough, extend it into a 14 × 5-inch/35 × 13 cm rectangle. Using your fingers, press 5 deep lengthwise ridges into the dough, being sure not to break the dough. Rub half of the flour paste over the surface and sprinkle with half of the nigella and sesame seeds.

**7.** Slide the dough and parchment onto the hot stone and bake until the bread has puffed up and is golden brown, about 18 minutes. Transfer the loaf to a wire rack, dispose of the parchment, and repeat the process to make the second loaf. Serve warm. Store any leftovers in an airtight plastic bag at room temperature for up to a couple of days.

# NAN-E-BARBARI PIZZA

**MAKES 2 (14-INCH/35 CM) PIZZAS; SERVES 4**

**NAN-E BARBARI DOUGH** (page 64), prepared through step 3

**BREAD FLOUR**

2 cups/500 g **GO-TO TOMATO SAUCE** (recipe follows) or store-bought

½ pound/225 g fresh **MOZZARELLA CHEESE**, torn into small pieces

3 **MARINATED ARTICHOKES**, thinly sliced

When I was a kid, we used to make pizzas on large Afghan flatbreads that we purchased at the grocery store (Toronto is a pretty multicultural city, and the bread aisle reflects that). We would cook a simple sauce to top the flatbreads, and sprinkle them with cheese and sometimes artichokes. When we first started making *nan-e barbari* at Hot Bread Kitchen, I remembered that childhood favorite and realized the dough would also make a great pizza.

**1.** Put a pizza stone on the lowest rack of the oven and preheat to 550°F/290°C. Let the stone heat up for at least 30 minutes.

**2.** Line the back of a baking sheet with parchment. Transfer one piece of dough to a lightly floured work surface. Press and stretch the dough into a thin round measuring about 14 inches/35 cm in diameter. Transfer the round to the baking sheet. Evenly spread 1 cup/250 g of the tomato sauce over the dough and scatter half of the mozzarella on top. Top the cheese with half of the artichokes.

**3.** Slide the parchment and dough onto the hot stone and bake until the crust is golden and crisp, the sauce is bubbling, the cheese is melted, and the artichokes are browned, 10 to 15 minutes.

**4.** While the pizza is in the oven, shape and top the second pizza using the remaining dough, sauce, cheese, and artichokes. When the first pizza is done, slide it onto a serving platter or a board and then slip the new one into the oven to bake.

**5.** Slice and serve the pizzas while they're hot.

# GO-TO TOMATO SAUCE

**MAKES 2½ CUPS/625 G**

I put it on pizza, I cook chicken in it, I throw it on pasta. This versatile tomato sauce, inspired by a Mario Batali recipe, is one that I always make in double batches.

2 tablespoons **EXTRA-VIRGIN OLIVE OIL**

1 small **CARROT**, peeled and coarsely grated

½ large **ONION**, finely diced

2 **GARLIC CLOVES**, thinly sliced

1 tablespoon **FRESH THYME LEAVES**, finely chopped

1 (28-ounce/795 g) can **WHOLE PEELED TOMATOES**

**KOSHER SALT**

Heat the olive oil in a large saucepan over medium heat. Add the carrot, onion, garlic, and thyme and cook, stirring now and then, until the vegetables are soft, about 10 minutes. Add the tomatoes, along with their juice, season with salt, and bring to a boil. Reduce the heat and simmer, stirring now and then and breaking the tomatoes up with your spoon as you go, until the sauce is thickened, about 30 minutes. Season to taste with salt and set aside to cool to room temperature. If you prefer a smooth sauce, puree in a blender or use an immersion blender to puree the sauce in the pot. Store in an airtight container in the refrigerator for up to 1 week or in the freezer for up to 2 months.

# NAN-E QANDI

MAKES 6 (5-INCH/13 CM) ROUNDS; SERVES 6

½ teaspoon **ACTIVE DRY YEAST**

¾ cup/180 g **WHOLE MILK**

3¼ cups/415 g **BREAD FLOUR**, plus
more for shaping

1 teaspoon **KOSHER SALT**

¾ teaspoon **BAKING POWDER**

9 tablespoons/125 g **UNSALTED
BUTTER**, melted and cooled

¼ cup plus 1 tablespoon/105 g
**HONEY**

**CANOLA OIL**

1 large **EGG**, beaten

1 tablespoon **SESAME SEEDS**

**NOTE:** If you are baking
double-size *nan-e qandis* for
muffuletta sandwiches
(page 77), the initial rising
time (8 hours) will remain the
same, but the second rising
time will increase to 3 hours
and the baking time will
increase to 25 minutes.

Rich with butter and milk and sweet from a bit of honey, *nan-e qandi* is an addictive bread from Iran. This dough has a long fermentation; it is the first dough we put in the mixer in the morning and the last one we bake. Serve *nan-e gandi* with coffee or tea, or use it to make a killer grilled cheese sandwich or, as we found out, muffuletta (page 77). Who would have thought?

**1.** Stir together the yeast and milk in the bowl of a stand mixer fitted with a dough hook. Add the bread flour, salt, baking powder, melted butter, and honey. Mix on low speed until all of the dry ingredients are combined and a loose dough forms, about 1 minute. Increase the speed to medium-high and mix until the dough is supple, smooth, and has some shine, about 5 minutes. Do the windowpane test (page 16) to ensure the gluten is fully developed.

**2.** Coat the inside of a large bowl with oil and transfer the dough to it. Cover the bowl with plastic wrap or put the whole bowl in a large plastic bag and let it stand at room temperature until the dough is softer than a firm balloon, is supple, and holds an indentation when pressed lightly, about 8 hours. Note that since there's so little yeast in this dough, this rising will happen very slowly.

**3.** Turn the dough out onto a lightly floured surface and divide it into 6 equal pieces (each weighing about 4.75 ounces/135 g). Form each piece into a roll (page 123),

cover loosely with plastic wrap, and let rest for 5 minutes. Use a rolling pin to form each roll into disks measuring 5 inches/13 cm across.

**4.** Evenly space the *nan-e qandis* on 2 parchment-lined rimmed baking sheets. Use a fork to make a few pricks on top of each one and then coat the tops with the beaten egg and sprinkle with the sesame seeds. Drape the *nan-e qandis* loosely with plastic wrap or a large plastic bag and let them rest for 20 minutes.

**5.** Meanwhile, preheat the oven to 350°F/180°C.

**6.** Bake the *nan-e qandis* until they're golden brown, rotating the trays halfway through baking so that the *nan-e qandis* brown evenly, about 20 minutes altogether. Serve warm or at room temperature. Store any leftovers in an airtight plastic bag at room temperature for up to a couple of days. Reheat in a 350°F/180°C oven for a few minutes before eating.

# NAAN

MAKES 12 (3 × 6-INCH/7.5 × 15 CM) PIECES; SERVES 12

1 teaspoon **ACTIVE DRY YEAST**

¼ cup/55 g **WATER**

5 cups minus 2 tablespoons/ 620 g **BREAD FLOUR**, plus more for shaping

1 tablespoon **KOSHER SALT**, plus more for serving

2 teaspoons **SUGAR**

½ teaspoon **BAKING POWDER**

¾ cup/180 g **WHOLE MILK**

¾ cup/180 g **PLAIN FULL-FAT YOGURT**

1 tablespoon **GHEE** (see Note, page 40) or **UNSALTED BUTTER**, melted, plus more as needed

Naan may be the paradigm of yeasted flatbreads. Fresh from a tandoor oven and served with curries and roasted meat, this Indian bread is a delicacy. Poor facsimiles made with chemical dough softeners are now available in grocery stores, but naan with a long shelf-life and a long list of ingredients is not the real deal. The yogurt and ghee in this version ensure that the dough is tart and toothsome. Eat naan hot out of the oven if you can.

**1.** Stir together the yeast and water in the bowl of a stand mixer fitted with a dough hook. Add the bread flour, salt, sugar, baking powder, milk, yogurt, and 1 tablespoon ghee to the bowl. Mix on low speed until all of the ingredients are combined, about 2 minutes. Increase the speed to medium-high and mix until the dough is smooth and leaves the sides of the bowl clean, about 5 minutes.

**2.** Coat the inside of a large bowl with some ghee and transfer the dough to it. Cover the bowl with plastic wrap or put the whole bowl into a large plastic bag and let the dough rise at room temperature until it is softer than a firm balloon, is supple, and holds an indentation when pressed lightly, about 2 hours.

**3.** Transfer the dough to a floured work surface and divide it into 12 equal pieces (each weighing about 3½ ounces/100 g). Roll each piece into a ball between the palms of your hands. Cover the dough balls with plastic wrap and let rise at room temperature until they're softer than firm balloons and hold indentations when pressed lightly, about 1 hour.

**4.** Put a pizza stone on the lowest rack of the oven and preheat to 500°F/260°C. Let the stone heat up for at least 30 minutes.

**5.** Working with one naan at a time (keep the rest covered with plastic), gently stretch and lightly press each piece of dough into an oblong shape, measuring about 3 × 6 inches/7.5 × 15 cm.

**6.** Using the back of a rimmed baking sheet, transfer the naan to the hot pizza stone, fitting as many as you can in a single layer. Bake until the edges are dry and the underside is browned, about 2 minutes. Use a large spatula to flip the naan, and bake until the underside is browned, another 2 minutes. Repeat the process with the remaining pieces of dough. Keep the baked ones warm in a towel-lined basket while you bake the rest.

**7.** Serve the naan warm, spread with ghee and sprinkled with salt, if desired. Any leftovers should be stored in an airtight plastic bag at room temperature. Reheat on both sides in a skillet over medium heat or in a 400°F/205°C oven.

# GARLIC NAAN WITH GREEN CHILE

MAKES 12 (4-INCH/10 CM) PIECES; SERVES 12

5 **GARLIC** cloves, minced

½ **GREEN CHILE**, seeded and minced

2 tablespoons finely chopped **FRESH MINT LEAVES**

2 tablespoons **NIGELLA SEEDS**

**NAAN DOUGH** (page 70), prepared through step 3

**ALL-PURPOSE FLOUR**

8 tablespoons/115 g **GHEE** (see Note, page 40), at room temperature

**KOSHER SALT**

Naan, especially when it's hot right out of the oven, is hard to beat, but studding it with a heady mix of garlic, chile, fresh mint, and oniony nigella seeds makes it pretty unforgettable.

**1.** Put a pizza stone on the lowest rack of the oven and preheat to 500°F/260°C. Let the stone heat up for at least 30 minutes.

**2.** Put the garlic, chile, mint, and nigella seeds in a small bowl and stir to combine.

**3.** Sprinkle each ball of naan dough with about 2 tablespoons of the garlic mixture and then fold the dough in half to encase the garlic mixture. Working with one naan at a time (keep the rest covered with plastic), gently stretch the dough into a rough circle about 4 inches/10 cm in diameter.

**4.** Using the back of a rimmed baking sheet, transfer the naan to the hot pizza stone, fitting as many as you can in a single layer. Bake

until the edges are dry and the underside is browned, about 2 minutes. Use the peel or the spatula to flip the naan and bake until the underside is browned, another 2 minutes. Repeat the process with the remaining pieces of dough. Keep the baked ones warm in a towel-lined basket while you bake the rest.

**5.** Serve the naan warm, spread with the ghee and sprinkled with salt. Any leftovers should be stored in an airtight plastic bag at room temperature. Reheat on both sides in a skillet over medium heat or in a 400°F/205°C oven until warm.

# PITA

**MAKES 16 (8-INCH/20 CM) ROUNDS**

2¼ teaspoons **ACTIVE DRY YEAST** (1 envelope)

3 cups/680 g **LUKEWARM WATER**

3 cups/380 g **BREAD FLOUR**, plus more for shaping

3 cups/390 g **WHOLE WHEAT FLOUR**

1 tablespoon **KOSHER SALT**

2 tablespoons **EXTRA-VIRGIN OLIVE OIL**, plus more as needed

In Arabic, pita is called just *khubz,* or "bread." The pita you find outside of homes and bakeries in the Maghreb (in northwest Africa) isn't great; even some of the best falafel joints use a disappointing machine-made cardboard-like bread. This recipe, which is easy to make at home, uses a one-to-one ratio of white to whole wheat flour. Use the pita for sandwiches or serve with a plate of fresh Hummus (page 76).

**1.** Stir together the yeast and water in the bowl of a stand mixer fitted with a dough hook. Add the bread flour, whole wheat flour, salt, and olive oil. Mix on low speed until the ingredients are combined, about 2 minutes.

**2.** Increase the speed to medium-high and mix until the dough is smooth, pulls away from the sides of the bowl (and leaves the sides clean), has a bit of shine, and makes a slapping noise against the sides of the bowl, about 6 minutes. Do the windowpane test (page 16) to ensure that the gluten is fully developed.

**3.** Coat the inside of a medium bowl with olive oil and transfer the dough to it. Cover the bowl tightly with plastic wrap (or put the entire bowl in a large plastic bag) and let the dough rise at room temperature until the dough is softer than a firm balloon, is supple, and holds an indentation when pressed lightly, about 1 hour and 30 minutes.

**4.** Put a pizza stone on the lowest rack of the oven and preheat to 475°F/245°C. Let the stone heat up for at least 30 minutes.

**5.** Transfer the dough to a lightly floured surface and divide it into 16 equal pieces (each weighing about 3 ounces/90 g). Roll each piece into a ball, cover the dough balls loosely with plastic wrap and let them rest for 10 minutes.

**6.** Working with one ball of dough at a time (keep the others covered) on a floured surface, press the ball into a disk with a rolling pin and then roll it into an 8-inch/20 cm round. It will be quite thin, about ⅛ inch/3 mm thick. Using the back of a rimmed baking sheet or a large spatula, transfer the dough to the hot pizza stone and bake until it's puffed up, about 2 minutes. Bake as many as you can fit on your pizza stone. Use a spatula to carefully turn the pita over and bake for an additional minute on the second side just to fully cook the pita. The pita should not take on much color.

**7.** Keep the pitas warm in a towel-lined basket while you bake additional pieces of dough. Serve warm. Leftovers can be stored in an airtight bag at room temperature for a few days. Reheat on a hot pizza stone for a minute on each side.

# HUMMUS

SERVES 4 TO 6

1 cup/230 g **DRIED CHICKPEAS**

¼ teaspoon **BAKING SODA**

¼ cup/55 g **TAHINI**

¼ cup/55 g fresh **LEMON JUICE,** or more to taste

1 large **GARLIC CLOVE,** minced

1½ teaspoons **KOSHER SALT,** or more to taste

¼ cup/55 g **ICE-COLD WATER**

**EXTRA-VIRGIN OLIVE OIL**

> **NOTE:** This hummus is best consumed immediately. If you are going to keep it in the fridge (for up to 3 days) and serve it later, increase the water to ½ cup/110 g. This will ensure that your hummus keeps its luxurious texture and doesn't turn into spackle.

If you're going to take the time to make your own Pita (page 74), the best thing to do while the dough is rising is to cook a pot of chickpeas for homemade hummus. This is something I make often and it comes together quickly and easily, so long as you soak your chickpeas the night before. Feel free to tweak the amounts of tahini, lemon, garlic, and salt to your taste, but be sure to follow the directions about how long to puree the hummus to achieve a smooth, creamy, light texture. I had been trying to achieve creamy Israeli-style results for twenty years. Then, a talented chef from Palestine told me the secret: baking soda in the chickpeas. Turns out, this is common knowledge in the Middle East, but rarely translated.

1. Put the dried chickpeas in a large pot (at least 4-quart/1-liter capacity) and add enough cold water to cover by at least 4 inches/10 cm. Let the chickpeas soak at room temperature for at least 6 hours or overnight.

2. Drain and rinse the chickpeas. Return the drained chickpeas to the pot. Sprinkle the baking soda over the chickpeas and set the pot over high heat. Cook the chickpeas, stirring with a wooden spoon, until the skins start to break and the pot is dry, 4 to 5 minutes. The skins should be starting to stick a little to the bottom of the pot. Add enough cold water to cover the chickpeas by 4 inches/10 cm and bring to a boil. Reduce the heat and simmer until the chickpeas are very soft and can be easily squished between your fingers, but are not completely breaking down, about 45 minutes (the cooking time will vary depending on how old the chickpeas are and how long you soaked them—monitor closely to make sure that you don't overcook). As the chickpeas are cooking, skim off and discard any scum and skins that float to the top.

3. Drain the cooked chickpeas into a colander and rinse with cold water. Pick out and discard the skins as you see them, but don't drive yourself crazy—it's okay if you don't get each and every one out.

4. Put the chickpeas in a food processor and pulse for a minute to turn the chickpeas into a thick, chunky paste. Add the tahini, lemon juice, garlic, and salt and pulse a few times to distribute the ingredients well and then let the machine run until the mixture is smooth, about 2 minutes. With the machine still running, slowly drizzle in the ice-cold water and process until the hummus is completely smooth, creamy, and light, another 2 full minutes. Taste and adjust for seasoning, adding more lemon juice and/or salt if you'd like.

5. Let the hummus sit at room temperature for 30 minutes before serving. Serve warm drizzled with olive oil.

# MUFFULETTA
## WITH OLIVE SPREAD

SERVES 4

¼ cup/40 g pitted **GREEN OLIVES**

¼ cup/40 g **GIARDINIERA**, drained and roughly chopped

1 marinated **ARTICHOKE**, roughly chopped

2 **CORNICHONS**, roughly chopped

1 tablespoon brined **CAPERS**, drained

1 **ANCHOVY FILLET**

½ **CELERY STALK**, finely chopped

Pinch of **RED PEPPER FLAKES**

½ cup/110 g **EXTRA-VIRGIN OLIVE OIL**

2 **NAN-E QANDIS** (page 69), halved horizontally

¼ pound/115 g thinly sliced **PROVOLONE CHEESE**

¼ pound/115 g thinly sliced **MOZZARELLA CHEESE** (see Note)

¼ pound/115 g thinly sliced **MORTADELLA**

¼ pound/115 g thinly sliced **SOPPRESSATA**

¼ pound/115 g thinly sliced **COPPA**

**NOTE:** Packaged (as opposed to fresh) mozzarella is fine in this sandwich—preferable, even, since it has a lower water content and won't make the sandwich mushy.

*Muffuletta* is the name of both a Sicilian bread and one of the world's greatest sandwiches. The latter originated at the Central Grocery shop in New Orleans when Italian farmers sold their produce at the neighboring market. Combining the farmers' produce with the shop's sliced meats and cheeses on their loaves of muffuletta bread, the iconic sandwich was born. My take on the classic sandwich uses our *nan-e qandi* bread to make delicious staff meals. You can make the sandwiches on two regular *nan-e qandis* or make one that's double the standard size (see Note, page 69), which more accurately mimics the sandwiches you get in New Orleans (they're generally so huge that you buy a wedge, not an entire sandwich). Focaccia Rounds (page 80) make another good bread substitution here.

**1.** Put the olives, giardiniera, artichoke, cornichons, capers, anchovy, celery, and pepper flakes in a food processor and pulse a few times until everything is coarsely chopped; do not make a smooth paste. Add the olive oil and give it one or two more pulses to incorporate.

**2.** Divide the olive spread among the 4 cut sides of the *nan-e qandis* and spread to the edges (this way each bite will have a thin layer of olive spread next to the fillings).

Layer the provolone, mozzarella, mortadella, soppressata, and coppa over 2 of the bread halves and close the sandwiches. Wrap each sandwich in plastic wrap, put a cutting board on top of them, and put something heavy (like a couple cans of beans or a pot) on the board. Let the sandwiches sit for at least 20 minutes at room temperature or for up to 6 hours in the refrigerator (bring to room temperature before serving).

**3.** Cut into quarters and serve.

# OLIVE OIL FOCACCIA

MAKES 1 (13 × 18-INCH/33 × 46 CM) FOCACCIA; SERVES 8

1 teaspoon **ACTIVE DRY YEAST**

2¾ cups/630 g **WATER**

5½ cups/700 g **BREAD FLOUR**

4 tablespoons/55 g **EXTRA-VIRGIN OLIVE OIL**, plus more for shaping and drizzling

1 tablespoon **KOSHER SALT**, plus more for sprinkling

¾ teaspoon **SUGAR**

Toppings (page 81; optional)

If you are new to baking yeasted breads, focaccia is a good place to start. Baked on a rimmed baking sheet and stretched to the edges, it requires little special shaping. With the olive oil and salt on top, it's a showstopper, especially when you pull it out hot from the oven at a dinner party. Serve this with cheese or dips, make sandwiches for a crowd (halve the focaccia horizontally, fill it, and then cut it into squares as you would a large sheet cake; then grill in a panini press, if desired), and turn leftovers into delicious croutons.

**1.** Stir together the yeast and water in the bowl of a stand mixer fitted with a dough hook. Add the flour and mix on low speed until the ingredients are well combined. Mix on medium speed until the dough looks like thick muffin batter, about 2 minutes. Turn the mixer off and allow the mixture to sit for 10 minutes to allow the flour to hydrate.

**2.** Add 2 tablespoons/30 g of the olive oil and the salt and sugar and mix on low speed until combined, about 1 minute. Turn the speed up just a notch and mix until the dough is quite thick and starting to pull away slightly from the sides of the bowl, about 3 minutes. It will be very sticky at this point. Increase the speed to high and let the dough mix until it comes together, makes slapping noises as it turns, the bowl is clean, and there's a slight sheen to the dough, about 6 minutes. Do a windowpane test (page 16) to ensure that the gluten is fully developed.

**3.** Coat the inside of a large bowl with olive oil and transfer the dough to it. Fold the dough over itself a couple of times, cover the bowl with plastic wrap (or put the

entire thing into a large plastic bag), and let rise at room temperature until it is 1½ times its original volume, about 2 hours.

**4.** Generously oil a 13 × 18-inch/33 × 46 cm rimmed baking sheet. Remove the dough from the container with oiled hands and press the dough into the pan with your fingers so it evenly covers the pan. If the dough resists, simply let it rest for 10 minutes and then stretch it a bit more. Repeat this process as many times as needed until the dough willingly stretches to cover the entire surface of the pan. Loosely cover the focaccia with plastic wrap and let it rest for 30 minutes.

**5.** Preheat the oven to 400°F/205°C.

**6.** Uncover the dough, use your fingers to firmly dimple the surface. Press down until you feel the hard surface below, being careful not to tear your dough. Use a pastry brush to paint the focaccia with 2 tablespoons/30 g olive oil and then sprinkle it evenly with 1 teaspoon salt. Note that if you opt for any of

*recipe continues*

## Focaccia Rounds

One of my favorite ways to make focaccia is to divide the dough into 10 pieces (each weighing about 4½ ounces/ 125 g) and form into rolls (page 123). Evenly space the balls on 2 parchment-lined rimmed baking sheets.

Let the rolls rise for 1 hour until they look puffy and supple.

Uncover the rounds and use your fingers to make 5 dimples on the surface of each. Press down firmly until you feel the baking sheet, being careful not to tear your dough. With a pastry brush, lightly cover each focaccia round with olive oil and top with a pinch of kosher salt and a pinch of herbes de Provence. Bake until they're browned on top, about 20 minutes.

Let cool, then halve each round horizontally and fill with anything from sliced ham and arugula to chicken parmesan, or use them for Muffuletta with Olive Spread (page 77).

the variations opposite, this is the moment to add them, on top of the oil and salt.

**7.** Bake the focaccia until it's nicely browned and the underside is crisp, about 30 minutes. Remove to a wire rack and let cool for at least 10 minutes before slicing and serving. Store leftovers in an airtight plastic bag at room temperature for up to 2 days. Reheat in a 300°F/150°C oven for a few minutes.

# Seasonal Focaccia Variations

We sell focaccia topped with all sorts of vegetables at our farmers' market stands, changing the toppings every few weeks to use what's in season. In the fall, the unexpected combination of sweet apple and sharp cheddar drives customers crazy—in a good way. During the coldest months, when the market can look a bit bleak, sliced potatoes and rosemary help eliminate winter blues; the starch-on-starch combination is comforting and incredibly satisfying. The start of spring in New York is always marked by ramps (thin wild leeks), and summer means gorgeous tomatoes that seem to nearly overflow from the market's tables. There is room for creativity: broccoli—yum; kale—perfect; sundried tomatoes—check. Cut vegetables in bite-size pieces so they cook with the dough and use your olive oil liberally.

Each of the following provides enough topping for one 13 × 18-inch/ 33 × 46 cm focaccia. Add the toppings right after the dough is oiled and salted as indicated in the recipe on page 79.

## Apple and Cheddar Focaccia

Seed and thinly slice 2 Honeycrisp apples and evenly shingle them over the surface of the oiled and salted focaccia. Sprinkle the apples with 1 cup/95 g coarsely grated sharp cheddar cheese. Bake until the exposed focaccia is browned, the underside is crisp, and the apples and cheese are browned and bubbling, about 20 minutes.

## Ramp and Pecorino Focaccia

Trim and roughly chop a bunch of ramps (use the greens!). Put them in a bowl and toss together with 3 tablespoons olive oil and ½ teaspoon kosher salt. Evenly scatter the ramps over the surface of the oiled and salted focaccia and sprinkle them with ½ cup/50 g coarsely grated pecorino cheese. Bake until the exposed focaccia is browned, the underside is crisp, the ramps are softened and browned in spots, and the cheese is melted and browned, about 20 minutes.

## Potato and Rosemary Focaccia

Using a mandolin, very thinly slice 6 Red Bliss potatoes and put them in a large bowl. Toss the potatoes with ⅓ cup/80 ml extra-virgin olive oil, 1 tablespoon kosher salt, and 2 teaspoons minced rosemary. Evenly shingle the potatoes over the surface of the oiled and salted focaccia and bake until browned and the underside is crisp, about 20 minutes.

## Tomato and Basil Focaccia

Slice 2 hefty heirloom tomatoes as thinly as possible. Evenly shingle them over the surface of the oiled and salted focaccia and drizzle with an additional 2 tablespoons olive oil and sprinkle with ½ teaspoon salt. Tear 6 large basil leaves over the top and bake until the exposed focaccia is browned, the underside is crisp, and the tomatoes are browned and bubbling, about 20 minutes.

# MASA Y MAS

## TORTILLAS AND MORE

In this chapter we move further afield from flour, water, yeast, and steam and take a trip to Mesoamerica where corn reigns supreme. Tortillas, gorditas, and tostadas are just a few of the delicious products made with masa—a dough of corn, water, and a little bit of slaked lime. Each microregion in Mexico and Central America cooks masa in a different way to create a variety of delicious foods. This chapter starts with the base dough recipe—blue, white, and yellow masa—because it is the mother dough that inspires the creations that follow.

The key point of this chapter is that masa from *nixtamal* can be made at home but rarely is. Processed corn flour—masa harina—made with dehydrated nixtamalized corn is widely available and is what most home cooks use to make tortillas. The good news is that varieties of masa harina with few additives and made with non-GMO corn are increasingly available. The not-so-good news is that the art of taking simple corn and turning it into a fresh fragrant dough is being lost. This chapter starts with the recipe for Masa from Nixtamal (page 89) because it yields the best results. Elidia, the first baker we hired, taught us how to nixtamalize corn: partially cook and soak it in lime, then grind it into masa. Nixtamal-ization allows for the conversion of dried corn kernels into a pliable dough. The secret lies in slaked lime—also known as calcium hydroxide, builders' lime, *cal*, or pickling lime—a white powder used in food preparation and also, believe it or not, to make cement. It is highly alkaline and is used to create a solution that softens corn and loosens the hull from the kernel. Nixtamalization also releases oils that help with

emulsification. The ancient process also harnesses the nutritional benefits of dried corn, extracting additional niacin, not to mention its terrific flavor, and aids in digestion.

The nixtamalized corn is then rinsed and milled. When I was staying with a family in Xela, Guatemala, I visited the community corn mill (*molino*) every morning with my host. She would take her *nixtamal* to be ground into masa on a big, noisy mill. It was a wonderful, fragrant scene—each woman having nixtamalized her corn a little differently. Early-rising mothers chatted while they waited in line to grind their corn for tortillas and other delicacies. I always thought it would be an ideal place to organize a revolution.

Alas, scenes like this are increasingly rare. More frequently, home chefs and commercial tortilla factories use masa harina—dehydrated and ground corn that is sold as a shelf-stable flour with the addition of preservatives. Similar to pancake mix, masa harina is the quickest way to fresh tortillas, even if they're not 100 percent from scratch.

At Hot Bread Kitchen, tortillas from *nixtamal* were the first product we sold, and we continue to make tortillas this way because they are just tastier. It also allows us to be exacting in our ingredient sourcing; we use only non-GMO corn and even integrate heritage and local varieties. In this chapter, I show you how you can accomplish the same thing at home. It takes a little extra commitment and planning, but the process pays off in many ways.

In addition to everything you need to know about making corn tortillas, you'll also find here more than a dozen recipes from our bakers that show you how to use tortillas and fresh masa. There's a lot of mixing and matching. The spaghetti squash mixture from Spaghetti Squash Tacos (page 100) can be rolled into tortillas with a bit of cheese and then fried, just as the chicken from Tinga Tostadas (page 101) can be used in Carnitas Cemitas (page 135). The carnitas—either the fast version on page 107 or the slow-and-low version on page 106—can be used in Gorditas (page 104), tostadas, tacos, a cemita, or can even be served alongside some Refried Beans (page 109) and rice. *¡Buen provecho!*

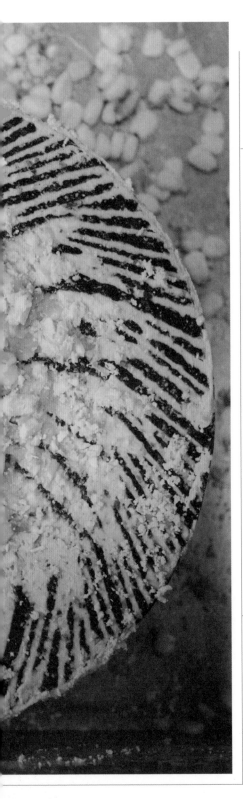

*Stones from our molino,
or corn grinder*

## Tips for Masa and Tortillas

Making tortillas from scratch, with the right ingredients, equipment, and knowledge, is a rewarding process. These tips will likely answer many of the questions you'll have along the way.

- Not all corn is created equal. I tried everything possible to make masa—including popcorn (nope, it doesn't work) and pozole (not a fit either). You want to seek out dent corn or field corn—the cheap stuff that is often used in animal feed. Make sure, however, that it has been cleaned for human consumption (see sources, page 291). Hot Bread Kitchen sources yellow, white, and blue corn. Red is also beautiful, although harder to find in the United States.

- Fresh masa can be stored in a sealed container in the refrigerator for up to 7 days. Masa made with blue corn might become more lavender in color, but it will still taste good. You will know if your masa has turned if it has a strong acidic smell.

- I recommend two methods for reheating tortillas.
  o **STEAMING:** Put a small round of parchment on the bottom of a bamboo steamer, add a stack of 6 or more tortillas, depending on the size of your steamer, and put the steamer into a pot that has 1 inch/2.5 cm or so of boiling water in it. Make sure the water does not touch the tortillas. Put the lid on the pot and steam the tortillas until soft, about 2 minutes.
  o **STOVETOP:** Heat a skillet over high heat, dip your index finger in water, and circle the outside of the tortilla with water. Put the tortilla in the skillet and heat just until soft, at most 30 seconds on each side.

- Transfer the heated tortillas to a bowl or basket lined with a clean kitchen towel. Serve immediately, wrapping the towel around the tortillas to keep them warm.

# MASA FROM NIXTAMAL

**MAKES 1 POUND/ABOUT 3 CUPS/455 G**

3 quarts/3 liters **WATER**

3 tablespoons **CALCIUM HYDROXIDE**

1½ cups/455 g **DRIED WHOLE KERNEL DENT CORN**

**NOTE:** If you have a manual corn grinder, you will need to find a sturdy place to attach it. If the clamp is wide enough, a kitchen counter is ideal. Grinding requires a lot of torque, and a shaky kitchen table won't support it—trust me, I've tried.

Tortillas (page 92), tamales (pages 95 and 97), Gorditas (page 104), and tostadas (page 101) are only as good as the masa from which you make them. For that reason, I am opening the chapter with the Cadillac of masa—masa from *nixtamal*. The difficult part about making this recipe is tracking down the corn, calcium hydroxide (*cal*), and a corn grinder (*molino*). You can order these from Hot Bread Kitchen or find them in large Latin markets and online (see sources, page 291). Once you have your ingredients and tools on hand, authentic homemade tortillas are well within reach. As an alternative, many tortillerias, including Hot Bread Kitchen, will sell you fresh masa. Just ask!

**1.** Bring the water to a boil in a large pot. Stir in the calcium hydroxide until it dissolves and then remove the pot from the heat. Add the corn to the pot, cover it, and let it sit for at least 8 hours or overnight.

**2.** Drain the corn in a colander and rinse it with fresh water to remove most of the loosened skins (but don't rinse it too much—a little bit of the softened hull will help keep the tortillas soft).

**3.** Set up your corn grinder according to the manufacturer's instructions. Grind the corn into a bowl, feeding a very thin stream of fresh water through the grinder with the corn. You may need help with this. This process will involve a bit of trial and error, as corn grinders have metal plates that don't have fixed settings. You want them to be close enough for the corn to be finely ground; ultimately you're looking for a consistency that's like Play-Doh—neither too wet nor too dry. The amount of water needed as you grind will depend on the type of corn and the fineness of the grind: You want enough to keep the ground corn moist, but not so much that the masa is too wet. If a whole or broken kernel falls into your masa, don't fret; I like the rustic look and feel of having a kernel or two in a tortilla. Collect the masa in a ball. If it is crumbly and dry, add a little more water as you bring the dough together. Use immediately in recipes such as tortillas or gorditas or refrigerate in a sealed plastic bag for up to 7 days.

# MASA FROM MASA HARINA

MAKES 1 POUND/ABOUT 3 CUPS/455 G

Scant 1 cup/215 g **WATER**, or more if needed

1½ cups/240 g **MASA HARINA** (preferably Bob's Red Mill), or more if needed

While we proudly make our own fresh masa at Hot Bread Kitchen, taking a shortcut at home by using masa harina (dehydrated, nixtamalized corn ground into flour) is acceptable. If it gets you making and enjoying fresh tortillas and gorditas, that's okay in my book. Like anything else, the raw ingredients are important here. Use a masa harina with as few ingredients as possible, ideally just corn and lime. The recipe below is a good guide, but do refer to the instructions on the bag, as different brands absorb water differently.

Pour the water into a large bowl. Add the masa harina and stir to integrate. Knead the dough for 30 seconds until it is firm and supple. It should not stick to your fingers when you touch it and should not crumble when you press it into a ball; it should have the texture of Play-Doh. Add more water or masa harina if necessary to achieve the right consistency. Cover the dough and let rest for 30 minutes before using. Masa from masa harina can be refrigerated for up to 3 days, but you may need to add some water to get it back to the desired consistency.

## NANCY MENDEZ, PRODUCT COORDINATOR, TORTILLAS

Nancy was born in Puebla, Mexico. When she was ten years old, her grandmother decided it was time for her to learn to make tortillas. Until then, her grandmother had made them by herself twice a day, grinding her own masa by hand on a *metate*, a mortar and pestle–style tool. Nancy resisted because, frankly, it's a lot of work. When her exasperated grandmother asked her how they'd eat what was a staple of the family diet if Nancy didn't learn to make tortillas, Nancy quickly replied, "I'll buy them!"

Decades later, the tables, not to mention the grinder, have turned. Nancy is Hot Bread Kitchen's tortilla maestro and believes that "you don't forget traditions if you make them." She's the person in charge of the masa grinder and the tortilla machine. Her day is long—we start tortillas at 4 a.m. If she's low on energy (or that brutal wake-up gets her down), she thinks of her grandmother and, in her words, "how my hard work at Hot Bread Kitchen helped pay for my grandmother's operation and how proud she was whenever I would call her and tell her about my tortillas."

The road to Hot Bread Kitchen started for Nancy after she left Puebla and moved to Queens in 2002. With an elementary school education and limited English, Nancy worked seasonal jobs in catering and retail—including selling food on the street—to help support her family. She found her way to Hot Bread Kitchen in 2009 through a friend who worked at the bakery. We hired her to head our tortilla production after she graduated from Hot Bread Kitchen's training program. Taught well by her grandmother, Nancy drew on her family knowledge and decades of experience to improve our product and streamline our production. Nancy has developed, and makes, the finest tortillas in New York City. Much of what Nancy does looks deceptively simple, yet her touch and intuition are key to the thousands of tortillas that our market and restaurant clients buy every week. The hardest part of her job is keeping up with the demand she's created! Perhaps the biggest compliment she's been paid is by her eight-year-old daughter, Alexa, who recently told Nancy that when she grows up, she wants to make tortillas just like her mom. Nancy's *abuela* would be *muy orgullosa* (so proud). Talk about continuing traditions.

# TORTILLAS

**MAKES 10 (6-INCH/15 CM) TORTILLAS**

1 pound/about 3 cups/455 g **MASA FROM NIXTAMAL** (page 89), **MASA FROM MASA HARINA** (page 90), or store-bought **FRESH MASA**

**NOTE:** A 6-inch/15 cm tortilla is a good size for a tostada, but for tacos you might prefer a smaller size (see page 110). Use this chart to find the perfect tortilla size for you.

| Tortilla Size | Recipe Yield | Weight of Masa |
|---|---|---|
| 4 in/10 cm | 30 | 1/2 oz/15 g |
| 5 in/13 cm | 12 | 1 oz/30 g |
| 7 in/18 cm | 8 | 2 oz/55 g |

I am a firm believer that the tortilla makes the taco. It is a travesty to slow cook meats and beans, source delicious cheeses, and chop fresh herbs, and throw them into stale, chemical-laden bread. Masa has no gluten to hold the dough together, so it may take a little practice to learn how to handle it. The good news is that there is no harm in balling the dough from a failed tortilla attempt back together and pressing it again. For this recipe, I recommend purchasing a tortilla press, though it is not necessary. You can readily scale up this recipe for a crowd—just enlist a strong helper for the pressing!

**1.** Roll your masa into a large ball. If the dough crumbles or feels dry, sprinkle some water on the outside and knead for 30 seconds to integrate. The dough should feel firm and supple—like fresh Play-Doh.

**2.** Roll the dough into a log about 1½ inches/4 cm thick and slice it crosswise into 10 equal pieces (each about 1½ ounces/45 g). Roll each piece into a small ball. Cover them loosely with plastic wrap or a damp towel to keep the dough from drying out as you press and cook each tortilla.

**3.** Put your tortilla press on a table at a comfortable height, so that you can use your body weight to assist in the pressing. A kitchen table might be better than a counter, depending on your height. If you don't have a tortilla press, you can use a heavy cutting board as the bottom and a heavy metal saucepan with a flat bottom as the top.

**4.** Set a griddle or large cast iron skillet over high heat. Line a basket or a shallow bowl with a clean cloth napkin. Cut a plastic produce bag at the seams, so that you have two pieces of thin plastic.

**5.** Put one piece of plastic on the tortilla press, then put one of the dough balls on top of the plastic, push down lightly with the heel of your hand so that it turns into a thick disk, and cover the top with the remaining plastic. Using a tortilla press (or your metal pan), flatten the tortilla. Open the press, turn the tortilla 180 degrees, and repeat the process so that you have a very thin circular tortilla that measures 6 inches/15 cm in diameter. When pressing, be sure to jiggle the handle a bit for extra force.

**6.** Hold the flattened tortilla in the palm of your hand. Peel off the top piece of plastic. Gently transfer the tortilla to the other hand with the plastic facing up and peel off that plastic. Now you will have only the masa disk in your hand with one side hanging slightly off your hand. Starting with the part that is hanging, gently lay the tortilla on the hot griddle by pulling your hand away. The tortilla should lie flat on the pan without any creases.

**7.** Cook the first side of the tortilla just until the edges begin to dry, about 1 minute. Flip and cook the tortilla until you start to see some steam puffing up inside of it and brown spots developing on the underside, about another 2 minutes. To encourage the steam, you can take your fingertips or a spatula and lightly press down on the tortilla. Flip it onto the first side one more time, and cook for just 30 seconds to get some brown spots. The cooking speed depends on the heat of your cooking surface. Hotter is better. A great tortilla will have two distinct layers, which develop when the heat is hot enough to create steam that puffs the dough and helps it separate. (Note that if the tortilla puffs up while cooking, it's said to mean that you're ready to get married!)

**8.** Transfer the cooked tortilla to the napkin-lined basket and cover with the napkin. Repeat the process until you've used up all of your dough, being sure to keep the cooked tortillas wrapped in the napkin. Serve warm.

When I was launching Hot Bread Kitchen, we made only a few dozen tortillas per shift—all by hand. We used a hand-powered *molino* (mill) to grind the corn for Masa from Nixtamal (page 89) and pressed each tortilla with a wooden tortilla press that Elidia, Hot Bread's first baker, had brought with her when she crossed the Rio Grande. As our production grew, so did the muscles in our right arms. Grinding 10 pounds of corn by hand takes a long time—pressing each tortilla, even longer.

At the time I was paying my bills by consulting for Amnesty International. Through that work, I met a young man and in the course of our conversation details of my fledgling nighttime tortilla business came out, as did my desperate need for a better corn-grinding machine. He mentioned that his dad, Peter Brock, an architect and inventor in Berkeley, California,

were seriously into bike machines. I was introduced to Peter, and we had just one conversation to discuss what a corn-grinding bike might look like. Two months later, voilà! A great big box arrived at my door: Peter had designed and built us an amazing corn-grinding bicycle that he dubbed the Jessa-Molino 2000.

And, soon enough, even though it was a huge advancement over our hand-powered grinder, we outgrew the bicycle-powered grinder and needed one that could handle larger amounts of corn. When Elidia went home to Mexico to visit family, she was also tasked with finding us an electric *molino*. I got one staticky call asking me to wire her $400. I did so happily and eagerly awaited the arrival of our *molino*—something I imagined would be the size of a food processor.

A few weeks later, a tractor-trailer showed up outside my Brooklyn brownstone apartment.

Inside was our new *molino*—and it was the size of a Volkswagen Bug. I had to pay neighbors in beer to lug it up the front steps and do some fast-talking when the landlord caught us bringing it inside. Needless to say, we turbo-charged our tortilla production. We used that grinder until we moved to La Marqueta, when all of a sudden we had a different obstacle: We could now grind hundreds of pounds of corn, but we were still balling and pressing it by hand.

So in 2011, I visited every *nixtamal* tortilleria in East Los Angeles looking for a solution. With the support of a visionary philanthropic investor, we purchased a combination *molino*/press/tunnel oven. We have a tank to prepare corn for nixtamalization and a stone grinder that flies through grain. The masa goes into a funnel at the top, which feeds the dough through a flattener. Then the machine cuts the dough into rounds and sends them through an oven that looks like a Rube Goldberg machine. Fully baked fluffy tortillas emerge, ready to be cooled on a rack before they get vacuum-sealed, labeled, and delivered all around New York. It has been hundreds of pounds of trial and error, but Nancy Mendez, our tortilla coordinator, has definitely mastered the process. Now we make thousands of fresh tortillas every week. That would probably be the equivalent of riding from New York to East L.A. if we had to grind it on the bike.

# TAMALES VERDES CON POLLO

MAKES 12 TAMALES; SERVES 6

15 **CORN HUSKS** (see Notes)

2 bone-in, skin-on **CHICKEN BREAST HALVES**

½ **YELLOW ONION**

4 **GARLIC CLOVES**

**KOSHER SALT**

½ pound/225 g **TOMATILLOS**, husked, rinsed, and roughly chopped

2 to 3 **JALAPEÑOS**, roughly chopped (seeded if you want less heat)

1 teaspoon **DRIED MEXICAN OREGANO** (see Notes)

½ teaspoon **CUMIN SEEDS**

3 **CLOVES**

3 **ALLSPICE BERRIES**

¼ cup/55 g **COLD WATER**

1 tablespoon **CANOLA OIL**

1 pound/about 3 cups/455 g **MASA FROM NIXTAMAL** (page 89), **MASA FROM MASA HARINA** (page 90), or store-bought **FRESH MASA**

½ cup/115 g **RENDERED LARD** or additional **CANOLA OIL**

Olga Luna, a bakery trainee, taught me how to make tamales with a spicy tomatillo sauce. Ideally they should be prepared with fresh masa from *nixtamal* but also work well with masa made from masa harina. When I asked Olga how she handles leftovers, she looked at me like I was from another planet. She told me that her son can eat nine tamales for dinner! Needless to say, these are so good that leftovers usually aren't an issue, though they can be reheated in a pinch.

1. Soak the corn husks in cold water for at least 30 minutes and up to overnight.

2. Put the chicken, onion, and 2 of the garlic cloves in a large pot and cover with cold water. Add a large pinch of salt and bring to a boil. Skim off and discard any foam that rises to the top. Reduce the heat and simmer until the chicken is firm to the touch, about 30 minutes. Transfer the chicken to a plate and reserve the broth. Once the chicken is cool enough to handle, shred the meat (discard the skin and bones).

3. Meanwhile, put the remaining 2 garlic cloves, tomatillos, jalapeños, oregano, cumin, cloves, and allspice in a blender. Add the water and a large pinch of salt and blend until pureed.

4. Heat the canola oil in a large skillet over high heat until shimmering. Add the tomatillo mixture and ½ cup/120 ml of the reserved chicken broth. Bring the mixture to a rolling boil, then reduce the heat and simmer, stirring now and then, until the sauce is thickened and has lost its bright color (you're getting flavor in exchange!), about

10 minutes. Season the sauce to taste with salt.

5. Put the masa in a large bowl and add ½ teaspoon salt and the lard. Mix everything together with your hands. The mixture should be moist, but dry enough to hold a shape if you roll a small piece into a ball. Add some of the reserved chicken broth if it is dry. Another test to make sure you have the right ratio of masa to fat is to form a ball with a small handful of the mixture and inspect the surface when you touch it: It should be smooth and not have any cracks. Add more of the chicken broth if you're not there yet.

6. Drain the corn husks. Put a corn husk in the palm of one of your hands so that it forms a cup. Add a handful of masa mixture (about ⅓ cup/65 g) so that it rests toward the top of the corn husk—you want at least 3 inches/7.5 cm of empty corn husk beneath the masa mixture. Press the masa mixture down to flatten it and top with a few tablespoons of the tomatillo sauce and then add a small handful

*recipe continues*

**NOTES:** The filling is meant to be evenly distributed among 12 corn husks, but the ingredient list calls for 15 husks in case you have a few narrow husks and need to double them up or one is cracked. If you have extra corn husks at the end, you can tear a few into thin strips and use them to tie each tamale into a neat, tidy package. They don't, however, need to be tied to be cooked properly.

Olga suggests using Mexican oregano, which is stronger in flavor and a little bit less sweet tasting than standard dried oregano, which is most often from the Mediterranean. See page 291 for sources or simply substitute 1 tablespoon regular oregano instead.

(about ¼ cup/25 g) of the shredded chicken. Roll the corn husk around the mixture so that it forms a cylinder and then fold the bottom up so that the filling won't come out (leave the top open). Stack the filled and rolled tamales in a pile.

**7.** Set up a large steamer that will accommodate all of your tamales. There are specialty tamale steamers, but any type of steamer will work, as will a large heatproof colander set inside of a large pot filled with a few inches of water. Just make sure the water doesn't touch the tamales. Cover the steamer and bring the water to a boil over high heat.

**8.** Stack the tamales inside of the steamer like Lincoln Logs and cover tightly with foil or a lid. Steam the tamales, checking occasionally to make sure the water

has not evaporated and adding more as needed, until the masa is cooked through, about 1 hour. To check if they're cooked through, unwrap one tamale and check the masa: It should be firm and moist. When you break off a piece of masa with your hand or a fork, it should break off cleanly and easily and appear almost like a steamed cake. If the masa mixture is still too soft, continue steaming the tamales for a little longer. Note that the masa mixture will continue to firm as the tamales cool a little.

**9.** Serve the tamales immediately in the husks, letting everyone unwrap them at the table. Leftovers can be reheated, in their husks, on a comal (griddle) or in a dry cast iron skillet over high heat until dark brown on both sides (which will give them an extra toasty, nutty flavor).

## Vegetarian Tamales

For an excellent vegetarian variation, Olga suggests making spicy tomato tamales with cheese. Heat 2 tablespoons canola oil in a large skillet over medium-high heat. Add 5 roughly chopped tomatoes, 1½ thinly sliced garlic cloves, and 2 thickly sliced seeded jalapeños. Sauté until softened, about 10 minutes, then add ½ cup/115 g vegetable broth and simmer until the mixture is stewed and soft, about 10 minutes more. Season to taste with salt and set aside to cool. Fill each tamale with about ⅓ cup/65 g of the masa mixture (use canola oil instead of lard to keep it vegetarian), a spoonful of the tomato mixture (being sure to get a piece of jalapeño in each tamale), and add a slice of cheese (preferably *queso de freír,* see Note, page 98, but you can substitute Monterey Jack cheese). Roll the tamales and steam them as directed.

# FLAUTAS DE QUESO

**MAKES 24 FLAUTAS; SERVES 8**

1 (16-ounce/455 g) block **QUESO DE FREÍR** (see Note)

24 (6-inch/15 cm) **CORN TORTILLAS**, homemade (page 92) or store-bought

**CANOLA OIL**

**KOSHER SALT**

2 cups/475 g **REFRIED BEANS** (page 109), warmed

1 cup/75 g shredded **ICEBERG LETTUCE**

½ cup/120 g **MEXICAN CREMA**, homemade (page 108) or store-bought

½ cup/50 g grated **COTIJA** or crumbled **FETA CHEESE**

**SALSA VERDE** (page 108)

> **NOTE:** *Queso de freír* is a chewy white Mexican cheese made for frying; you can substitute Monterey Jack or halloumi instead.

A flauta, also known as a taquíto, is a rolled taco that's fried until crisp. Flautas make great appetizers or can be a meal on their own served alongside extra refried beans, rice, and a fresh avocado salad. Cheese is the simplest filling, but experiment with cooked mashed potatoes or the *tinga* from Tinga Tostadas (page 101). Spicy Salsa Verde (page 108) is a must.

**1.** Cut the block of cheese into 24 sticks: To do this, cut the block of cheese in half horizontally, through the middle. Then cut each of the two resulting rectangles crosswise into 12 pieces so that you end up with 24 sticks of cheese.

**2.** Working with one tortilla at a time (keep the rest covered with plastic), roll a piece of cheese inside the tortilla and use a toothpick to securely close the tortilla. You can do this a few hours in advance; wrap the flautas with plastic wrap or drape with a damp kitchen towel to keep the tortillas from drying out.

**3.** Pour 2 inches/5 cm of canola oil into a large pot or a deep skillet. Heat over medium-high heat until a frying thermometer reads 350°F/180°C (or when you add a flauta and the oil bubbles vigorously). Add as many flautas as you can fit in a single layer, seam side down. Fry them, pressing down with tongs or a spatula to keep them submerged, turning once or twice, until browned and crisp, about 2 minutes total. Transfer the flautas to a baking sheet lined with paper towels and sprinkle with salt. Fry the remaining flautas, adding more oil if necessary and letting it come back up to temperature between batches.

**4.** Discard the toothpicks and serve the flautas on a warm serving platter. Top with the refried black beans, shredded lettuce, *crema*, cheese, and salsa verde. Serve immediately.

# SPAGHETTI SQUASH TACOS

**MAKES 12 TACOS; SERVES 4**

1 (3-pound/1.4 kg) **SPAGHETTI SQUASH**, halved lengthwise and seeded

1 tablespoon **EXTRA-VIRGIN OLIVE OIL**

Juice of 1 **LIME**

½ teaspoon **CHILE POWDER**

½ teaspoon ground **CUMIN**

½ teaspoon ground **CORIANDER**

**KOSHER SALT**

12 (5-inch/13 cm) **CORN TORTILLAS**, homemade (page 92) or store-bought

2 cups/475 g **REFRIED BEANS** (page 109), warmed, or 1 (15-ounce/425 g) can black beans, rinsed and drained

¼ **RED ONION**, thinly sliced

½ cup/50 g grated **COTIJA** or crumbled **FETA CHEESE**

Small handful of finely chopped **FRESH CILANTRO**

Selling our products at New York City's farmers' markets keeps us in close proximity to tons of wonderful local produce. We're always looking for ways to incorporate all sorts of fruits and vegetables into our recipes so that we can collaborate with our farmer friends. These tacos, great for vegetarians (and vegans if you forgo the cheese), are a fun way to use a favorite fall vegetable.

**1.** Preheat the oven to 400°F/205°C.

**2.** Rub the cut sides of the squash halves with the olive oil, put them cut side up on a rimmed baking sheet, and roast until tender, about 45 minutes.

**3.** Use a fork to shred the flesh into spaghetti-like strands into a large bowl (discard the skin). Add the lime juice, chile powder, cumin, and coriander. Season to taste with salt.

**4.** Heat the tortillas in a dry skillet set over medium high or directly over the flames on your stove. Divide the beans, spaghetti squash, onion, cheese, and cilantro among the tortillas and serve immediately.

# TINGA TOSTADAS

MAKES 12 TOSTADAS; SERVES 4

## TINGA

2 bone-in, skin-on **CHICKEN BREAST HALVES**

1 **YELLOW ONION**, halved

4 **GARLIC CLOVES**, crushed and peeled

**KOSHER SALT**

3 **TOMATOES**

1 to 2 canned **CHIPOTLE PEPPERS IN ADOBO SAUCE** (to taste)

3 tablespoons **EXTRA-VIRGIN OLIVE OIL**

4 sprigs **FRESH THYME**

**NOTE:** As mentioned, the chicken *tinga* (pulled chicken) is versatile. For tacos, where the filling should be less saucy, you can make *tinga* in the style of carnitas: Poach the chicken with the flavors in the sauce (onion, garlic, tomatoes, and chipotles), then shred the flavorful meat and fry it until the pieces are browned and crisp.

*Tostadas de tinga* are a classic Mexican street food made with saucy chicken. Because the crispy tostada (fried tortilla) inevitably breaks when you bite into it, all over Mexico City you can see people next to tostada stands bent forward to avoid shirt stains from a falling piece of this delicious pulled chicken. Tostadas make a great appetizer, snack, or light lunch and are also one of the best ways that I know to use leftover *nixtamal* tortillas. The *tinga*, chicken braised in a spicy chipotle and tomato sauce, is worth making ahead of time, since its flavor improves if it sits overnight and then gently reheats. The *tinga* is incredibly versatile—you can use it in tacos (see Note), Carnitas Cemitas (page 135), or on Gorditas (page 104). If you prefer pork, you can definitely substitute either carnitas recipe (page 106 or 107) in this tostada.

**1.** To make the *tinga*, put the chicken breasts in a large pot and cover with cold water. Add one of the onion halves, 2 of the garlic cloves, and 1 teaspoon salt. Bring to a boil over high heat, skimming off and discarding any foam that rises to the top. Reduce the heat and simmer until the chicken is firm to the touch, about 30 minutes. Transfer the chicken to a bowl and set aside until cool enough to handle. Reserve the chicken broth (discard the onion and garlic). Once the chicken is cool, shred the chicken meat with your hands (discard the skin and bones).

**2.** Meanwhile, bring a large pot of water to a boil. Score the bottom of each tomato with an "X" and drop into the boiling water. Cook until the skin starts to peel, about 1 minute, and use a slotted spoon to transfer the tomatoes to a bowl or a plate. When they're cool enough to handle, peel the tomatoes and transfer to a blender with

the remaining 2 garlic cloves, the chipotles, and ½ teaspoon salt. Blend until smooth.

**3.** Slice the remaining onion half into thin half-moons. Heat the olive oil in a large pot over medium-high heat and add the onion, thyme, and a large pinch of salt. Cook, stirring now and then, until the onion just begins to soften, about 10 minutes.

**4.** Add the shredded chicken and the tomato mixture to the pot along with 1 cup/240 ml of the reserved chicken broth (save the rest for something else or freeze it for future use). Bring the mixture to a boil, reduce the heat, and simmer until the chicken is very tender and all of the flavors are well developed, about 20 minutes. Season to taste with salt. Keep the *tinga* warm.

*recipe continues*

## TOSTADAS

**CANOLA OIL**

12 (6-inch/15 cm) **CORN TORTILLAS**, homemade (page 92) or store-bought

1½ cups/360 g **REFRIED BEANS** (page 109), warmed

½ head **ICEBERG LETTUCE**, shredded

1 **TOMATO** finely diced

½ cup/120 g **MEXICAN CREMA**, homemade (page 108) or store-bought

½ cup/50 g grated **COTIJA** or crumbled **FETA CHEESE**

**5.** Meanwhile, to make the tostadas: Pour 1 inch/2.5 cm of canola oil into a large pot or a deep skillet and heat over medium-high heat. Once the oil is hot (when you add a tortilla, the oil should bubble vigorously), add as many tortillas as you can fit in a single layer and fry them, pressing down with tongs or a spatula to keep them flat, until browned and crisp, about 1 minute per side. Transfer the crisp tortillas to a baking sheet lined with paper towels to cool. Fry the remaining tortillas, adding more oil to the pot if necessary and waiting for the oil to get hot in between batches.

**6.** To assemble the tostadas, spread each one with 2 tablespoons refried black beans, top with a large spoonful of *tinga*, a small handful of shredded lettuce, some diced tomato, a drizzle of *crema,* and a generous sprinkling of cheese.

# GORDITAS

MAKES 6 GORDITAS; SERVES 3

1 pound/about 3 cups/455 g **MASA FROM NIXTAMAL** (page 89) or **MASA FROM MASA HARINA** (page 90)

¼ cup/55 g rendered **LARD** or **VEGETABLE OIL**, plus more for frying

**KOSHER SALT**

¾ cup/180 g **REFRIED BEANS** (page 109)

½ cup/130 g **SALSA VERDE** (page 108)

¼ cup/60 g **MEXICAN CREMA**, homemade (page 108) or store-bought

¼ cup/25 g grated **COTIJA** or crumbled **FETA CHEESE**

Elidia, our first baker, and I have worked together for hundreds of hours in our rental kitchen in Queens, becoming close friends. She helped me with everything from finding recipes to finding a husband and, of course, running a business. One day, early on, a group of potential investors was coming to visit and I asked her to make something special using our masa. Elidia prepared gorditas—savory corn cakes made by frying small disks of masa so that they're crispy on the outside and tender inside. They're the greatest little boats for all sorts of toppings, including carnitas (pages 106 and 107) and *tinga* (page 101). Needless to say, we got the investment.

**1.** Put the masa in a large bowl with the lard and ½ teaspoon salt and mix together. Knead the dough with your hands to a soft Play-Doh consistency, adding warm water if necessary. Divide the dough into 6 equal pieces (each weighing about 2½ ounces/75 g), and roll each into a ball. Gently press each one down to make a flat disk about ½ inch/1.5 cm thick and about 4 inches/10 cm in diameter. If the edges are cracked when you form the first disk, add a little bit more water, a tablespoon at a time, to the remaining masa before continuing.

**2.** Set a large cast iron skillet or griddle over high heat. Working in batches if necessary, add the gorditas to the pan in a single layer and cook, turning once, until lightly browned on both sides, about 2 minutes per side. Transfer a gordita to a platter and use your fingers or the back of a spoon to make a small indentation (½ inch/1.5 cm deep) in the top (only do this on one side). Repeat for all the disks.

**3.** Heat ¼ inch/6 mm fat (lard or oil) in a cast iron skillet set over medium high until it's shimmering. Working in batches, cook the gorditas in the hot fat, turning once, until golden brown and crisp on both sides, about 2 minutes per side. Transfer the gorditas to a plate lined with paper towels and sprinkle each one with a little bit of salt.

**4.** Top the indentation of each gordita with refried beans, salsa verde, *crema*, and cheese and serve immediately.

# SLOW-AND-LOW CARNITAS

**MAKES ENOUGH FILLING FOR 24 TACOS OR 8 TO 10 CEMITAS; SERVES 8 TO 10**

4 pounds/1.8 kg **BONELESS PORK SHOULDER**, skin and excess fat trimmed, cut into 2-inch/5 cm pieces

**KOSHER SALT**

5 tablespoons/70 g **CANOLA OIL**

1 tablespoon **FRESH THYME LEAVES**, chopped

6 **GARLIC CLOVES**, minced

1 teaspoon ground **CHILE POWDER**

1 teaspoon ground **CUMIN**

Grated zest and juice of 1 **ORANGE**

1 (12-ounce/355 ml) **BOTTLE BEER**, preferably a dark beer like Negra Modelo

1 cup/225 g **WATER**

Carnitas is, in my estimation, the gold standard for taco fillings. This version of carnitas takes nearly 4 hours to cook, but most of the cooking is unattended and the results are delicious. Except for crisping the meat at the end, you can make the braised pork in advance; in fact, it's even better if you do. This is an ideal filling for tacos (see page 110), Carnitas Cemitas (page 135), tostadas, or Gorditas (page 104). Whichever way you make it, do not forget to top it with the Salsa Verde (page 108).

**1.** Preheat the oven to 300°F/150°C.

**2.** Generously season the pork all over with 1½ teaspoons salt and let it sit at room temperature for about 1 hour so that it comes to room temperature.

**3.** Heat 2 tablespoons of the oil in a wide, heavy pot over medium-high heat. Working in batches if necessary, add the pork in a single layer. Cook, turning now and then, until well browned on each side, about 15 minutes. Transfer the pork to a large plate.

**4.** Add the thyme, garlic, chile powder, and cumin to the skillet and cook, stirring a bit, until the aromatics are fragrant, about a minute. Add the orange zest, orange juice, beer, and water and bring the mixture to a boil. Reduce the heat and simmer for 2 minutes, scraping the bottom with a wooden spoon, until you've released all the tasty bits of browned pork. Return the pork and any juices that have accumulated on the plate to the pot.

**5.** Transfer the pot, uncovered, to the oven and oven-braise the pork, turning it every 30 minutes or so, until much of the liquid has evaporated and the pork is falling-apart tender, about 4 hours. Transfer the pork to a platter or a baking dish and let it rest until it's cool enough to handle. Reserve the cooking liquid.

**6.** Use your hands to shred the meat into bite-size pieces, discarding any huge chunks of fat along the way.

**7.** Heat the remaining 3 tablespoons oil in a large, heavy skillet over medium-high heat. Working in batches if necessary, put a single layer of shredded pork in the skillet along with a little of its cooking liquid, and cook, turning the pieces now and then, until they're browned and crispy in places, about 10 minutes. Serve hot.

# FAST CARNITAS

**MAKES ENOUGH FILLING FOR 24 TACOS OR 8 TO 10 CEMITAS; SERVES 8 TO 10**

4 pounds/1.8 kg **BONELESS PORK SHOULDER**, skin and excess fat trimmed, cut into 2-inch/5 cm pieces

**KOSHER SALT**

½ cup/110 g **CANOLA OIL**

Leaves from 8 sprigs **FRESH OREGANO**

Nancy recently taught me how to make a fast carnitas, a savory porky filling that's great for Gorditas (page 104), tacos, tostadas, and even Carnitas Cemitas (page 135). There are two important details in this method. First, bring the pork to room temperature before starting the recipe so that the meat cooks quickly and evenly. Second, be patient while browning the pork—let it go past the point of being browned to getting really very dark brown. Nancy describes it as the color of shoe leather; I prefer mahogany.

**1.** Generously season the pork all over with 1½ teaspoons salt and let it sit at room temperature for about 1 hour so that it comes to room temperature.

**2.** Heat the oil in a large, heavy skillet over medium-high heat. Working in batches if necessary, add the pork and oregano in a single layer. Cook, turning now and then, until the pork is well browned on all sides, about 15 minutes.

**3.** Once all of the pork has been browned, return it all to the pan and reduce the heat to medium-low. Put a lid slightly ajar on the pan and cook the pork, stirring occasionally, until even more browned and tender, a further 15 minutes.

**4.** Use tongs to remove the pork from the skillet and set it aside on a plate until it's cool enough to handle. Reserve the oil and oregano in the pan.

**5.** Cut the pork into ½-inch/1.5 cm cubes. Put the skillet back over medium-high heat and return the pork to the skillet. Cook, seasoning with salt to taste, until the cubes are crisp, about 10 minutes. Serve hot, garnished with the fried oregano.

# SALSA VERDE

**MAKES 2 CUPS/480 G**

1½ pounds/680 g **TOMATILLOS**, husked and rinsed

1 to 2 **JALAPEÑOS** or **SERRANO CHILES** (to taste)

3 **GARLIC CLOVES**, peeled but whole

½ packed cup/20 g **FRESH CILANTRO LEAVES**

1 tablespoon **KOSHER SALT**, or more to taste

This makes a simple and delicious sauce for nearly every recipe in this chapter. Elidia, my first employee, taught me how to make this version and I like it so much I could drink it as a soup. It's really about the freshness of the tomatillos and having the cojones to salt them enough to offset their acidity. In fact, lots of salt is the simple difference between okay salsa verde and terrific salsa verde. Don't hold back.

**1.** Bring a large pot of water to a boil. Add the tomatillos and chiles and cook until the vegetables are softened, the skin from the tomatillos begins to split, and they go from bright green to more of an olive green, about 10 minutes. Use a slotted spoon to transfer the vegetables to a cutting board. Cut out and discard the cores of the tomatillos and the chile stems. Reserve ½ cup/120 ml of the cooking liquid.

**2.** With a food processor running, drop the garlic through the feed tube. Add the tomatillos and chiles, the reserved cooking liquid, and the cilantro. Puree until smooth and season assertively with salt. Serve at room temperature. Store in an airtight container in the refrigerator for up to 5 days.

# MEXICAN CREMA

**MAKES ¾ CUP/180 G**

½ cup/120 g **SOUR CREAM**

¼ cup/60 g **WHOLE MILK**

½ teaspoon **KOSHER SALT**

While sour cream comes with just about every Tex-Mex dish, real Mexican *crema* isn't the same thing; it's a bit saltier and thinner, too, so it's very easy to drizzle on top of things. It's readily available in Latin American grocery stores and increasingly available at big supermarkets. But if you can't find it, substitute this mixture.

Whisk together the sour cream, milk, and salt in a small bowl. Cover and refrigerate until needed, or for up to 1 week.

# REFRIED BEANS

MAKES 8½ CUPS/2 KG; SERVES 8

1 pound/455 g **DRIED BLACK BEANS**

3 tablespoons **CANOLA OIL**

1 large **YELLOW ONION**, finely diced

3 **GARLIC CLOVES**, minced

1 tablespoon **FRESH OREGANO LEAVES**, finely chopped

**KOSHER SALT**

These beans are an ingredient in many of Hot Bread Kitchen's favorite dishes, including Carnitas Cemitas (page 135) and tostadas (page 101), and also make a meal when served with a pot of perfectly cooked rice. They aren't really "refried"—more like well reduced to intensify the flavors. Serve drizzled with Mexican Crema (page 108) and scattered with chopped cilantro and grated Cotija cheese.

**1.** Put the beans in a bowl and add enough cold water to cover by at least 2 inches/5 cm. Let soak overnight.

**2.** Drain the beans, transfer to a large pot, and cover with 5 cups/ 1.1 liters cold water. Bring to a boil, reduce the heat, partially cover, and simmer until the beans are tender, 1 to 2 hours depending on their age.

**3.** Measure out 2 cups/475 ml of the cooking liquid and set aside. Drain the beans and return them to the pot along with the reserved liquid. Using an immersion blender (or a regular blender or food processor), puree the mixture until very smooth.

**4.** Meanwhile, heat the oil in a large pot over medium-high heat. Add the onion, garlic, oregano, and a large pinch of salt and cook, stirring now and then, until the aromatics are soft, about 10 minutes. Add the pureed beans to the pot and bring the mixture to a boil. Reduce the heat, season to taste with salt, and simmer until the mixture is really thick and all of the flavors are well blended, about 10 minutes. The mixture should be thick but pourable. If it's too thick, add a little cooking liquid or water. Serve warm. You can make these ahead and store them in an airtight container in the refrigerator for up to 1 week. Reheat over low heat, adding a little water if necessary.

# HOW TO MAKE LEGIT TACOS

Tacos shouldn't be overstuffed, complicated, or hard to eat. You want to build tacos that celebrate your beautiful tortillas.

- Start with fresh, warm corn tortillas. If you're working with tortillas that have cooled down, reheat them (see page 87). Traditionally tacos in Mexico use two 4-inch tortillas stacked for every taco. When serving shoddy commercial tortillas, this ensures you don't end up with a broken tortilla and carnitas in your lap, and provides back-up if any of the meat is left on the plate. If you are enjoying handmade tortillas, they will be thicker, more flavorful, and sturdier, so you don't really need to double up. We recommend one 5-inch/13 cm tortilla per taco for these recipes.

- Tacos should be limited to a single protein, such as carnitas (pages 106 and 107) or the chicken mixture from Tinga Tostadas (page 101), or a vegetarian option like the filling for Spaghetti Squash Tacos (page 100). Whatever your filling, add only a small amount (¼ cup/60 g) so that the taco can be easily handled—and you can eat more of them and your delicious tortillas.

- Tacos should be topped simply. Typically, tacos get a little bit of finely diced raw white onion and roughly chopped cilantro. That's it. Sliced or whole radishes can be served alongside, along with pickled jalapeños, lime wedges, and Salsa Verde (page 108). Of course a little Cotija cheese on top never hurt anyone . . . If you can't find Cotija, crumbled feta cheese works as a good substitute.

Spaghetti Squash Taco (page 100), blue corn tortilla with tinga (page 101), yellow corn tortilla with Slow-and-Low Carnitas (page 106), served with Guacamole (page 113), Refried Beans (page 109), Mexican Crema (page 108), and Salsa Verde (page 108)

# BAKED CHILE, CUMIN, AND LIME
# TORTILLA CHIPS

**MAKES 6 CUPS**

12 (6-inch/15 cm) blue, white, or yellow **CORN TORTILLAS**, homemade (page 92) or store-bought

3 tablespoons **COCONUT OIL**, melted, or **OLIVE** or **CANOLA OIL**

¼ cup/55 g fresh **LIME JUICE**

1 teaspoon ground **CHILE POWDER**

1 teaspoon ground **CUMIN**

1 teaspoon **KOSHER SALT**

### Fried Tortilla Chips

Fry the naked tortilla wedges in a generous amount of 375°F/190°C canola oil until browned and crisp, turning once, about 4 minutes total. Transfer to paper towels to drain and then toss with the lime juice, chile powder, cumin, and salt.

We don't usually sell tortilla chips because they're hard to prepare in large quantities by hand, but we make an exception for Super Bowl Sunday. When I make these at home, I like to bake them—they're a bit healthier and cleanup is easier. While there's nothing boring about regular, salted chips, this combination of chile, cumin, and lime is really delicious. For added visual appeal, use a combination of blue, white, and yellow corn tortillas. (*See photograph on page 111.*)

**1.** Preheat the oven to 375°F/190°C.

**2.** Stack the tortillas and cut them into 8 wedges. Divide the wedges between 2 rimmed baking sheets and arrange them in a single layer.

**3.** Whisk together the oil, lime juice, chile powder, cumin, and salt in a small bowl. Use a brush to lightly coat the chips on one side with the mixture.

**4.** Transfer the baking sheets to the oven and bake until the chips are beginning to get crisp and brown, about 7 minutes. Remove the baking sheets from the oven, turn each chip over, and brush with a little more fat. Return to the oven, switching the baking sheets from top to bottom, until the chips are crisp and just barely browned, another 5 to 7 minutes.

**5.** Let the chips cool to room temperature (they will get even crispier as they cool) before serving.

# GUACAMOLE

**SERVES 8 TO 10**

4 **HASS AVOCADOS**, peeled and pitted (reserve the pits)

8 **PLUM TOMATOES**, finely diced

1 small bunch **CILANTRO**, leaves and tender stems finely chopped (about 1½ cups/60 g)

1 small **WHITE ONION**, finely diced

1 to 3 **SERRANO CHILES** (to taste), seeded and thinly sliced

Juice of 1½ **LEMONS**

**KOSHER SALT** and freshly ground **BLACK PEPPER**

There are many schools of thought when it comes to guacamole, but this version—studded with lots of cilantro, onion, tomatoes, and serrano chiles and seasoned with lemon—is Nancy's specialty. Sometimes when her shift is over at Hot Bread Kitchen, she'll fry a bunch of tortillas into chips and make a batch of this guacamole and everyone goes crazy for it. The key to really good guacamole is choosing avocados at the perfect ripeness; you want ones with skin that is entirely black but still a little firm to the touch. I also check that the stem is still intact, which is a good way to ensure that they aren't overripe.

**1.** Put the avocados, tomatoes, cilantro, onion, chiles, and lemon juice in a large bowl. Use a fork to combine the ingredients. Ultimately you want the guacamole to be smooth enough so that it's easy to scoop up with a chip, but not so smooth that every bite is the same; there should be some pieces of avocado intact for texture. Season the guacamole to taste with salt and pepper.

**2.** If you're not serving the guacamole immediately, insert the avocado pits into it and cover with plastic wrap, pressing it directly onto the surface of the guacamole, to keep it from browning. Store it this way at room temperature for no longer than 1 hour. After that, refrigerate for up to 1 day.

# TAMALES DULCES
## WITH CINNAMON AND PINEAPPLE

**MAKES 24 TAMALES**

30 **CORN HUSKS** (see Notes, page 97)

2 **CINNAMON** sticks

½ cup/100 g **SUGAR**

3 cups/680 g **WATER**

3 cups/390 g **MASA HARINA** (preferably Bob's Red Mill), or more if needed

16 tablespoons/225 g **UNSALTED BUTTER**, melted and cooled

2 drops **RED FOOD COLORING** or **BEET JUICE** (optional)

1 (20-ounce/565 g) can **SLICED PINEAPPLE**, drained

½ cup/65 g **RAISINS**

These sweet tamales make a beautiful dessert at the end of a Mexican meal or a welcome snack. Drizzle them with a little condensed milk when you serve them if you really want to gild the lily. Tamales dulces are usually pink like Olga's. The pink color makes them easier to identify in the pot (and makes them appealing to kids, perhaps), but since it doesn't affect the taste, I have made the coloring optional.

1. Soak the corn husks in cold water for at least 30 minutes and up to overnight.

2. Put the cinnamon sticks, sugar, and water in a saucepan, bring to a boil, and stir to dissolve the sugar. Remove from the heat and set aside to cool.

3. Put the masa harina in a large bowl and add the melted butter and food coloring. Strain the cinnamon syrup into the bowl (discard the cinnamon sticks) and mix everything together vigorously with a wooden spoon. The mixture should be moist but dry enough to hold a shape if you roll a small piece into a ball. Another test to make sure you have the right ratio of masa to fat and water is to form a ball with a small handful of the mixture and inspect the surface when you touch it: It should be smooth and not have any cracks. Add a little warm water if you're not there yet. If you've added too much liquid, simply add more masa harina until you achieve the right consistency.

4. Assembly time! Drain the corn husks. Put a corn husk in the palm of one of your hands so that it naturally forms a cup. Add a handful of masa mixture (about ⅓ cup/45 g) so that it rests toward the top of the corn husk—you want at least 3 inches/7.5 cm of empty corn husk beneath the masa mixture. Press the masa mixture down and top with a half slice of pineapple and a couple of raisins. Roll the corn husk around the mixture so that it forms a cylinder and then fold the bottom up so that the filling won't come out. Stack the filled and rolled tamales in a pile.

5. Steam the tamales as directed on page 97.

# THE DARK, CRUSTY LOAF

## LEAN BREADS AND ROLLS

The breads in this chapter use the same basic ingredients discussed throughout the book: grain, water, salt, and steam. But here we deepen our relationship with a critical ingredient of good bread: time. Artisan bakers let water, flour, and salt rest, raise, activate, and proof into crusty, tangy, edible art. It is an age-old process that optimizes fermentation (the linchpin of much delicious food and drink, such as bread, wine, and cheese) to transform hearty grains. As flour and water sit for enough time for naturally occurring yeast to multiply, the gas produced by the gluttonous yeast expands the dough, transforming a tightly formed mass into an air-filled loaf. Fermentation adds huge amounts of flavor; think about the difference between shredded raw cabbage and sauerkraut. The process creates a similar depth of flavor in bread.

Because, as the saying goes, "time is money," baking scientists have developed ways to produce breads more quickly. By adding large quantities of commercial yeast, removing natural pre-ferments, adding sugar and fats, and utilizing high-protein flours, commercial bakeries can make faster, cheaper, and more standardized products—but their loaves are not nearly as healthful or delicious as artisanal bread.

"Yeast: Use it responsibly" is a mantra of Karen Bornath, our training director, and that is what we do at Hot Bread Kitchen. We introduce as little yeast as possible, so that the flavor of the grain has time to develop and shine. In the bakery, we use wild-yeast levains and pre-fermented dough to encourage a long and slow fermentation. We have the benefit

of six different pre-ferments and more than eighteen hours a day of production time to make our line of seventy artisanal products. Keeping multiple levains is feasible for a large-scale artisanal bakery, but it isn't always practical for the home baker. This book presents one versatile pre-fermented dough, or *pâte fermentée*, which provides a simple way to use less yeast, give fermentation more time, and achieve consistent and delicious results The *pâte fermentée* uses a pinch of commercial yeast and should be mixed at least eight hours before you bake. It becomes an ingredient in your final dough and contributes the benefits of slow fermentation. While I am a strong proponent of maintaining a levain or starter for home baking, I made the decision to omit it from this book because it is complicated for the home baker to control. It adds another level of variability that stands between you and beautiful lean loaves. If you have or can procure a levain or starter, you can substitute a white levain at the same hydration for the *pâte fermentée* in these lean doughs. (We are happy to share a bit of ours at Hot Bread Kitchen; see United Nations of Bread, page 139.)

The breads that you make from these doughs will impress everyone who eats them. They take some forethought and planning but are well worth it. And just think of the yummy sandwiches you can make!

*Cibatta Squares (page 141),*
*Focaccia Rounds (page 80),*
*Pepita Multigrain Square (page 155)*

# Tips for Shaping Breads

Like sourcing the right ingredients (see page 12), mixing correctly (see page 15), and letting your dough rise (see page 16), learning to create the various shapes is essential to baking delicious breads at home. Here are a handful of techniques you need to know, plus some general tips. Many of the breads in the book use these shapes, so you may want to fold the corner down on this page—you may be referring to it a lot.

- When shaping doughs into loaves, one fundamental goal is to create a taut skin on the outside. This is important because that structure encourages loaves to expand upward and not just outward (the latter yields a flat loaf). Most shapes hide the seam or crease on the bottom (Ciabatta, page 141, is one beautiful exception), allowing you to pull toward the bottom, tightening the skin on top, kind of like a face-lift. As you shape rolls or a batard, think about pulling tightly toward the bottom. You will know that you have the desired surface tension when you poke a loaf before it rises and it resists your finger. It should feel about as firm as a balloon filled with helium. Note that after the bread is shaped, once it has risen and is filled with carbon dioxide, it will have more give when poked.

- Shaping dough requires the right firm-but-light touch. If your dough sticks to your hands or to the table, you are treating your dough too firmly. It is never good to knock all of the gas out of a dough; punching down your doughs is very 1990s. On the other side of the spectrum, if your seams are opening up on the bottom, you may want to start

applying a little more pressure in your shaping.

- Some recipes ask you to **pre-shape** your dough either as a log roll or boule (both explained below). We do a preshape to get a better-looking bread with nice internal structure, or crumb. A preshape allows you to start your final shaping from a predictable place—a nice smooth bundle. Try to use as little flour as you can during this stage. Then let the dough rest for at least 10 minutes before the final shaping.

- The **log roll** (see photographs opposite), as we've termed it, is the most common shape in this book and is used either as the final shape (Pepita Multigrain, page 153) or as a preshape. Folding the dough over itself a few times creates a taut skin and develops structure and a clean seam. It also helps to make sure that your loaves are of uniform density so they rise and bake evenly. Working with one piece of dough at a time, lightly flatten the dough with your hands so it forms a rough rectangle. With a short side facing you, fold the top of the dough toward its center. Press down with the pads of your fingers to create the "roll."

Seal the seam and create a taut surface and tight roll. Fold the new top edge over the center so it aligns with the bottom edge and press this seam down, again being mindful of creating surface tension. There should now only be one seam on one side of your dough. Give it a few rolls on the floured surface so that your folded dough forms a cylinder, the log. The length and height will depend on the amount of dough.

- To form a **Pullman loaf** (any bread baked in a loaf pan, such as Grindstone Rye, page 150), first form a log roll, then give the dough a few extra rolls on the floured surface so that it forms a loaf to fit your pan, usually 8 to 10 inches/20 to 25 cm. Put the roll into the pan, seam side down.

- To form a **batard** (a free-form loaf that is wide at the center and slightly tapered at the edges, such as New Yorker Rye, page 142), first preshape as a boule (opposite). Let rest for 10 minutes. Turn the dough seam side up, flatten it slightly, then form a log roll. Lengthen your loaf to the desired length by rocking it on the table. With the outer sides of your to hands, apply pressure to the ends of the dough to taper them.

- To form a **boule, roll,** or **bun** such as for Hamburger Buns (page 182), Corn Rye (page 147), or a round preshape, divide the dough evenly and gently form the pieces into rough rectangles. With the dough lying flat on the work surface, gather the corners to the center of the dough—you'll have a little bundle. Pinch the place where the 4 corners meet. Once you have done that, gather the new edges to your pinch, creating more surface tension. You will have a little beak where your corners came together and, when you pick it up, you should have a nice, smooth round ball. Put the bundle beak side down on the work surface and use your palm to lightly round the ball. Use the pinky edge of your hand to tighten the surface tension even more.

# Baking Tips

Here are some tips for handling fermentation and these satisfying breads:

- *Pâte fermentée* (page 126) is a fully formed, simple dough that bakers mix into the final dough to kick-start the fermentation process. Making a *pâte fermentée* is simple, but it requires forethought. If you save a little bit of dough (that doesn't have any fat or add-ins like raisins or seeds) from previous bread baking, you can use it in recipes that call for a *pâte fermentée*. Store in a bowl covered with plastic wrap for up to 24 hours in the fridge or freeze it for up to 2 weeks in an airtight plastic bag. Cut the *pâte fermentée* into walnut-size pieces and use them straight out of the fridge.

- You'll see instructions in this chapter and others to **slash** or **score** the shaped loaves before baking them. These slits allow steam to escape during baking and help control the direction the bread will expand in. Scoring is done right before breads go in the oven. It can feel intimidating when you have to take a blade to your pristine loaf, but the best results come from a fast, confident, smooth slash. Don't tear it by moving too slowly or not applying enough pressure. The blade should cut about ⅛ to ¼ inch/3 to 6 mm into the loaf.

- The best tool for **scoring bread** is a **bread lame**, a small, thin, extremely sharp, razor-like blade that's attached to a handle. Paring knives just don't, pardon the pun, cut it as well. Bread lames are inexpensive (see

page 291 for sources) and useful if you begin baking a lot of bread at home. Note that certain loaves, like Ciabatta (page 141), are not scored. On those loaves, the trapped gases find the weakest point and escape, leaving an irregular, more rustic pattern on the top of the loaves.

- "Oven spring" is a desirable effect that happens in the first 5 minutes when your loaf is placed in the oven. It is a rapid expansion created by the evaporation of water in the dough and a sort of last hurrah for the yeast before they are killed off by the rising internal temperature of the dough. If your score was done right, this is when you'll see your bread open beautifully and the "ear" will form.

- For some breads that have lots of grains and seeds, like the Pepita Multigrain (page 153) or Grindstone Rye (page 150), you will create a soaker. This step is started at least 8 hours before to soften seeds and grains and prevent them from drying out when they bake. The soaker also starts to ferment, which adds to the flavor and enzymatic activity of the bread. Be sure to drain soakers well before you add them to the dough or you will be adding too much moisture to the loaf.

# PÂTE FERMENTÉE

**MAKES ABOUT 1¼ CUPS (RISEN AND DEFLATED)/300 G**

½ cup plus 1 teaspoon/120 g
**LUKEWARM WATER**

⅔ teaspoon **ACTIVE DRY YEAST**

1⅓ cups plus 1 tablespoon/180 g
**BREAD FLOUR**

1 teaspoon **KOSHER SALT**

*Pâte fermentée* is an ingredient in many recipes in the lean and enriched doughs chapters. You need to make it 8 to 24 hours before you bake your bread. This extra step extends fermentation time and allows you to achieve a light, flavorful loaf with less yeast. *Pâte fermentée* contains the ingredients of simple French bread dough—flour, water, yeast, and salt—so, in a pinch, you could bake and eat it. Unlike other types of pre-ferments, such as levain, *pâte fermentée* does not impart a sour flavor to the bread. Instead it adds depth of flavor and extends the shelf life of your bread. If you make bread often, you can save the trimmings from lean doughs to use in your *pâte fermentée*. More likely, if you are making a Rustic Batard (page 128), Traditional Challah (page 175), or any number of the breads in this book, you will mix a batch of the *pâte fermentée* the day before, then refrigerate it until you are ready to bake.

**1.** Put the water and yeast in the bowl of a stand mixer fitted with a dough hook, then add the flour and salt. Mix on low speed for 2 minutes until combined into a shaggy dough. Cover the bowl with plastic wrap and let stand at room temperature for 30 minutes.

**2.** Refrigerate the mixture for a minimum of 8 hours and a maximum of 24. (There is no need to return it to room temperature before using.)

**3.** If you're measuring the *pâte fermentée* rather than weighing it, be sure to deflate it with a wooden spoon or with floured fingertips before measuring.

# RUSTIC BATARD

**MAKES 1 (12-INCH/30 CM) LOAF**

1¼ cups/285 g **WATER**

2¾ cups/340 g **BREAD FLOUR**, plus more for shaping

⅔ cup/80 g **WHOLE WHEAT FLOUR**

Scant ½ cup/105 g **PÂTE FERMENTÉE** (page 126), cut into walnut-size pieces

2½ teaspoons **KOSHER SALT**

⅛ teaspoon **ACTIVE DRY YEAST**

**CANOLA OIL**

**NOTE:** This dough, with its long fermentation, is used in several other breads in this book. Once you master it, you will be able to play with many variations.

This is a perfect place to start your adventures in slow fermentation. The rustic batard made with a coarse whole wheat flour is a versatile, hearty, crusty bread. The way to coax the most flavor out of your flour is to plan ahead and make this over three days. The schedule could go something like this: Friday morning: mix your *pâte fermentée,* about 45 minutes start to finish; Saturday morning: mix the dough, about 1 hour, including some leisurely resting; Sunday morning: wake up early, take your dough out of the fridge, preshape, rest, shape again, long rest, and bake. By lunchtime on Sunday you will have a glorious golden loaf to serve with cheeses, meats, or a delicious bowl of soup. This bread is perfect in Ribollita (page 284) or a bread salad (page 279 or 280).

1. Combine the water, bread flour, and whole wheat flour in a stand mixer fitted with a dough hook. Mix on low speed until all of the ingredients are combined, 2 minutes. Let rest for 20 minutes to hydrate the flours.

2. Add the *pâte fermentée,* salt, and yeast. Mix on low speed until all of the ingredients are combined, 2 minutes. Increase the speed to medium to medium-high and mix until the dough is smooth, pulls away from the sides of the bowl (and leaves the sides clean), has a bit of shine, and makes a slapping noise against the sides of the bowl, about 4 minutes. Do the window-pane test (page 16) to ensure that the gluten is fully developed.

3. Coat the inside of a large bowl with oil and transfer the dough to it. Cover the bowl tightly with plastic wrap (or put the whole bowl in a large plastic bag) and let stand at room temperature until the dough is puffy and supple and has increased in volume, 1½ to 2 hours at room temperature. Alternatively (for slower fermentation and more flavor), let rise at room temperature for 45 minutes until you start to see the dough getting softer and rising slightly. Fold the dough in half in the bowl, cover tightly with plastic wrap, and refrigerate for a minimum of 4 hours and a maximum of 12.

4. Turn the dough out onto a lightly floured work surface. Preshape into a boule (see page 123). Let rest for 10 minutes. If the dough is cold, let rest for 45 minutes. Shape the dough into a batard (see page 122) measuring about 12 inches/30 cm long, 4 inches/10 cm wide, and about 3 inches/7.5 cm tall. There should be one long seam along the bottom of the loaf. Apply slight downward pressure with the pinky sides of your hands to taper the ends slightly and ensure that they are well sealed.

*recipe continues*

**5.** Line the back of a baking sheet with parchment and put the loaf, seam side down, on the pan. Put the entire baking sheet in a large plastic bag or cover the loaf loosely with plastic wrap and let rise until soft and plump, about 1 hour. If you touch the loaf lightly, your finger will leave an indentation.

**6.** Meanwhile, put a pizza stone on the middle rack of the oven and pre-heat to 500°F/260°C. Set a baking dish in the bottom of the oven.

**7.** Use a bread lame or very sharp paring knife to score 1 long slash down the length of the loaf. Leave ½ inch between the tip of the loaf and the end of the score. Slide the loaf onto the pizza stone in one swift movement with the parch-ment. Put 10 ice cubes in the baking dish at the bottom of the oven (this will create steam) and reduce the oven temperature to 450°F/235°C.

**8.** Bake until the bread is browned on top (the "ear," or the place where the score opens, should be a darker brown) and the loaf sounds hollow when you tap it on the bottom, about 45 minutes. Transfer to a wire rack to cool completely.

**9.** Store bread that will be con-sumed within 24 hours in a paper or cloth bag. After that, store in a plastic bag at room temperature.

# PAN BAGNAT

SERVES 4

¼ medium **RED ONION**, finely diced

**KOSHER SALT**

1½ tablespoons **SHERRY VINEGAR**

¼ pound/115 g **GREEN BEANS**, topped and tailed, cut into 1-inch/2.5 cm lengths

4 small **YELLOW CREAMER POTATOES** (about ⅓ pound/ 150 g), cut into ½-inch/1.5 cm dice (optional)

2 teaspoons **DIJON MUSTARD**

¼ cup/55 g **EXTRA-VIRGIN OLIVE OIL**, plus more for drizzling

Freshly ground **BLACK PEPPER**

1 (7-ounce/198 g) jar **OLIVE OIL–PACKED TUNA**, drained

½ **ENGLISH CUCUMBER**, cut into small dice

½ small bulb **FENNEL**, thinly sliced

½ **RED BELL PEPPER**, cut into small dice

2 tablespoons minced **FLAT-LEAF PARSLEY**

Small handful of **GREEN AND BLACK OLIVES**, pitted and roughly chopped

1 (12-inch/30 cm) loaf **CRUSTY BREAD**, such as Ciabatta (page 141) or Rustic Batard (page 128)

4 hard-boiled **EGGS**, sliced

2 **TOMATOES**, sliced

6 **ANCHOVY FILLETS**

This classic sandwich from the South of France is essentially a niçoise salad served on a roll instead of a plate. The key to a great *pan bagnat* is in the ingredients; fresh, snappy green beans and oil-packed tuna sold in glass jars make a huge difference. Traditionally, these sandwiches don't include potatoes, but if you like starch with your starch (like me), go ahead and include them. These sandwiches improve as they rest, which makes them great for picnics. In fact, every spring at our annual Hot Bread Kitchen Family Picnic, the *pans bagnats* always fly off the table.

**1.** Put the onion in a small bowl and add a pinch of salt and the vinegar. Stir together and let sit while you prepare the green beans and potatoes (if using).

**2.** Bring a large pot of water to a boil and salt it generously. Add the green beans and cook until they're bright green and just tender, about 2 minutes. Use a handheld strainer or slotted spoon to transfer the green beans to a bowl. Put the potatoes in the water and boil until they're tender, about 20 minutes. Drain the potatoes and transfer them to the bowl with the green beans. Set aside to cool.

**3.** Meanwhile, whisk the mustard into the onion and then, while whisking, slowly drizzle in ¼ cup/ 60 ml olive oil to make a dressing. Season to taste with salt and plenty of pepper. Pour the dressing over the green beans and potatoes and add the tuna, cucumber, fennel, bell pepper, parsley, and olives. Stir to combine and taste for seasoning, adding more salt and pepper if necessary.

**4.** Halve the bread horizontally and use your hands to scoop out the fluffy interior bread (use for Bread Crumbs, page 281). Drizzle the interior of each half of the bread generously with olive oil and lay the sliced eggs on one side and the sliced tomatoes on the other. Season the eggs and tomatoes with plenty of salt and pepper. Put the tuna mixture on top of one half of the sandwich and then lay the anchovies in a long strip on top of the tuna mixture. Close with the other half of the bread and then wrap the sandwich very tightly in plastic wrap. Put something heavy on top of the sandwich (such as a baking sheet or a cutting board with a few cans of beans or something else heavy on top) and let the sandwich sit for at least 1 hour at room temperature or up to 6 hours in the refrigerator.

**5.** Before unwrapping, bring to room temperature if necessary, slice into 4 sandwiches, and serve.

## Cemita Rolls

MAKES 9 ROLLS

You can form the rustic batard dough into *cemitas*—Mexican sandwich rolls with sesame seeds that are used in the Carnitas Cemitas (page 135) and whenever you'd use a kaiser roll—like, perhaps, a turkey sandwich with tomato and lots of mayonnaise.

Line 2 rimmed baking sheets with parchment paper. After the first rise, turn the dough out onto a lightly floured surface. Divide it into 9 equal pieces (each weighing about 3 ounces/80 g). Work each piece of dough into a roll (see page 123). Transfer the rolls, seam side down, to the baking sheets, evenly spacing the rolls apart. Cover with plastic wrap and let stand at room temperature until the rolls are soft and puffy, about 1½ hours.

    Meanwhile, preheat the oven to 400°F/205°C.

    Uncover the rolls and lightly mist them with water from a spray bottle. Sprinkle a pinch of sesame seeds on top of each one. Bake, rotating the trays halfway through the baking, until the *cemitas* are beautifully browned, about 20 minutes. Transfer the rolls to a wire rack to cool completely.

## Rustic Rolls

MAKES 12 ROLLS

Proving the versatility of the rustic batard dough, you can use it to make crusty dinner rolls, too.

Line 2 rimmed baking sheets with parchment paper. After the first rise, turn your dough onto a lightly floured surface. Flatten the dough evenly so it's 1½ inches/4 cm thick, and use a bench scraper or large chef's knife to divide the dough into 12 equal pieces (each weighing about 2 ounces/60 g). They do not need to be the same shape: Some can be squares, others triangles; sometimes we even have trapezoids. Put them on the baking sheets, leaving ½ inch/1.5 cm between the rolls. Cover the rolls with plastic wrap and let stand at room temperature until they are puffy and soft to the touch, about 1 hour and 30 minutes.

    Meanwhile, preheat the oven to 450°F/235°C.

    Remove the plastic wrap from the dough and score each roll with one swift slash. Bake the rolls, rotating the trays halfway through the baking, until they're golden brown, about 15 minutes. Transfer the rolls to a wire rack to cool completely.

*Cemita Roll,*
*Bolillo Roll (page 193)*

# CARNITAS CEMITAS

**MAKES 4 SANDWICHES**

½ cup/110 g **MAYONNAISE,** homemade (page 167) or store-bought

1 **CHIPOTLE IN ADOBO SAUCE,** or to taste

1 teaspoon **DISTILLED WHITE VINEGAR**

¼ teaspoon **KOSHER SALT**

4 **CEMITA ROLLS** (page 132) or **OTHER CRUSTY ROLLS WITH SESAME SEEDS** on top, halved horizontally

½ cup/120 g **REFRIED BEANS** (page 109), warm

2 cups/500 g **FAST CARNITAS** (page 107)

½ medium **WHITE ONION,** thinly sliced

1 plum **TOMATO,** thinly sliced

½ cup/60 g shredded **QUESO OAXACA** or **MOZZARELLA CHEESE**

**NOTE:** You can substitute for the carnitas chicken *tinga* (page 101) or even sautéed mushrooms and avocado.

*Cemita* refers to both the name of this delicious sandwich and the type of roll the sandwich comes on. This recipe uses my favorite combination of traditional ingredients, but feel free to riff on it and make the *cemita* with other fillings. For a *torta* sandwich (on the right in the photograph opposite), swap the *cemita* roll for a Bolillo Roll (page 193), use regular mayonnaise instead of the chipotle mayo, and add pickled chiles. No matter how you fill them, assemble the sandwiches while the meat and beans are hot, so that the cheese melts and the bread absorbs the juices. Serve these with cold Mexican beer.

**1.** Combine the mayonnaise, chipotle, vinegar, and salt in a food processor and puree until smooth. (Alternatively, finely chop the chipotle and whisk it together with the other ingredients.)

**2.** Divide the chipotle mayonnaise among the cut sides of the rolls and spread to cover the surface. Evenly divide the refried beans among the rolls and spread to cover. Scoop the carnitas or chicken on top of the bottom halves of the rolls and top each one with onion, tomato, and cheese. Close the sandwiches with the top halves, push down on them firmly, and cut in half and serve.

# OLIVE BOULES

**MAKES 2 (ROUGHLY 6-INCH/15 CM) ROUND LOAVES**

**RUSTIC BATARD DOUGH** (page 128), prepared through step 2

1 cup/65 g pitted and halved **KALAMATA OLIVES**

1 teaspoon **HERBES DE PROVENCE**

**CANOLA OIL**

**ALL-PURPOSE FLOUR**

When I was learning to bake at Daniel, I spent at least six months halving kalamata olives for their sourdough. I dreamt kalamatas. I devised a home decor scheme based on their color palette. Mark, the head baker, told me that they sliced the already pitted olives to ensure no pit fragments made it into the bread. That's attention to detail—the kind I strive to instill at Hot Bread Kitchen. This loaf is irresistible. The salty, briny olives and savory herbes de Provence transform our rustic dough into a Mediterranean bread worthy of any special occasion. Try serving toasted slices spread with ricotta and topped with roasted tomatoes with drinks before dinner.

**1.** Once the dough is smooth and the gluten is developed, add the olives and herbes de Provence, mixing as briefly as possible to distribute, less than a minute.

**2.** Coat the inside of a large bowl with oil and transfer the dough to it. Cover the bowl tightly with plastic wrap (or put the whole bowl into a large plastic bag) and let stand until the dough is puffy and supple and has increased in volume, 1½ hours to 2 hours at room temperature. Alternatively (for slower fermentation), let rise at room temperature for 45 minutes until you start to see the dough getting softer and rising slightly. Fold the dough in half, cover tightly with plastic wrap, and refrigerate for a minimum of 4 hours and a maximum of 12. Allow the dough to come to room temperature before proceeding.

**3.** Turn the dough out onto a lightly floured work surface and divide it into 2 equal pieces (each weighing about 15 ounces/420 g). Preshape each piece of dough as a boule (see page 123). Let rest for 10 minutes.

Working with one piece at a time (and leaving the other under loose plastic wrap), flatten your dough slightly and reshape as a boule (see page 123). Repeat the process with the second piece of dough.

**4.** Line the backs of two baking sheets with parchment. Put the loaves, seam side down, on the pans. Put the baking sheets into large plastic bags or cover the loaves loosely with plastic wrap and let them rise at room temperature until the loaves are soft and plump, about 1 hour. If you touch a loaf lightly, your finger will leave an indentation.

**5.** Meanwhile, put a pizza stone on the middle rack of the oven and preheat to 500°F/260°C. Let the stone heat up for at least 30 minutes. Set a baking dish in the bottom of the oven.

**6.** Use a bread lame or very sharp paring knife to score 4 slashes around the periphery of one of the boules. (*See photograph on page 125.*) Slide the loaf, with the parchment paper, onto the pizza stone in one swift movement. Put 10 ice cubes in the baking dish at the bottom of the oven (this will create steam) and reduce the oven temperature to 450°F/235°C. Put the other loaf on the baking sheet, covered tightly, in a cool place.

**7.** Bake until the bread is browned on top and the loaf sounds hollow when you tap it on the bottom, about 30 minutes. Transfer to a wire rack to cool completely. Meanwhile, score and bake the second loaf.

**8.** Store bread that will be consumed within 24 hours in a paper or cloth bag. After that, store in a plastic bag at room temperature.

# CRACKED PEPPER AND CHEDDAR BATARD

**MAKES 2 (ROUGHLY 10-INCH/25 CM) LOAVES**

**RUSTIC BATARD DOUGH** (page 128), prepared through step 2

2 teaspoons coarsely ground **BLACK PEPPER**

2 cups/190 g grated **EXTRA SHARP CHEDDAR CHEESE**

**CANOLA OIL**

**ALL-PURPOSE FLOUR**

This was a Greenmarket favorite for many years. We use a sharp cheddar for this that we purchase from an Amish farmer's neighboring stall. The other layer of flavor comes from black pepper. The key is to not grind it too finely—keeping it coarse allows for real bites of peppery flavor. Hot out of the oven with a lot of butter, this bread needs nothing else. Even without the butter, you'll want to eat the whole thing.

**1.** Continue mixing the dough and, once it is smooth, add the pepper and cheddar, mixing as briefly as possible until evenly distributed, less than a minute.

**2.** Coat the inside of a large bowl with oil and transfer the dough to it. Cover the bowl tightly with plastic wrap (or put the whole bowl into a large plastic bag) and let stand until the dough is puffy and supple and has increased in volume, 2 to 2½ hours at room temperature. Alternatively (for slower fermentation), let rise at room temperature for 45 minutes until you start to see the dough getting softer and rising slightly. Fold the dough in half inside the bowl, cover tightly with plastic wrap, and refrigerate for a minimum of 4 hours and a maximum of 12. Allow the dough to come to room temperature before proceeding.

**3.** Turn the dough out onto a lightly floured work surface and divide it into 2 equal pieces (each weighing about 18 ounces/500 g).

Preshape each piece of dough into a boule (see page 123). Let rest for 10 minutes.

**4.** Working with one piece at a time (and leaving the other under loose plastic wrap), flatten your dough slightly and reshape into a log roll, and then into a batard (see page 122) measuring about 10 inches/25 cm long, 4 inches/10 cm wide, and about 3 inches/7.5 cm tall. Repeat the process with the second piece of dough.

**5.** Line the backs of 2 rimmed baking sheets with parchment. Put the loaves, seam side down, on the pans. Put the baking sheets in large plastic bags or cover the loaves loosely with plastic wrap and let them rise until they are soft and plump, about 1 hour. If you touch the loaf lightly, your finger will leave an indentation.

**6.** Meanwhile, put a pizza stone on the middle rack of the oven and preheat to 450°F/235°C. Let the stone heat up for 30 minutes. Set a baking dish in the bottom of the oven.

**7.** Use a bread lame or very sharp paring knife to score 1 long slash down the length of one of the loaves. Leave ½ inch/1.5 cm between the tip of the loaf and the end of the score. Slide the dough onto the pizza stone, with the parchment, in one swift movement. Put 10 ice cubes in the baking dish at the bottom of the oven (this will create steam) and reduce the oven temperature to 425°F/220°C after 10 minutes. Put the other loaf on the baking sheet, covered tightly, in a cool place.

**8.** Bake until the bread is browned on top and the exposed cheese is really dark. The loaf will sound hollow when you tap it on the bottom, about 30 minutes. Transfer to a wire rack (discard the parchment) to cool completely. Meanwhile, score and bake the second loaf.

**9.** Store bread that will be consumed within 24 hours in a paper or cloth bag. After that, store in a plastic bag at room temperature.

# UNITED NATIONS OF BREAD

Last spring, Hot Bread Kitchen hosted a dinner for the Board of Trustees of the Rockefeller Foundation. It was quite an honor and a wonderful opportunity to show Hot Bread's hospitality to a supporter. It was also a riot to see La Marqueta dressed up with rented plants and stage lighting.

After cocktails, a tour, and a *m'smen* demonstration, we sat down to an elegant dinner. I was seated right between the foundation's remarkable president, Judith Rodin, and Ashvin Dayal, the foundation's managing partner for Asia. We talked about everything from the wind electrification of rural India to building resilient global cities. At a certain point, Ashvin, who lives in Singapore, mentioned that he was a baker and he had some pretty technical questions. Turns out, Ashvin isn't a dabbler; he is a skilled baker and, in fact, his wife's family owns a bakery in North India.

While our dinner companions continued to discuss the world at large, we jumped into flour, fermentation, and "oven spring," the expansion that happens to bread in the first few minutes of baking. He lamented that his starter had died recently because he had been traveling too much to feed it. Aileen, our head baker, packed Ashvin a to-go coffee cup with some of ours. We said bon voyage to our starter and it has been raising bread in Asia ever since.

# CIABATTA

**MAKES 2 (9-INCH/23 CM) LOAVES**

**RUSTIC BATARD DOUGH** (page 128), prepared through step 3

**ALL-PURPOSE FLOUR**

**NOTE:** To achieve an airy interior, do not refrigerate dough before shaping and baking.

## Ciabatta Squares

To make these rolls (see photograph on page 119), mix the ciabatta dough as instructed, then follow the shaping instructions for Pepita Multigrain Squares (page 155). Let rise until puffy and supple, about 2 hours. Bake and cool as instructed.

A fresh, airy, chewy ciabatta is perfect for sandwiches and also bread salads (see pages 279 and 280). Of all the loaves, it is easiest to shape because the shape is irregular. The great flavor comes from whole wheat flour and the *pâte fermentée*.

**1.** Heavily dust a rimmed baking sheet with flour.

**2.** Turn the dough out onto a lightly floured work surface. Without folding, form it into roughly a 10-inch square. This bread is different from others because the seam becomes the top of the bread.

**3.** Divide the dough down the middle into 2 equal rectangles. Work with one piece of dough at a time (leave the other loosely covered with plastic wrap). This is a rustic shaped dough and you want to create an overlapping three-way fold. Working with the short end of the rectangle facing you, fold the top edge to the center and press the edge lightly to seal. Then fold the bottom edge to the center and press lightly to seal. Put the folded dough seam side down (the seam will be the top of the loaf once you bake it) on the floured baking sheet. Repeat the process with the second rectangle of dough. Cover the loaves with plastic wrap and let them stand at room temperature until they are softer than firm balloons, are supple, and hold indentations when pressed lightly, about 1 hour 30 minutes.

**4.** Meanwhile, put a pizza stone on the middle rack of the oven and preheat to 500°F/260°C. Set a baking dish in the bottom of the oven.

**5.** Put a sheet of parchment on a pizza peel or the underside of a rimmed baking sheet. Use both hands to gently cradle one of the loaves and flip it over as you transfer it to the parchment (unless you have a really big pizza stone and then you can fit both; just make sure that you leave at least 3 inches/7.5 cm between the loaves). Slide the dough onto the pizza stone with the parchment in one swift movement. Put 10 ice cubes in the baking dish at the bottom of the oven (this will create steam) and reduce the oven temperature to 450°F/235°C. Put the other loaf, covered tightly, in a cool place.

**6.** Bake until the bread is browned on top and sounds hollow when you tap it on the bottom, 20 to 25 minutes. Transfer to a wire rack to cool completely. Meanwhile, bake the second loaf. Store in a paper or cloth bag for up to 1 day. After that, store in a plastic bag at room temperature.

# NEW YORKER RYE

MAKES 2 (10-INCH/25 CM) LOAVES

2¾ cups/345 g **BREAD FLOUR**, plus more for shaping

2¾ cups/360 g **RYE FLOUR**

Scant 2 cups/440 g **WATER**

1⅔ cups/400 g (risen and deflated) **PÂTE FERMENTÉE** (page 126), cut into walnut-size pieces (you'll need to double the recipe)

1 tablespoon plus 1 teaspoon **KOSHER SALT**

¼ teaspoon **ACTIVE DRY YEAST**

2 tablespoons **CARAWAY SEEDS**

**CANOLA OIL**

This is the rye bread that you find loaded with pastrami and spicy mustard in New York City's delis. Our version stands out from the crowd because of the flavor imparted by the *pâte fermentée* and the high percentage of coarse local rye flour. We developed a killer Reuben sandwich (page 148) to take advantage of this satisfying bread, though it's also great to use for a simple grilled cheese with sharp cheddar. The scoring on this bread is important for both structure development and aesthetic. Practice five firm, confident slashes to get the real New York bakery look on these classic loaves.

**1.** Combine the bread flour, rye flour, and water in a stand mixer fitted with a dough hook. Mix on low speed until combined, 2 minutes. Let rest for 20 minutes to give the flours time to hydrate.

**2.** Add the *pâte fermentée*, salt, and yeast. Mix on low speed until the ingredients are fully combined, about 2 minutes. Increase the speed to medium to medium-high and mix until the dough is smooth, pulls away from the sides of the bowl (and leaves the sides clean), has a bit of shine, and makes a slapping noise against the sides of the bowl, 5 to 6 minutes. The gluten should be fully developed; you are looking for a shiny and smooth dough. You will know it is ready when you lightly tug a piece of the dough and it doesn't pull right off—it snaps back. Add the caraway seeds and mix for 1 minute more to integrate.

**3.** Coat the inside of a large bowl with oil and transfer the dough to it. Cover with plastic wrap (or put the whole bowl into a large plastic bag) and let stand at room temperature until the dough is puffy, supple, and very soft to the touch, about

1 hour. (Note that because this dough has a lot of pre-ferment, it is not an ideal dough to let rise overnight in the fridge.)

**4.** Line a pizza peel or the underside of a rimmed baking sheet with parchment.

**5.** Turn the dough out onto a lightly floured work surface and divide it into 2 equal pieces (each weighing about 27 ounces/770 g). Preshape each piece of dough into a loose boule (see page 123). Let rest for 15 minutes.

**6.** Working with one at a time (and leaving the other under loose plastic wrap), seam side up, flatten your dough slightly and shape into a log roll. Now you want to make your log roll look like a batard with rounded ends (see page 122) measuring about 10 inches/25 cm long, 4 inches/10 cm wide, and about 3 inches/7.5 cm tall. There should be one long seam along the bottom of the loaf. Apply slight downward pressure with the pinky side of your hands to round the ends. Repeat the process with the second piece of dough.

*recipe continues*

**7.** Put the loaves, seam side down, on the lined baking sheet. Put the entire pan in a large plastic bag or cover the loaves loosely with plastic wrap and let them rise until the loaves are soft and plump, about 1 hour. If you touch a loaf lightly, it should hold an indentation.

**8.** Meanwhile, put a pizza stone on the middle rack of the oven and preheat to 500°F/260°C. Set a baking dish in the bottom of the oven.

**9.** Use a bread lame or very sharp paring knife to score 5 (2-inch/5 cm) long parallel slashes on an angle on the top of one loaf. Slide the dough and the parchment onto the pizza stone in one swift movement. Put 10 ice cubes in the baking dish at the bottom of the oven (this will create steam) and reduce the oven temperature to 450°F/235°C. Put the other loaf, covered tightly, in a cool place.

**10.** Bake until the bread is browned on top and darker brown along the score lines and the loaf sounds hollow when you tap it on the bottom, about 25 minutes. Transfer to a wire rack to cool completely. Meanwhile score and bake the second loaf.

**11.** Store bread that will be consumed within 24 hours in a paper or cloth bag. After that, store in a plastic bag at room temperature.

*Gloria with a Corn Rye
(page 147).*

# RYE BREAD AND MY FAMILY

In this photograph, my great-grandfather is proudly taking out of a then-modern gas oven a rye bread with *kimmel; kimmel* is Yiddish for caraway seeds. The shape of Hot Bread Kitchen's rye breads takes inspiration from the ones he used to bake. Unfortunately, Laibish "Louis" Perlmutter shuttered his bakery in downtown Toronto long before I was born, but his style of rye remained my family's go-to bread. As a kid, I always preferred rye bread without *kimmel*, but no matter how many times I asked, my parents wouldn't buy unseeded rye. When I got old enough, I realized that I could avoid *kimmel* if I went with them to the bakery—they'd let me order whatever I wanted. Now I run my own bakery and can make—and eat—the breads I want!

# CORN RYE

**MAKES 3 (7-INCH/18 CM) LOAVES**

**NEW YORKER RYE DOUGH**
(page 142), prepared through
step 3

**ALL-PURPOSE FLOUR**

¼ cup/40 g **CORNMEAL**

The name of this variation on traditional rye bread derives from the word *korn,* which is what Eastern European bakers called grains and kernels, especially rye. Corn rye bread is distinguished by its soft texture, rich flavor, and traditional round shape. We started baking it because we knew it was an endangered—but delicious—bread. The cornmeal on the outside adds a nice crunchy layer.

**1.** Transfer the dough to a floured work surface. Divide the dough into 3 equal pieces (each weighing about 17½ ounces/500 g). Working with one piece of dough at a time (keep the rest covered with plastic), preshape each piece of dough into a loose boule (see page 123). Let rest for 15 minutes.

**2.** Working with one piece of dough at a time (and leaving the others under loose plastic wrap), flatten your dough slightly and reshape again into a tight boule. The diameter of each boule should be approximately 5 inches/13 cm.

**3.** Now you will give the corn rye its unique "corny" top. Put the cornmeal on a plate. Mist the top of your loaves with water using a spray bottle and then gently invert the top of each loaf into the cornmeal, rolling it around to get full coverage on the dome of the loaf.

**4.** Line the backs of 2 rimmed baking sheets with parchment. Evenly space 2 loaves on one of them and put the third loaf on the second sheet. Put the baking sheets in large plastic bags or loosely cover them with plastic wrap, and let stand in a cool place until soft and an indentation remains in the dough when you gently press on it, about 1 hour.

**5.** Meanwhile, put a pizza stone on the middle rack of the oven and preheat to 500°F/260°C. Let the stone heat for at least 30 minutes. Set a baking dish in the bottom of the oven.

**6.** Using a bread lame or sharp paring knife, score the tops of the 2 loaves three times in parallel lines about 2 inches/5 cm long. Carefully open the oven and slide the loaves onto the pizza stone in one swift movement with the parchment. Put 10 ice cubes in the baking dish at the bottom of the oven (this will create steam) and reduce the oven temperature to 450°F/235°C. Put the remaining loaf, covered tightly, in a cool place.

**7.** Bake until the bread is well browned on top and sounds hollow when you tap it on the bottom, about 30 minutes. Transfer to a wire rack to cool completely. Meanwhile, score and bake the remaining loaf. Store in a paper or cloth bag at room temperature for up to 1 day. After that, store in a plastic bag at room temperature.

# REUBENS WITH SRIRACHA SPECIAL SAUCE

**SERVES 4**

½ cup/110 g **MAYONNAISE,** homemade (page 167) or store-bought

2 tablespoons **KETCHUP**

1 tablespoon **SRIRACHA SAUCE**

1 tablespoon minced **FRESH PARSLEY**

1 tablespoon minced **RED ONION**

1 **DILL PICKLE,** finely diced

A few dashes of **WORCESTERSHIRE SAUCE**

**KOSHER SALT** and freshly ground **BLACK PEPPER**

8 thin slices **NEW YORKER RYE** (page 142) or store-bought **RYE BREAD**

8 slices **SWISS CHEESE**

1 pound/455 g thinly sliced **CORNED BEEF**

¾ cup/255 g drained **SAUERKRAUT**

2 tablespoons/30 g **UNSALTED BUTTER**

My cousin Dave Ward has always been a big supporter of Hot Bread Kitchen and an avid consumer of good bread. He also knows a lot about sandwiches. A long time ago, he showed me his technique for the classic sandwich, and my relationship with our rye bread has never been the same. While Dave says it's not traditional to use a seeded rye, he agrees it makes a worthwhile difference in flavor. If you can, purchase the corned beef from a good deli. Using quality meat will make a big difference in this sandwich.

**1.** Stir together the mayonnaise, ketchup, Sriracha, parsley, onion, pickle, and Worcestershire sauce in a small bowl. Season to taste with salt and pepper.

**2.** Set a medium skillet that will accommodate 2 sandwiches over high heat, and let it get really hot while you prepare the bread.

**3.** Put the slices of bread on a work surface. Spread one side of each slice of bread with the sauce (make sure you use all of it) and put a slice of cheese on each piece of bread.

**4.** Put the corned beef in the hot skillet and cook, stirring now and then, until its edges are crispy, about 2 minutes. Take the corned beef out of the pan and immediately divide it among 4 of the slices of bread and spoon the sauerkraut on top. Close the sandwiches with the remaining 4 slices of dressed-and-cheesed bread.

**5.** Reduce the heat to medium and melt half the butter in the skillet. Put 2 sandwiches in the skillet and cook, pressing down with a spatula, until the bottom is browned and crisp, 4 to 5 minutes. Carefully turn each sandwich over and cook until the second side is browned and crisp and the cheese is completely melted, another 4 minutes. Repeat with the remaining 2 sandwiches and serve immediately.

# GRINDSTONE RYE

## SOAKER

¼ cup/35 g **WHEAT BERRIES**

¼ cup/35 g **RYE BERRIES** or additional **WHEAT BERRIES**

2 tablespoons **CORNMEAL**

¼ cup/40 g **ROLLED OATS**

¼ cup/40 g **SUNFLOWER SEEDS**

¼ cup/40 g **SESAME SEEDS**

⅔ teaspoon **SALT**

½ cup plus 2 tablespoons/ 140 g **WATER**

## DOUGH

1½ cups plus 2 tablespoons/360 g **VERY WARM WATER**

2½ cups/325 g **RYE FLOUR**

1 cup plus 3 tablespoons/150 g **BREAD FLOUR**, plus more for shaping

½ cup/55 g **WHOLE WHEAT FLOUR**

¾ cup plus 2 tablespoons/210 g (risen and deflated) **PÂTE FERMENTÉE** (page 126), cut into walnut-size pieces

1 tablespoon plus ¼ teaspoon **KOSHER SALT**

1 teaspoon **BROWN SUGAR**

1½ teaspoons **ACTIVE DRY YEAST**

1 tablespoon plus 2 teaspoons **LEMON JUICE**

3 tablespoons **CANOLA OIL**

3⅓ cups/145 g **STEEL-CUT OATS** or **ROLLED OATS**

This loaf is a dense, German-style rye, filled with seeds, grains, and a small amount of white flour. It's the first rye bread that we developed, and it now has a cult following. Come to think of it, I might be its biggest fan. I especially love it for Avocado and Ramp Toasts (page 152) or with smoked salmon and butter. There are a number of seeds and grains in the soaker; feel free to substitute and simplify. For example, if you really love sunflower seeds, you can replace the sesame seeds with extra sunflower seeds. Note that the soaker needs to be made a day before to allow the raw seeds to soften.

**1.** To prepare the soaker: Rinse the wheat berries and rye berries with cold water. Put them in a large heavy pot and add enough water to cover by at least 2 inches/5 cm. Bring to a boil over high heat, then reduce the heat, cover, and simmer gently, stirring occasionally, for 1 hour. Add more water to keep the soaker covered. The berries should still have the skin intact but be soft on the inside.

**2.** Drain the wheat berries and rye berries and combine in a large bowl with the cornmeal, rolled oats, sunflower seeds, sesame seeds, salt, and water. Cover with plastic wrap and let stand at room temperature for 8 hours or in the refrigerator for up to 24 hours.

**3.** To make the dough: Combine the water, rye flour, bread flour, whole wheat flour, *pâte fermentée*, salt, sugar, yeast, and lemon juice in a stand mixer fitted with a dough hook. Mix on low speed to integrate the ingredients, about 2 minutes. Increase the speed to medium to medium-high and mix until you can see some shininess to the dough,

6 minutes. This dough is heavy, almost sticky, so you can't look for the normal gluten clues. You will know it is ready when you lightly tug a piece of the dough and it doesn't pull right off—it snaps back.

**4.** Drain all water from the soaker and add the seeds and grains to the dough. Mix until they are distributed, about 2 minutes. Coat the inside of a large bowl with 1 tablespoon of the canola oil and transfer the dough to the bowl. Cover the bowl with plastic wrap (or put the whole bowl in a large plastic bag) and let stand at room temperature until the dough is softer and supple. This heavy dough will not puff up a lot like other doughs with more white flour. Give it about 1 hour.

**5.** Coat 2 (9 × 5-inch/23 × 13 cm) loaf pans with the remaining 2 tablespoons oil. Put the steel-cut oats on a platter or in a baking dish near your work surface. Dust the work surface with flour and turn the dough onto it. Gently push down the dough and divide it into 2 equal pieces.

**6.** Working with one piece of dough at a time (keep the other covered with plastic), form a log roll (see page 120). Using both hands, roll each log to 8 inches/20 cm long and 4 inches/10 cm wide with a long seam running along the bottom.

**7.** Spray the top of each loaf with water from a spray bottle and then roll the dampened top in the oats. Put the loaves, oat-coated side up and seam side down, into the prepared loaf pans.

**8.** Cover the loaves loosely with plastic wrap and let stand until the dough nearly fills the loaf pan, about 2 hours.

**9.** Meanwhile, preheat the oven to 400°F/205°C.

**10.** Bake until the breads are browned and the top is crusty, about 45 minutes. Turn out of the pans onto a wire rack to cool completely, at least 2 hours (because of the density of the bread). Store in a paper or cloth bag at room temperature for up to 1 day. After that, store in a plastic bag at room temperature. This bread freezes well.

# AVOCADO AND RAMP TOASTS ON GRINDSTONE RYE

**MAKES 4 TOASTS; SERVES 2 TO 4**

2 tablespoons **EXTRA-VIRGIN OLIVE OIL**

1 bunch **RAMPS** (about a dozen), trimmed but left whole

**KOSHER SALT**

2 tablespoons **SALTED BUTTER**, at room temperature

4 thick slices **GRINDSTONE RYE** (page 150), toasted

1 **HASS AVOCADO**, pitted, quartered, and peeled

½ **LEMON**

When I want a healthy lunch that's not a grilled cheese sandwich (which is what I eat too many days), I make avocado toast. I use Grindstone Rye because it's a healthy option and because its sour notes offset the avocado's creaminess. When ramps are in season, they are delicious on this sandwich. I substitute scallions the rest of the year.

**1.** Heat the olive oil in a large skillet over medium-high heat. Add the ramps and cook, stirring now and then, until charred in spots and wilted, about 5 minutes. Season the ramps to taste with salt and remove from the heat.

**2.** Butter one side of each slice of toast. Top each slice with a quarter of the avocado and use a fork to mash it so that it adheres to the bread. Sprinkle the mashed avocado generously with salt. Evenly divide the sautéed ramps among the toasts and squeeze the lemon half on top. Serve immediately.

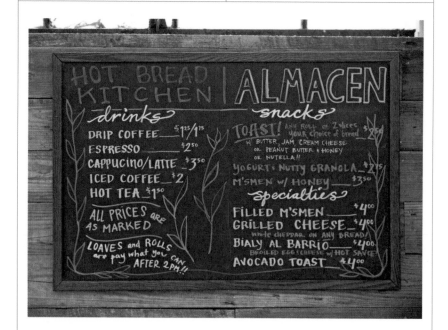

# PEPITA MULTIGRAIN

MAKES 2 (8-INCH/20 CM) LOAVES

## SOAKER

2 tablespoons **CRACKED WHEAT**

2 tablespoons **CORNMEAL**

2 tablespoons **ROLLED OATS**

2 tablespoons **MILLET**

2 tablespoons **FLAXSEEDS**

3 tablespoons **SESAME SEEDS**

3 tablespoons **SUNFLOWER SEEDS**

2 tablespoons **PEPITAS** (hulled
pumpkin seeds)

1 cup/225 g **BOILING WATER**

## DOUGH

1⅓ cups/305 g **COOL WATER**

1 cup/125 g **WHOLE WHEAT FLOUR**

2 cups/265 g **BREAD FLOUR**, plus
more for shaping

⅓ cup/45 g **RYE FLOUR**

½ tablespoon **CANOLA OIL**, plus
more for the bowl and pans

1 tablespoon **DARK BROWN SUGAR**

1 tablespoon **KOSHER SALT**

1¼ teaspoons **ACTIVE DRY YEAST**

½ cup/50 g **ROLLED OATS**

This is the consummate sandwich bread. I love the pepitas, which is what they call pumpkin seeds in Mexico. They feature prominently in the Mexican food that you find in Spanish Harlem, where our bakery is located. There are a lot of grains in this bread, which, if you are having trouble sourcing or have an aversion to, can be substituted for one another. For example, use all millet and no flaxseeds or double your pepitas as a real celebration of El Barrio. You should note that this is bread that takes its time. In addition to a soaker, there is an 8- to 24-hour rest in the fridge, so plan ahead.

1. To prepare the soaker: Combine the cracked wheat, cornmeal, oats, millet, flaxseeds, sesame seeds, sunflower seeds, pepitas, and boiling water in a large bowl and let soak at room temperature for at least 8 hours.

2. To make the dough: Combine the water, whole wheat flour, bread flour, and rye flour in a stand mixer fitted with a dough hook. Mix on low speed to integrate the ingredients, about 2 minutes. Let sit for 20 minutes to hydrate the flours.

3. Add the canola oil, the brown sugar, salt, and yeast. Mix on low speed until all of the ingredients are combined, just 1 to 2 minutes. Increase the speed to medium to medium-high and mix until the dough is smooth, pulls away from the sides of the bowl, and has a bit of shine. You will know the dough is ready when you lightly tug a piece of the dough and it doesn't pull right off—it snaps back.

4. Drain the soaker and add to the dough. Mix on low until everything is distributed, about 2 minutes.

5. Coat the inside of a large bowl with oil and transfer the dough to it. Cover the bowl with plastic wrap (or put the whole bowl into a large plastic bag) and let stand at room temperature until the dough is soft and puffy, about 1 hour. Fold the dough over itself, cover the bowl tightly with plastic wrap and refrigerate for at least 8 hours and up to 24 hours. Bring the dough to room temperature before proceeding.

6. When you are ready to shape the dough, coat 2 (8 × 4-inch/20 × 10 cm) loaf pans with canola oil. Spread the oats on a platter or in a baking dish near your work surface.

7. Turn the cold dough out onto a lightly floured work surface. Divide it into 2 equal pieces. Working with one piece at a time (keep the other covered with plastic), form a loose log roll (see page 120). Let the dough rest, covered, for 30 minutes.

*recipe continues*

**8.** Lightly flatten with hands and form a Pullman (see page 120). This time, roll out until 8 inches/20 cm long and 4 inches/10 cm wide. There should be a long seam running along the bottom. Repeat with the second piece of dough.

**9.** Spray the top of each loaf with water from a spray bottle and then roll the dampened top in the oats. Put the loaves, oat-coated side up and seam side down, into the prepared loaf pans. Cover the loaves loosely with plastic wrap and let stand until they nearly fill the loaf pans, about 2 hours.

**10.** Meanwhile, preheat the oven to 375°F/190°C.

**11.** Bake until the breads are browned and the oats have started to darken slightly, 40 to 45 minutes. Transfer to wire racks to cool completely. Store in a paper or cloth bag for up to 1 day. After that, store in a plastic bag at room temperature.

## Pepita Multigrain Squares

**MAKES 16 (4-INCH/10 CM) SQUARES**

Prepare the dough and let it rise in the refrigerator as instructed. When you are ready to shape, turn out the cold dough onto a lightly floured work surface and pat it into a large 16-inch/40 cm square. Use a bench scraper or a chef's knife to cut the dough into 16 (4-inch/10 cm) squares (each weighing about 2 ounces/60 g). Transfer them to 3 parchment-lined rimmed baking sheets, leaving at least 1 inch/2.5 cm between the squares—you should have 5 or 6 per tray. Dust the tops with flour, cover loosely with plastic wrap (or a plastic bag), and let them rest until they're supple and puffy, 3 to 4 hours.

Preheat the oven to 385°F/195°C.

Lightly mist the squares with water from a spray bottle. (Omit the oats used in the main recipe.) Bake, rotating the pans halfway through, until the squares are lightly browned. Transfer the squares to a wire rack to cool completely.

# PECAN CURRANT BATARD

**MAKES 2 (8-INCH/20 CM) LOAVES**

¾ cup/85 g **PECAN HALVES**, toasted

1 cup/160 g **DRIED CURRANTS**

5 cups/635 g **BREAD FLOUR**, plus
more for shaping

1¾ cups plus 2 tablespoons/415 g
**WARM WATER**

1 tablespoon plus 2 teaspoons
**KOSHER SALT**

¼ teaspoon **ACTIVE DRY YEAST**

⅔ cup/155 g (risen and deflated)
**PÂTE FERMENTÉE** (page 126),
cut into walnut-size pieces

**CANOLA OIL**

This loaf livens things up in a market crowded with raisin loaves. It's an elegant addition to any cheese board. This loaf gets scored five times on each side in a sort of ladder pattern. If you are less than confident in your scoring, five lines as described in the New Yorker Rye (page 142) also work perfectly well.

**1.** Put the pecans and currants in a large bowl and cover with hot water.

**2.** Combine the bread flour and warm water in a stand mixer fitted with a dough hook. Mix on low speed until well combined, about 2 minutes. Let rest for at least 20 minutes.

**3.** Add the salt, yeast, and *pâte fermentée* and mix on low speed to integrate, about 2 minutes, Increase the speed to medium to medium-high and mix until the dough is smooth, pulls away from the sides of the bowl (and leaves the sides clean), has a bit of shine, and makes a slapping noise against the sides of the bowl, about 5 minutes. You will know the dough is ready when you lightly tug a piece of the dough and it doesn't pull right off—it snaps back.

**4.** Drain the pecans and currants (discard the soaking liquid) and add them to the dough. Mix on low speed until just combined.

**5.** Coat the inside of a large bowl with oil and transfer the dough to it. Cover the bowl with plastic wrap (or put the whole thing into a large plastic bag) and let stand at room temperature until the dough is softer than a firm balloon, is supple, and leaves an indentation when pressed lightly, about 2 hours.

**6.** Turn the dough out onto a lightly floured work surface and divide it into 2 equal pieces (each weighing about 25 ounces/720 g). Preshape each piece of dough using a loose log roll (see page 120). Let rest for 10 minutes. Working with one piece at a time (and leaving the other under loose plastic wrap), flatten your dough slightly and reshape using another log roll. Now you want to make your roll look like a batard with rounded ends (see page 122). There should be one long seam along the bottom of the loaf. Apply slight downward pressure with the pinky sides of your hands to round the ends slightly. Repeat the process with the second piece of dough.

**7.** Line the backs of 2 rimmed baking sheets with parchment and put the loaves, seam side down, on the pans. Put the baking sheets in large plastic bags or cover the loaves loosely with plastic wrap and let them rise until the loaves are soft and plump, about 1 hour. If you touch the loaf lightly, your finger will leave an indentation.

**8.** Meanwhile, put a pizza stone on the middle rack of the oven and preheat to 500°F/260°C. Set a baking dish in the bottom of the oven.

**9.** Use a bread lame or very sharp paring knife to score 5 (1½-inch/4 cm) slashes on each side of one loaf (10 slashes in all). Slide the dough onto the pizza stone in one swift movement. Put 10 ice cubes in the baking dish at the bottom of the oven (this will create steam) and reduce the oven temperature to 425°F/220°C after 10 minutes. Put the other loaf on the baking sheet, covered tightly, in a cool place.

**10.** Bake until the bread is browned on top, the exposed currants are slightly charred, and the loaf sounds hollow when you tap it on the bottom, 20 to 25 minutes. Transfer to a wire rack (discard the parchment) to cool completely. Meanwhile, score and bake the second loaf.

**11.** Store bread that will be consumed within 24 hours in a paper or cloth bag. After that, store in a plastic bag at room temperature.

# TRADITIONAL ONION BIALYS

MAKES 12 (5-INCH/13 CM) BIALYS

## BIALY DOUGH

1⅓ cups/320 g **LUKEWARM WATER**

3½ cups plus 2 tablespoons/
465 g **BREAD FLOUR**, plus more
for shaping

½ cup plus 2 tablespoons/
150 g (risen and deflated)
**PÂTE FERMENTÉE** (page 126),
cut into walnut-size pieces

¾ teaspoon **ACTIVE DRY YEAST**

1 tablespoon **KOSHER SALT**


## FILLING

3 tablespoons **EXTRA-VIRGIN
OLIVE OIL**

4 medium **YELLOW ONIONS**, finely
diced (6 cups/900 g)

½ cup/60 g fine dried **BREAD
CRUMBS** (page 281)

1½ tablespoons **POPPY SEEDS**

½ teaspoon **KOSHER SALT**

You can't talk about bialys without talking about my friend Mimi Sheraton, the former *New York Times* restaurant critic. Her book *The Bialy Eaters* is the most captivating piece of food writing I've ever read. Within the parameters she outlines, I set off to make the best bialy in New York. While I'm proud that our bialys have become one of our signature breads and received critical acclaim, the best compliment came a year after we started making them, when Mimi called to say she liked ours. I hope you do, too.

**1.** To make the bialy dough: Put the water and flour in the bowl of a stand mixer fitted with a dough hook, and mix for 2 minutes. Let rest for 20 minutes.

**2.** Add the *pâte fermentée*, yeast, and salt and mix on low speed until the dry ingredients are completely combined. Add a little more water if this hasn't happened in 3 minutes. Increase the speed to medium to medium-high and mix until the dough is smooth, pulls away from the sides of the bowl (and leaves the sides clean), has a bit of shine, and makes a slapping noise against the sides of the bowl, 5 to 7 minutes. Do the windowpane test (page 16) to check to see if the gluten is fully developed.

**3.** Dust a clean bowl lightly with flour and transfer the dough to it. Cover the bowl with plastic wrap (or put the whole bowl in a large plastic bag) and let stand at room temperature until doubled in volume, about 1 hour and 30 minutes.

**4.** Meanwhile, to prepare the filling: Heat the oil in a large skillet set over medium-low heat. Add the

onions and cook, stirring now and then, until they just begin to brown and have reduced to about a third of their original volume, about 20 minutes. Transfer the onions to a bowl and stir in the bread crumbs, poppy seeds, and salt. Set aside to cool.

**5.** Transfer the dough to a lightly floured surface. Divide the dough into 12 equal pieces (each weighing about 2¾ ounces/80 g). Form each piece into a small bun (see page 123), cover with plastic wrap, and let rest for 5 minutes. Proceeding in the same order in which you shaped the pieces into balls, flatten each ball with the heel of your hand into a disk about 4 inches/10 cm in diameter.

**6.** Line the backs of 2 rimmed baking sheets with parchment. Put the disks on the baking sheets, evenly spaced and at least an inch apart. Loosely cover with plastic wrap. Let stand until the rolls are very soft and hold an indentation when you touch them lightly, 1 hour to 1 hour and 30 minutes.

*recipe continues*

**7.** Put a pizza stone on the middle rack of the oven and preheat to 500°F/260°C. Let the stone heat up for at least 30 minutes.

**8.** Uncover the bialys and, using the pads of both your index and middle fingertips, make a depression in the center of each disk of dough. Put about 2 tablespoons filling in the center of each bialy, spreading it out so it fills the center.

**9.** In one swift motion, slide the bialys and the parchment onto the pizza stone. Bake until golden brown, 12 to 15 minutes. Transfer to a wire rack to cool for a few minutes (discard the parchment).

**10.** Serve immediately. Leftovers can be kept in an airtight plastic bag at room temperature for 2 days.

## Mini Cheese Bialys

MAKES 24 (3-INCH/8 CM) BIALYS; SERVES 12

Hot Bread Kitchen's cheese bialys were born out of necessity. When I was head baker and hungry late at night with nothing open nearby, I would often take a bialy—the last thing to come out of the oven on most nights—and throw some cheese on it while it was still hot. These are smaller than our regular bialys because then you don't feel guilty if you eat a few of them! Use the sharpest cheddar you can find.

Traditional Onion Bialys dough and filling (page 159)
2 cups/95 g coarsely grated sharp cheddar cheese

Prepare the dough through the first rise and prepare the filling as directed.

Turn the dough out onto a lightly floured surface. Divide the dough into 24 equal pieces (each weighing about 1½ ounces/40 g). Form each into a disk measuring 2 inches/5 cm across as described in the Traditional Onion Bialys recipe.

Continue with the Traditional Onion Bialys recipe up to the point of topping them. Top each bialy with 1 heaping tablespoon of onion filling and a small handful of cheese. Bake the bialys as described.

# BIALY AL BARRIO

**SERVES 1**

1 tablespoon **UNSALTED BUTTER**

1 large **EGG**

**KOSHER SALT** and freshly ground
**BLACK PEPPER**

3 tablespoons coarsely grated
**SHARP WHITE CHEDDAR CHEESE**

1 **TRADITIONAL ONION BIALY**
(page 159), halved horizontally

A few drops of **VALENTINA HOT
SAUCE**

We developed this breakfast sandwich when we opened Hot Bread Almacen, our retail store at the front of La Marqueta. Our East Harlem neighborhood, known as El Barrio, inspired the name as well as our choice of Valentina hot sauce, a Mexican brand that lends vinegary spice to the classic egg-and-cheese combination. If you can't find Valentina hot sauce, substitute Cholula or any vinegar-based pepper sauce. Once you realize that the divot in a bialy is the perfect size for a large egg, your bialy breakfast will never be the same. Just one caveat before you dig in: This can be a messy sandwich to eat. Serve it with a steak knife and a fork for those who care about that kind of thing.

**1.** Melt the butter in a small non-stick skillet over medium-high heat. Crack the egg into the pan and season with salt and pepper. Cover the pan and cook the egg until the white is firm but the yolk is still runny, about 2 minutes.

**2.** Meanwhile, sprinkle half of the cheddar on the bottom half of the bialy and put it, along with the top half, into a toaster oven or under a hot broiler. Heat until the cheese is melted.

**3.** Put the egg on top of the melted cheese and sprinkle with the remaining cheese. Return the bialy to the toaster oven or broiler until the cheese melts. Drizzle with hot sauce, top with the top half of the bialy, and serve immediately.

# SMOKED MACKEREL SALAD ON BIALYS

**SERVES 6**

½ small **RED ONION**, finely diced

**KOSHER SALT**

7 ounces/200 g **SMOKED MACKEREL FILLETS**, skin removed

1 large **CELERY STALK**, finely diced

½ cup/110 g **MAYONNAISE**, homemade (page 167) or store-bought

2 tablespoons fresh **LEMON JUICE**

1 tablespoon prepared **HORSERADISH**

Freshly ground **BLACK PEPPER**

6 **TRADITIONAL ONION BIALYS** (page 159), halved horizontally

6 large **BOSTON LETTUCE LEAVES**, torn into bite-size pieces

One of my favorite sandwiches is a bialy filled with whitefish salad, lettuce, and a squeeze of lemon. You can use a whole smoked whitefish and perform the satisfying task of picking the meat from the bones, but it's easier to use smoked mackerel fillets, which are sold in most grocery stores and are simpler to handle. You could also substitute smoked trout or chub. If some of your bialy onions fall out when you slice them, simply collect them off the cutting board and sprinkle them on the fish salad.

**1.** Put the onion in a fine-mesh sieve and sprinkle with a large pinch of salt. Set the sieve in your sink or over a bowl and let the onion sit while you prepare the rest of the salad. This will help remove some of the pungency from the onion.

**2.** Meanwhile, put the mackerel in a large bowl and use your hands and a fork to break it up into small flakes. Make sure to remove any small bones as you go (there are inevitably some even if the package says they've been removed). Add the salted onion, celery, mayonnaise, lemon juice, and horseradish and stir to combine. Season to taste with plenty of black pepper.

**3.** Divide the mackerel salad among the bottom halves of the bialys and top with the lettuce. Top with the top halves of the bialys, slice each sandwich in half, and serve immediately.

## OLIVE OIL MAYONNAISE

**MAKES 1 GENEROUS CUP/300 G**

This mayonnaise adds richness to whatever it goes on. I love the spicy flavor that olive oil adds, but if you're not a fan of it, simply substitute canola oil for some or all of the olive oil.

1 large **EGG**

½ teaspoon **MUSTARD POWDER** or 1 teaspoon **DIJON MUSTARD**

2 tablespoons fresh **LEMON JUICE**, or more to taste

1 cup/225 g **EXTRA-VIRGIN OLIVE OIL**

**KOSHER SALT** and freshly ground **BLACK PEPPER**

Combine the egg, mustard, and lemon juice in a large bowl or in a blender. Vigorously whisk together until smooth. While whisking, slowly drizzle in the olive oil. Pour slowly at first, increasing to a more generous pour after the mayonnaise starts to come together. Once a thick mayonnaise forms, taste for seasoning and add a bit more lemon juice if you'd like, and plenty of salt and pepper. Store covered in the refrigerator for up to 3 days.

## RICE VINEGAR MAYONNAISE

**MAKES ABOUT 1 CUP/225 G**

This is great for bahn mi sandwiches (page 194). For extra flavor, add 1 teaspoon soy sauce and/or 1 teaspoon toasted sesame oil to the finished mayonnaise. For spicy mayonnaise, whisk in 1 teaspoon prepared wasabi paste, horseradish, or hot sauce (such as Sriracha). The possibilities are endless.

2 large **EGG YOLKS**

2 tablespoons **RICE VINEGAR**

¾ cup/170 g **CANOLA OIL**

Pinch of **KOSHER SALT**

Follow the same procedure as for Olive Oil Mayonnaise, substituting the ingredients above.

# CHALLAH AND BEYOND

ENRICHED BREADS, ROLLS, AND BUNS

The lean doughs from the last chapter create breads with crisp crusts and airy interiors. This chapter's recipes combine the flavor and the lift those doughs get from slow fermentation with the richness from fats like whole eggs, butter, and milk. Added fats not only make the breads delicious but also inhibit crust development, so these breads stay soft.

The first recipe in this chapter, Traditional Challah, is a versatile enriched bread that I have a personal connection to. The breads we bake at Hot Bread Kitchen are inspired by our bakers, and challah is one of my contributions to our repertoire. When I was three years old, my family lived on a farm in rural Ontario, in a small town called Gananoque, hundreds of miles away from the closest Jewish bakery. My family celebrated Shabbat on Fridays and my mother, who was finishing her PhD at the time, made a challah every week for dinner.

I don't have many memories from those years, but I can distinctly remember the smell of the dough after rising and how it felt to roll the dough into braids with my little hands. My love of challah started with those dense, flavorful loaves. Home-baked challah is different from the commercially produced, over-yeasted, fast challah that's now ubiquitous in many supermarkets. At Hot Bread Kitchen, we use a minimum amount of yeast, take our time to let flavor develop naturally, and create a nice chewy loaf.

Challah carries a lot of historical significance. The nuances that distinguish different types of challah tell us a lot about where the breads come from and who has made them. Ashkenazi Jews, from Central and Eastern Europe, make challah (page 175) rich with abundant eggs. Sephardic Jews from North Africa and the Middle East, on the other hand, leave out the eggs and incorporate spices like caraway and cumin into their version (page 190). Sweet challahs, with more honey than usual, or challahs baked with raisins (page 178), are made on holidays to symbolize bringing about joy and happiness.

Additionally, challah's shape carries tremendous symbolism. A braid, with all of its arms intertwined, is said to represent love. A three-strand braid stands for truth, peace, and justice coming together, and a large, twelve-strand braid is meant to represent the twelve tribes of Israel. Round, coiled loaves represent continuity. Learning to make these shapes can be a bit tricky at first, but once you get the hang of it, the process is almost meditative. You can try practicing with pieces of rope first to get comfortable with the challah-braiding process—that's what we do at the bakery.

Beyond the cultural and historical importance of challah, we love making it at Hot Bread Kitchen because it's a highly versatile dough that serves as the base for many other breads. Just as the rustic batard dough informed many breads in the lean breads chapter, the challah dough is used for our Mexican *conchas* (page 185) and to make hamburger and hot dog buns (page 182). Our dough is rich and is an apt substitute for brioche, but is quicker and easier to work with, since it doesn't use butter (and dairy wouldn't be kosher with a Sabbath meat dinner, if you're counting). Needless to say, leftover challah is great in all sorts of delicious dishes, including Tres Leches Bread Pudding (page 272) and Grilled Cheese French Toast with Caramelized Peaches (page 271).

Along with the challahs, this chapter has recipes for many of the derivations of challah dough, plus other breads made with doughs enriched with fats like whole milk, butter, and eggs, including Bahn Mi Baguettes (page 194) and Pain au Lait Pullman (page 192).

# Tips for Braids

Beautiful challahs can be made by simply coiling a strand of dough or interweaving three strands of dough to make the kind of plait that girls wear in their hair in grade school. But this chapter shows you how we make some of the more showy braids at Hot Bread Kitchen, creating different styles of challah for each dough. To achieve the best results, weigh each strand to make sure they are the same size and, thus, length. I also recommend doing a quick log roll preshape so that each strand has a consistent density.

- From the log roll (see page 120), you can then roll the dough into a **rope** or **long snake** for strands for challah. This move isn't like rolling out clay when you were a kid—pressing down and then pulling apart. Instead, using a gentle firmness, put your hands together in the center of the dough with your palms resting on the log and roll the dough gently back and forth as you slowly move your hands apart. To get to your desired length, you can repeat that rolling motion several times, resting 5 minutes between each one to relax the gluten. Do not just pull it; be mindful that you need to preserve the smooth surface.

- To form a **three-strand braid,** divide the dough into 3 equal pieces, do a log roll on each piece, then roll each one into a rope measuring about 15 inches/38 cm long. Press one end of each of the ropes together so that the 3 are connected at the top. Braid the 3 ropes together, as you would braid hair. Squeeze together at the second end of the braid and then tuck both ends under the loaf.

- To make a **single-strand braid,** you are essentially creating a fancy figure eight with the tails tucked in. To accomplish this, curl one end of the rope into an open circle; tuck the end of the circle under the rope, about 6 inches/15 cm away from the rope's opposite end. Bring the 6-inch/15 cm tail up and then tuck it under the dough circle at the 12 o'clock mark. Tug the circle and twist it once to make it into a figure eight. Thread the end of the tail through the newly formed open circle.

- To form a **turban** for Raisin Challah (page 178) or Sephardic Challah (page 190), form a log roll (page 120) and then roll it into a rope that's 32 inches/80 cm long as instructed on the previous page. Wind the rope into a coil, starting at the center and working outwards. Once the whole piece is coiled tightly, tuck the end underneath and apply a bit of pressure to ensure that it sticks.

# TRADITIONAL CHALLAH

**MAKES 2 (12-INCH/30 CM) LOAVES**

2½ cups/315 g **BREAD FLOUR**, plus more for shaping

1 tablespoon plus 2 teaspoons **SUGAR**

3¼ teaspoons **KOSHER SALT**

1¼ teaspoons **ACTIVE DRY YEAST**

1¼ cups/300 g (risen and deflated) **PÂTE FERMENTÉE** (page 126), cut into walnut-size pieces

3 large **EGG YOLKS**, beaten

2½ tablespoons **HONEY**

3 tablespoons **WATER**, or more if needed

3 tablespoons **CANOLA OIL**, plus more for coating the bowl

2 large **EGGS**, beaten

Most widely available challahs are loaded with commercial yeast. That quickly makes a great-looking puffy loaf, but the flavor suffers. Our challah is different—we use a high proportion of *pâte fermentée* and give it a lot of time to rise, which makes for a beautiful loaf that's also deeply flavorful and toothsome. This recipe includes directions and step-by-step photos to make a two-strand braid. If you are a fan of the more common three-strand braid, simply divide your dough into three strands and braid away. This dough is the base of many other recipes, so if your mixer is big enough, you may want to double it.

**1.** Put the bread flour, sugar, salt, and yeast in the bowl of a stand mixer fitted with a dough hook. Add the *pâte fermentée*, egg yolks, honey, water, and oil and mix on low speed until the dry ingredients are completely incorporated (i.e., you can't see any flour) and the yeast has disappeared into the dough. Add a little extra water if this hasn't happened in 3 minutes. Increase the speed to medium to medium-high and mix until the dough is smooth, pulls away from the sides of the bowl (and leaves the sides clean), has a bit of shine, and makes a slapping noise against the sides of the bowl, about 5 minutes. Do the windowpane test (page 16) to check to see if the gluten is fully developed. The dough will look smooth and feel slightly tacky.

**2.** Coat the inside of a large bowl with oil and transfer the dough to it. Lightly dust the top of the dough with flour and cover the bowl with plastic wrap or put the whole bowl in a large plastic bag. Let stand at room temperature until the dough is puffy and supple, about 1 hour and 30 minutes.

**3.** Tip the dough out onto a lightly floured surface. Flatten slightly and divide it into 4 equal pieces (each weighing about 7½ ounces/215 g). Working with one piece at a time (keep the rest covered with plastic), form a tight log roll (see page 120). Then, with two hands, give the piece a few rolls on the floured surface so that it forms a thick rope about 18 inches/45 cm long (see page 172). Repeat to make 4 ropes.

**4.** Leave 2 ropes loosely covered with plastic. Take the first 2 ropes and form a two-strand braid (see photographs on pages 176 and 177). Form an "X" in front of you with one rope going from the upper right to the lower left on the bottom, and the other on top, going from the upper left to the lower right on top. Fold the top right arm of the X down over the center so it's now facing down toward you. Fold the bottom left arm of the X up over the center so it's now where the top right arm used to be. Do the same with the top left arm and the bottom right arm. Keep building your braid in this fashion until you

*recipe continues*

have no dough left to cross. Turn the braid on its side so that what was the base is now one end of the loaf and squeeze the small end pieces of dough firmly together and tuck them under the braid. Set the braided loaf on a parchment-lined rimmed baking sheet and repeat the process with the remaining 2 ropes of dough to form a second loaf. Evenly space the loaves apart on the baking sheet.

**5.** Carefully brush the challahs with the beaten eggs, reserving whatever egg is left over for a second egg wash. Put the entire baking sheet in a large plastic bag or cover the challahs loosely with plastic wrap, and let them stand at room temperature until they have risen, are supple, and hold indentations when pressed lightly, about 1 hour.

**6.** Meanwhile, preheat the oven to 350°F/180°C.

**7.** Uncover the challahs and gently brush them again with the reserved egg. Bake the loaves until they're mahogany colored and sound hollow when you tap on the bottom of the loaves, 45 minutes to 1 hour. Insert a thin knife in between the strands to make sure that the dough is firm—it should have the density of a well-baked cake.

**8.** Transfer the breads to a wire rack to cool completely, at least 1 hour. Store leftovers in a plastic bag at room temperature or freeze.

# RAISIN CHALLAH

**MAKES 2 (7-INCH/18 CM) ROUND LOAVES**

**TRADITIONAL CHALLAH DOUGH**
(page 175), prepared through
step 1

1 cup/150 g **THOMPSON RAISINS**

**CANOLA OIL**

**BREAD FLOUR**

2 large **EGGS**, beaten

Our raisin challah is made with Traditional Challah dough but studded with raisins and shaped as a turban, not a braid. We sell the most of this satisfying bread during Rosh Hashanah and Yom Kippur (the holiest Jewish holidays), when it is traditional to eat round challah. That said, we make it year-round because it's so popular. After 2 p.m. at Hot Bread Almacen, our retail store in La Marqueta, our breads are pay-what-you-can and the other stall vendors race to our stand to see if there is any raisin challah left. It's also our staff's favorite bread. On Thanksgiving we take staff orders and the raisin challah is always the overwhelming favorite—the bakers' choice.

**1.** Once the dough is smooth (and still in the mixer), add the raisins, mixing as briefly as possible until they're evenly distributed, about 1 minute.

**2.** Coat the inside of a large bowl with oil and transfer the dough to it. Cover the bowl with plastic wrap (or put the whole bowl in a large plastic bag) and let stand until the dough is supple and puffy, about 1 hour at room temperature.

**3.** Turn the dough out onto a lightly floured work surface. Divide into 2 equal pieces (each weighing about 15 ounces/430 g). Leave one piece covered under plastic while you shape the other as a turban (see page 173). Repeat the process with the second piece of dough. Set the coiled loaves on a parchment-lined rimmed baking sheet, evenly spacing them apart.

**4.** Carefully brush the challahs with the beaten eggs, reserving what-ever egg is left over for a second egg wash. Put the entire baking sheet in a large plastic bag or cover the challahs loosely with plastic wrap and let them stand until they're softer than firm balloons, are supple, and hold indentations when pressed lightly, about 1 hour.

**5.** Meanwhile, preheat the oven to 350°F/180°C.

**6.** Uncover the challahs and gently brush them again with the reserved egg. Bake the loaves until they're mahogany colored and sound hollow when you tap on the bottom of the loaves, 30 to 40 minutes. Insert a thin knife between the strands to make sure that the dough is firm—it should have the density of a well-baked cake.

**7.** Transfer the breads to a wire rack to cool completely, at least 1 hour. Store leftovers in a plastic bag at room temperature or freeze.

# PARKER HOUSE ROLLS

**MAKES 30 (2-INCH/5 CM) ROLLS**

**TRADITIONAL CHALLAH DOUGH**
   (page 175), prepared through
   step 2

**BREAD FLOUR**

2 large **EGGS**, beaten

**SESAME SEEDS** (optional)

Parker House rolls are an American classic, especially at Thanksgiving. Their combination of deliciously browned exterior and soft, pillowy interior makes them predestined for mopping up turkey gravy. Note that the techniques for shaping and baking them—dividing the dough, forming each piece into a roll, and baking them so that they rise into each other and stick together—work with just about any bread dough (and are essentially the same for Chocolate Cherry Rolls, page 257). You can use this process with the other challah doughs (pages 175 to 190) or even the dough for Pecan Currant Batard (page 156).

**1.** Line a rimmed baking sheet with parchment paper.

**2.** Turn the dough out onto a lightly floured work surface. Divide the dough into 30 equal pieces (each weighing about 1 ounce/30 g). Then, working with one piece at a time (keep the rest loosely covered with plastic), shape each into a roll (see page 123). Put the rolls on the baking sheet, gathered sides down. Leave about ½ inch/1.5 cm between the rolls. The rolls look best when they're arranged in straight lines. Brush the rolls with the eggs (reserve any left over) and put the entire baking sheet in a large plastic bag or cover the rolls loosely with plastic wrap and let them rest at room temperature until they've risen and filled the pan, 45 minutes to 1 hour.

**3.** Meanwhile, preheat the oven to 350°F/180°C.

**4.** Uncover the rolls and gently brush them with the remaining eggs. Top each roll with a pinch of sesame seeds, if desired. Bake the rolls until they're really browned, a good dark mahogany color, and glossy, about 18 minutes. To see if they're baked, lightly separate the rolls and check that the dough is fully cooked, not gummy.

**5.** Transfer the rolls to a wire rack to cool completely. Store any leftovers in a plastic bag at room temperature for up to 4 days.

# HOT DOG AND HAMBURGER BUNS

**MAKES 12 (6-INCH/15 CM) HOT DOG BUNS OR 10 (4-INCH/10 CM) HAMBURGER BUNS**

**TRADITIONAL CHALLAH DOUGH** (page 175), prepared through step 2 (see Note)

**BREAD FLOUR** for shaping

2 large **EGGS**, beaten

**SESAME SEEDS** (optional)

**NOTE:** You can substitute Whole Wheat Challah dough (page 188) in this recipe.

At Hot Bread Kitchen, many of our breads are inspired by the countries that our bakers come from. I realized early on, though, that having the bakery in New York City means that we also need staples for homegrown New Yorkers. That's where these buns and rolls come in. And New Yorkers eat a lot of them, especially in the summertime.

1. Line a rimmed baking sheet with parchment paper.

2. Turn the dough out onto a lightly floured surface. For hot dog buns, divide the dough into 12 equal pieces (each weighing about 2½ ounces/70 g). For hamburger buns, divide the dough into 10 equal pieces (each weighing about 3 ounces/90 g). For hot dog rolls, shape each piece of dough using a log roll (see page 120). Then roll into ropes measuring about 6 inches/15 cm long. For hamburger buns, work each piece of dough into a roll (see page 123) measuring about 4 inches/10 cm in diameter.

3. Transfer the buns to the baking sheet, seam side down. For hot dog buns, pack them tightly so that their edges touch one another. For hamburger buns, leave a couple of inches (about 5 cm) between each of them. Brush them with the eggs (reserve any that's left over). Put the entire baking sheet in a large plastic bag or cover the buns loosely with plastic wrap and let them stand at room temperature until they're softer than firm balloons, are supple, and hold indentations when pressed lightly, about 1 hour.

4. Meanwhile, preheat the oven to 350°F/180°C.

5. Uncover the rolls and gently brush them with the remaining eggs. Top each roll with a pinch of sesame seeds if desired. Bake the rolls until they're really browned, a good dark mahogany color, and glossy, about 18 minutes. To check if the hot dog buns are baked, lightly separate the rolls and check that the dough is fully cooked, not gummy.

6. Transfer the rolls to a wire rack to cool completely. Store any leftovers at room temperature in a plastic bag for up to 4 days.

# VANILLA OR CHOCOLATE CONCHAS

MAKES 12 (3-INCH/7.5 CM) CONCHAS; SERVES 12

**TRADITIONAL CHALLAH DOUGH** (page 175), prepared through step 2

**CHOCOLATE OR VANILLA TOPPING**

3½ cups/445 g **BREAD FLOUR**

½ teaspoon **BAKING POWDER**

½ teaspoon **KOSHER SALT**

¼ cup/20 g **UNSWEETENED COCOA POWDER,** for chocolate buns

½ pound plus 6 tablespoons/ 310 g **UNSALTED BUTTER,** at room temperature

2½ cups/300 g **CONFECTIONERS' SUGAR**

2 teaspoons **VANILLA EXTRACT,** for vanilla buns, or ½ teaspoon **ALMOND EXTRACT,** for chocolate buns

A *concha* is a small, sweet roll, topped with a sugary crust that resembles a seashell (*concha* means "shell" in Spanish). They're ubiquitous in Mexico, where they are huge and sold in a variety of lurid colors, including nearly neon red and green. We developed ours to be pretty faithful to the genre, but not dyed or oversized. We use our challah dough for the base, which is untraditional, but it works well and is very similar to the egg-rich dough used in Mexico.

**1.** While the dough is rising, make the *concha* topping. Whisk together the flour, baking powder, and salt in a bowl. If making chocolate *conchas*, whisk in the cocoa powder. Put the butter and confectioners' sugar in the bowl of a stand mixer fitted with a whisk attachment and beat on medium speed until creamy, about 4 minutes. Beat in the extract. Add the flour mixture, and beat until just combined.

**2.** Put the topping between two large rectangles of parchment paper on a work surface. Roll the topping out until it's about ½ inch/1.5 cm thick. Remove the top parchment and, using a glass, cut out 12 rounds. (Save scraps to reroll if you make *conchas* again within a week or bake them in a 350°F/180°C oven for 10 minutes for a delicious cookie.) Using a sharp knife, score each round with a hash mark—do not cut through the topping. Let rest at room temperature, preferably somewhere cool.

**3.** Line a rimmed baking sheet with parchment paper.

**4.** Turn the challah dough out onto a lightly floured work surface and divide it into 12 equal pieces (each weighing about 2½ ounces/70 g). Form each piece into a roll (see page 123). Transfer the rolls to the baking sheet, leaving space between them. Gently top each one with a scored round and cover loosely with plastic wrap. Let the *conchas* stand at room temperature until they're softer than firm balloons, are supple, and hold indentations when pressed lightly, about 1 hour. As they rise, the topping will bend and start to cover the top of the dough.

**5.** Meanwhile, preheat the oven to 350°F/180°C.

**6.** Bake until the base is golden brown and the topping is firm to the touch, about 15 minutes.

**7.** Transfer the *conchas* to a wire rack to cool completely. Store in a plastic bag for up to 4 days.

# MONKEY BREAD

**MAKES 2 (9-INCH/23 CM) LOAVES; SERVES 8**

1 cup/200 g **GRANULATED SUGAR**

1 packed cup/220 g **DARK BROWN SUGAR**

1 teaspoon ground **CINNAMON**

½ teaspoon ground **NUTMEG**

**TRADITIONAL CHALLAH DOUGH** (page 175), prepared through step 2

**ALL-PURPOSE FLOUR**

**COOKING SPRAY**

This is a cinnamony, sweet pull-apart bread that we make to use up extra challah dough. Prepare to be swarmed by children and neighbors.

**1.** Whisk together the granulated sugar, brown sugar, cinnamon, and nutmeg in a small bowl.

**2.** Divide the dough in half. On a lightly floured work surface, use your hands to roll each half into an 18-inch/45 cm rope and then cut each rope into 18 (1-inch/2.5 cm) pieces. Transfer the pieces to a rimmed baking sheet, sprinkle them with half of the sugar mixture, and toss to coat.

**3.** Generously coat 2 (9 × 5-inch/ 23 × 13 cm) loaf pans with cooking spray. Divide the dough pieces between the pans, sprinkling them with the remaining sugar mixture as you go. Put the loaf pans in large plastic bags or cover them loosely with plastic wrap, and let them rest until they are softer than firm balloons, are supple, and fill the pans, about 1 hour.

**4.** Meanwhile, preheat the oven to 350°F/180°C.

**5.** Bake the monkey breads until they're browned and the sugar is bubbling, about 25 minutes. Let the breads cool in the pans on a rack for 20 minutes before unmolding. Serve warm or at room temperature. Store any leftovers in an airtight plastic bag for up to a couple of days at room temperature.

# WHOLE WHEAT CHALLAH

MAKES 2 (12-INCH/30 CM) LOAVES

¼ cup plus 1 tablespoon/65 g **WATER**

1¾ cups/220 g **WHOLE WHEAT FLOUR**, preferably coarsely ground

⅔ cup/85 g **BREAD FLOUR**, plus more for shaping

3 large **EGGS**

⅓ cup/75 g **CANOLA OIL**, plus more for coating the bowl

2½ tablespoons **HONEY**

1 tablespoon plus 2 teaspoons **SUGAR**

2 teaspoons **KOSHER SALT**

1¼ cups/300 g (risen and deflated) **PÂTE FERMENTÉE** (page 126), cut into walnut-size pieces

1¼ teaspoons **ACTIVE DRY YEAST**

1 tablespoon **SESAME SEEDS**

While I grew up eating Traditional Challah (page 175), this whole wheat version is the one I now eat on most Friday nights with my family. The large percentage of hearty local whole wheat flour makes me feel less guilty about eating most of the loaf myself.

This challah is formed into a one-strand braid, which requires some practice. If you are impatient or a traditionalist, form it into a typical three-strand loaf instead.

**1.** Combine the water, whole wheat flour and bread flour in the bowl of a stand mixer fitted with a dough hook. Mix on low speed until combined, about 2 minutes, then let rest for 20 minutes to hydrate the flours.

**2.** Lightly beat 2 of the eggs in a medium bowl and whisk in the oil, honey, sugar, and salt. Add to the mixer along with the *pâte fermentée* and yeast and mix on low until integrated, about 2 minutes, and turn up to medium to medium-high speed until the dough is smooth, pulls away from the sides of the bowl (and leaves the sides clean), has a bit of shine, and makes a slapping noise against the sides of the bowl, 5 to 6 minutes. Do the windowpane test (page 16) to check to see if the gluten is fully developed.

**3.** Coat the inside of a large bowl with oil and transfer the dough to it. Cover with plastic wrap (or put the whole thing in a large plastic bag) and let stand at room temperature until the dough is soft and supple, and holds an indentation when pressed lightly, 1½ to 2 hours.

**4.** Divide the dough into 2 equal pieces (each weighing about 16½ ounces/475 g). Working with one piece at a time (keep the other covered with plastic), form a log roll (see page 120). Then roll each piece on the floured surface so that it forms a rope about 18 inches/45 cm long (see page 172). Shape into a single-strand braid (see page 172). Set the loaves on a parchment-lined rimmed baking sheet.

**5.** Lightly beat the remaining egg. Carefully brush the challahs with the egg, reserving whatever egg is left over for a second egg wash. Put the entire baking sheet in a large plastic bag or cover the challahs loosely with plastic wrap and let them stand at room temperature until they're softer than firm balloons, are supple, and hold indentations when pressed lightly, about 1 hour.

**6.** Meanwhile, preheat the oven to 350°F/180°C.

**7.** Uncover the challahs and gently brush them again with the reserved egg. Sprinkle with the sesame seeds and let dry, uncovered, for 10 minutes.

**8.** Bake the loaves until they're mahogany colored and sound hollow when you tap on the bottom of the loaves, 20 to 25 minutes. Insert a thin knife between the strands to make sure that the dough is firm—it should have the density of a well-baked cake.

**9.** Transfer the loaves to a wire rack to cool completely, at least 1 hour. Store leftovers in a plastic bag at room temperature or freeze.

# SEPHARDIC CHALLAH

MAKES 2 (12-INCH/30 CM) ROUND LOAVES

1 tablespoon **SESAME SEEDS**

2 teaspoons **CARAWAY SEEDS**

2 teaspoons **CUMIN SEEDS**

2 cups/455 g **LUKEWARM WATER**

5 cups/635 g **BREAD FLOUR**, plus
    more for shaping

2¼ teaspoons **ACTIVE DRY YEAST**
    (1 envelope)

2½ tablespoons **EXTRA-VIRGIN
    OLIVE OIL**, plus more as needed

1 tablespoon **KOSHER SALT**

2 tablespoons **HONEY**

In North Africa and the Middle East, where Sephardic Jews come from, the Sabbath bread is filled with spices and seeds. The only complaint we've ever heard about our Sephardic challah is that it's not available year-round. This bread is dense with seeds and is, therefore, a little crumbly in texture. It makes delicious toast and exotic croutons that are especially great with the arugula salad on page 276.

**1.** Put the sesame seeds, the caraway seeds, and cumin seeds in a dry skillet and set it over medium heat. Cook, stirring, until the seeds smell fragrant and are lightly toasted, about 2 minutes. Transfer the seeds to a plate and let them cool.

**2.** Mix together the water and flour in the bowl of a stand mixer fitted with a dough hook. Mix for 2 minutes until integrated and let rest 20 minutes for the flour to hydrate.

**3.** Add the yeast, olive oil, salt, and honey and mix on low speed until the ingredients are thoroughly combined, about 2 minutes. Mix on medium-high speed until the dough is smooth, pulls away from the sides of the bowl (and leaves the sides clean), has a bit of shine, and makes a slapping noise against the sides of the bowl, about 5 minutes. Do the windowpane test (page 16) to check to see if the gluten is fully developed. Add the toasted seeds and mix on low to integrate, about 1 minute.

**4.** Coat the inside of a large bowl with olive oil, coat your hands with a little oil, and transfer the dough to the bowl. Cover the bowl with plastic wrap (or put the whole bowl in a large plastic bag) and let stand at room temperature until the dough is puffy and soft, about 1 hour.

**5.** Turn the dough out onto a lightly floured work surface. Divide into 2 equal pieces (each weighing about 1½ pounds/650 g). Leave one piece loosely covered with plastic while you shape the other as a turban (see page 173). Repeat the process with the second piece of dough. Set the coiled loaves on a parchment-lined rimmed baking sheet, evenly spacing them apart. Put the entire baking sheet in a large plastic bag or cover the loaves loosely with plastic wrap and let them stand until they are softer than firm balloons, are supple, and hold indentations when pressed lightly, about 1 hour.

**6.** Meanwhile, preheat the oven to 400°F/205°C.

**7.** Bake the loaves until they are mahogany colored and sound hollow when you tap on the bottom of the loaves, about 30 minutes. Insert a thin knife between the strands and make sure that the dough is firm—it should have the density of a well-baked cake.

**8.** Transfer the loaves to a wire rack to cool completely. Any leftovers can be stored in an airtight plastic bag at room temperature for a few days.

# PAIN AU LAIT PULLMAN

MAKES 2 (9-INCH/23 CM) LOAVES

2¼ teaspoons **ACTIVE DRY YEAST** (1 envelope)

2 cups/500 g **WHOLE MILK**, at room temperature

5½ cups/710 g **BREAD FLOUR**, plus more for shaping

2 tablespoons **SUGAR**

1 tablespoon plus 2 teaspoons **KOSHER SALT**

3½ tablespoons **UNSALTED BUTTER**, melted and cooled

**CANOLA OIL**

White bread has gotten itself a bad name—shorthand for insipid, industrial bread. This classic loaf has lots of soul and flavor and will put white bread back in your good graces. While this dough can be formed into many shapes, we often sell it as a Pullman loaf, a traditional sandwich bread. The one pictured here is made in the bakery for food service, but your home version will have a domed top. The milk in the dough adds softness and extends the bread's shelf life; the butter keeps it moist.

1. Mix together the yeast and milk in the bowl of a stand mixer fitted with a dough hook. Add the flour, sugar, salt, and melted butter and mix on low speed until the ingredients are combined, 1 to 2 minutes. Increase the speed to medium-high and mix until the dough is smooth, pulls away from the sides of the bowl (and leaves the sides clean), has a bit of shine, and makes a slapping noise against the sides of the bowl, about 6 minutes. Do the windowpane test (page 16) to check to see if the gluten is fully developed.

**2.** Put the dough in a large clean bowl and cover with plastic wrap (or put the whole bowl in a large plastic bag). Let stand at room temperature until tripled in size, about 1½ hours.

**3.** Coat 2 (9 × 5-inch/23 × 13 cm) loaf pans with oil.

**4.** Turn the dough out onto a lightly floured work surface. Divide into 2 equal pieces (each weighing about 23 ounces/650 g). Working with one piece at a time (keep the other covered with plastic), form a pullman (see page 120). Roll the dough on the floured surface so that it forms a loaf that measures 9 inches/23 cm long. Repeat the process with the second piece of dough. Put the loaves, seam side down, into the prepared loaf pans. Cover loosely with plastic wrap and let stand until they fill the pans by about three-quarters, about 1 hour.

**5.** Meanwhile, preheat the oven to 400°F/205°C.

**6.** Brush the loaves lightly with water or lightly mist them with a spray bottle. Bake until the breads are golden brown and sound hollow when tapped, 30 to 40 minutes. Let the loaves cool in the pans for 5 minutes. Then loosen the loaves and turn them out on their sides onto wire racks. Let them cool completely on their sides. Store in a paper or cloth bag for up to 1 day. After that, store in a plastic bag at room temperature.

## Bolillo Rolls

**MAKES 8 ROLLS**

This is a Mexican hoagie roll used for tortas. It has a soft interior, ideal for absorbing the delicious drippings from carnitas (pages 106 and 107).

Pain au Lait Pullman dough (opposite), prepared through step 2
¼ cup/60 g water
1 teaspoon cornstarch

Line a rimmed baking sheet with parchment paper. Turn the dough out onto a lightly floured surface. Divide it into 8 equal pieces (each weighing about 5¼ ounces/150 g). Work each piece of dough into a roll (see page 123). Gently roll 2 opposing ends of the roll to taper them and form the dough into an oval shape. Transfer the rolls to the baking sheet, evenly spacing them apart. Put the entire baking sheet in a large plastic bag or cover the rolls loosely with plastic wrap and let them rest at room temperature for 1 hour.

Meanwhile, preheat the oven to 350°F/180°C.

Combine the water and cornstarch in a small saucepan. Cook, stirring, over medium heat until the mixture is thickened, about 2 minutes. Set aside to cool.

Uncover the rolls, brush them with the cornstarch mixture, and, using a bread lame or sharp paring knife, slash each oval down the middle stopping ½ inch/1.5 cm from each end. Bake the bolillos, rotating the pans front to back halfway through baking, until the rolls are beautifully browned, about 25 minutes. Transfer to wire racks to cool completely.

# BAHN MI BAGUETTES

**MAKES 5 (ROUGHLY 10-INCH/25 CM) LOAVES, ENOUGH FOR 5 LARGE SANDWICHES**

3 cups/380 g **BREAD FLOUR**

1 cup minus 1 tablespoon/210 g
   **WATER**

¾ cup plus 2 tablespoons/
   205 g (risen and deflated)
   **PÂTE FERMENTÉE** (page 126),
   cut into walnut-size pieces

1 tablespoon **KOSHER SALT**

½ teaspoon **ACTIVE DRY YEAST**

1½ tablespoons **UNSALTED BUTTER**,
   at room temperature

**CANOLA OIL**

Adding butter to a classic baguette dough gives it a flaky crust, which gives these sandwich-friendly breads the same satisfying mouthfeel of a baguette, but they won't cut the roof of your mouth.

**1.** Combine the flour and water in a stand mixer fitted with a dough hook. Mix on low speed until combined, 1 to 2 minutes. Let rest for 20 minutes to hydrate the flour.

**2.** Add the *pâte fermentée*, salt, yeast, and butter. Mix on low speed until all of the ingredients are combined, just 1 to 2 minutes. Increase the speed to medium to medium-high and mix until the dough is smooth, pulls away from the sides of the bowl (and leaves the sides clean), has a bit of shine, and makes a slapping noise against the sides of the bowl, 4 to 6 minutes. Do the windowpane test (page 16) to check to see if the gluten is fully developed.

**3.** Coat the inside of a large bowl with oil and transfer the dough to it. Cover the bowl tightly with plastic wrap (or put the whole bowl into a large plastic bag) and let stand at room temperature until it is puffy and soft, about 2 hours.

**4.** Line the undersides of 2 baking sheets with parchment paper. Turn the dough out onto a lightly floured surface. Divide it into 5 equal pieces (each weighing about 6 ounces/165 g). Working with one piece of dough at a time, form a log roll (see page 120). Then roll each piece of dough into a cylinder mea-

suring about 7 inches/17.5 cm long. The ends should not be tapered. Put the loaves on the baking sheets at least 2 inches/5 cm apart. Cover the loaves with plastic wrap and let them stand until they're soft and supple, and hold indentations when pressed lightly, about 2 hours.

**5.** Meanwhile, put a pizza stone on the middle rack of the oven and preheat to 500°F/260°C. Set a baking dish in the bottom of the oven.

**6.** Using a bread lame or sharp paring knife, slash each loaf three times across the top. Put the breads from one baking sheet on the pizza stone in one swift movement, letting the parchment slide off the sheet and onto the stone. Put 10 ice cubes in the baking dish at the bottom of the oven (this will create steam) and reduce the oven temperature to 450°F/235°C.

**7.** Bake until the breads are lightly browned on top and sound hollow when you tap them on the bottom, 12 to 16 minutes. Transfer to a wire rack to cool completely and discard the parchment paper. Meanwhile, bake the remaining loaves in the same manner.

**8.** Store bread that will be consumed within 24 hours in a paper or cloth bag. After that, store in a plastic bag at room temperature.

# ROAST PORK BELLY BAHN MI
## WITH "THE WORKS"

**MAKES 4 LARGE SANDWICHES; SERVES 6 TO 8**

**KOSHER SALT**

1 teaspoon **DARK BROWN SUGAR**

¼ teaspoon **5-SPICE POWDER**

¼ teaspoon ground **WHITE PEPPER**

1 (1-pound/455 g) piece bone-in, skin-on **PORK BELLY**

4 **BAHN MI BAGUETTES** (page 194) or other crusty hero rolls

14 ounces/400 g **PORK LIVER PÂTÉ**, homemade (page 197) or store-bought

¾ cup/170 g **MAYONNAISE**, homemade (such as **RICE VINEGAR MAYONNAISE**, page 167) or store-bought, preferably Kewpie

1½ cups/150 g **QUICK CARROT AND DAIKON PICKLES** (page 198)

1 **ENGLISH CUCUMBER**, cut into thin strips 3 inches/7.5 cm long

1 to 2 **JALAPEÑOS** (to taste), seeded and thinly sliced

Large handful of **FRESH CILANTRO LEAVES**

**SRIRACHA SAUCE**

Thuy Nguyen, our former farmers' market manager, is Vietnamese and made these delicious sandwiches for our staff. Even though we come from so many different places, everyone seems to love them. The method for seasoning and roasting the pork belly is a little time consuming but worth having in your repertoire. The resulting meat is great on its own or alongside rice and cooked greens. If you don't eat pork, rub the seasoning mixture on chicken thighs, steak, or even tofu, and grill or broil; omit the pâté.

1. In a small bowl, stir together 1 teaspoon salt, the brown sugar, 5-spice powder, and white pepper.

2. Fill a large skillet with 1 inch/ 2.5 cm of water and bring to a boil. Reduce the heat and, using tongs, quickly dip the skin side of the pork belly into the water just until the skin itself is hot, about 30 seconds. Try to keep the meat above the water during this time. Transfer the pork to a cutting board, skin side up. Pierce the skin about a dozen times across the surface with the tip of your knife, being careful to pierce just the skin and fat and not the meat below. Rinse the pork under cold water and dry completely with paper towels.

3. Rub the reserved seasoning mix all over the pork meat, avoiding the top skin layer. Rub ¼ teaspoon salt into the skin. Cover the pork meat with plastic wrap but leave the skin exposed to the air (so that it can further dry out); then put it on a plate and refrigerate overnight or for up to 3 days.

4. On the day you are ready to roast the pork, take it out of the fridge and let it sit on the counter for an hour, so that it comes to room temperature.

5. In the meantime, preheat the oven to 425°F/220°C. Set a wire rack on a rimmed baking sheet.

6. Put the pork belly, skin side up, on the rack. Roast the pork until the exterior is browned, about 30 minutes.

7. Reduce the oven temperature to 350°F/180°C and roast the pork until the meat is tender, about 30 minutes more. (Thuy's father taught her to poke it with something blunt like a chopstick, and if it's soft, you know it's done.) Remove from the oven and drain the fat from the baking sheet (discard or reserve for another use, such as sautéing onions).

8. Preheat the broiler.

*recipe continues*

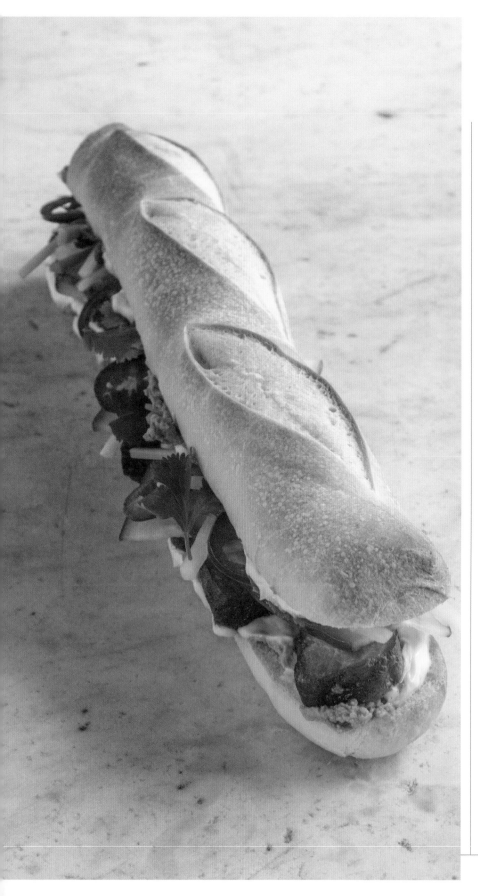

**9.** Broil the pork until the skin is crispy and bubbling, just a few minutes depending on the strength of your broiler. Transfer the pork to a cutting board and let it cool for at least 15 minutes. Remove the bone and then thinly slice the pork belly.

**10.** Reheat the oven to 400°F/205°C.

**11.** Put the bread on a rimmed baking sheet and put it in the oven until the bread is warm and the crust feels dry and crisp, about 4 minutes.

**12.** Once the bread is cool enough to handle, slice each roll in half horizontally, but don't cut it all the way through. Open each baguette as you would a book.

**13.** Working with one roll at a time, spread ¼ cup/100 g pâté on the cut sides of the bread. Spread 3 tablespoons of the mayonnaise on top. Evenly put one-quarter of the sliced pork belly on one side of the bread and then add one-quarter of the pickles, cucumber, jalapeño, and cilantro. Close the sandwiches, cut them in half, and serve immediately with Sriracha on the side.

# PORK LIVER PÂTÉ

**MAKES 1 POUND 5 OUNCES/600 G**

While making your own pâté sounds impressive and maybe even impossible, this recipe couldn't be easier. Note that this recipe yields more than you need for the sandwiches. You can either use extra on the sandwiches for additional porky deliciousness or spread it on toasted bread and serve with cornichons for a snack.

1 pound/455 g **PORK LIVER**, cleaned and trimmed of any excess tissue, cut into 1-inch/2.5 cm pieces

1 cup/240 g **WHOLE MILK**

6 tablespoons/85 g **UNSALTED BUTTER**, at room temperature

2 **GARLIC CLOVES**, minced

2 **SHALLOTS**, finely chopped

**KOSHER SALT** and freshly ground **BLACK PEPPER**

1 tablespoon **COGNAC** or other brandy

2 tablespoons **HEAVY CREAM**

Put the liver and milk in a bowl and cover tightly with plastic wrap. Refrigerate for at least 1 hour or up to 1 day. Discard the milk. Rinse and drain the liver with cold water and dry it with paper towels. This step helps to tame the liver's strong taste.

Melt 2 tablespoons/30 g of the butter in a large skillet over medium-high heat. Add the garlic and shallots and cook, stirring, until the aromatics are fragrant, about a minute. Add the liver and season with salt and pepper. Cook the liver, turning the pieces once, until they're browned on both sides, 1 to 2 minutes per side. Add the Cognac to the pan (be careful—if you have a gas flame it might burst into flame, but don't worry, it will extinguish itself quickly) and cook until the liquid is completely evaporated, about a minute. At this point the pieces of liver should be just firm to the touch.

Transfer the contents of the pan, making sure you scrape the bottom well, into a food processor. Pulse the liver a few times until roughly chopped. While the machine is running, add the remaining 4 tablespoons/60 g butter, 1 tablespoon/15 g at a time, and then pour in the cream. Taste the mixture for seasoning, adding more salt and pepper if necessary. At this point, if you want the mixture to be extra smooth, use a rubber spatula to press it through a fine sieve into a clean bowl (it's okay to skip this step).

Transfer the pâté to a ramekin and cover it tightly with plastic wrap. Chill the pâté in the refrigerator for at least 2 hours or for up to 3 days. Taste the pâté again before serving—it might need more salt and pepper, as chilling it will slightly diminish the seasoning.

# QUICK CARROT AND DAIKON PICKLES

**MAKES ABOUT 3 CUPS/300 G**

These easy pickles make a refreshing, crunchy, bright accompaniment to sandwiches, tacos, grilled cheese sandwiches, and cured meat platters. Thuy likes them on a bowl of rice topped with a fried egg. I can't think of a better breakfast!

1 cup/225 g **DISTILLED WHITE VINEGAR**

½ cup/100 g **SUGAR**

½ teaspoon **KOSHER SALT**

2 medium **CARROTS**, peeled and cut into small matchsticks (about 2 cups/200 g)

½ small **DAIKON**, peeled and cut into small matchsticks (about 1 cup/100 g)

2 cups/450 g **COLD WATER**

Put the vinegar, sugar, and salt in a large nonreactive bowl and whisk until the sugar is dissolved. Add the carrots, daikon, and water to the bowl. Stir everything together and cover the bowl tightly with plastic wrap. Refrigerate for at least 30 minutes and up to 2 days before serving.

# ICED VIETNAMESE COFFEE

SERVES 1

1 generous tablespoon **CONDENSED MILK**

¾ cup/170 g **BOILING WATER**

2 tablespoons ground **CHICORY COFFEE**, preferably Café Du Monde

The combination of strongly brewed chicory coffee, sweet condensed milk, and lots of ice is a bahn mi's best friend. Traditionally, each cup is made by filling a glass with ice and condensed milk and putting a small Vietnamese-style coffee percolator right on top of the glass so that the hot coffee pours down directly on the milk and ice. These percolators are available widely online (see sources, page 291), but if you don't have individual percolators, simply brew a strong pot of chicory coffee, mix ½ cup/120 ml of it with the condensed milk, and enjoy.

1. Put the condensed milk in the bottom of a heatproof glass or measuring cup. Set a small coffee percolator on top of the glass. Fill the percolator with the ground coffee according to the manufacturer's instructions. Slowly pour the boiling water over the grounds so that the coffee drips directly onto the condensed milk.

2. When the coffee stops dripping, remove the percolator and stir the coffee and milk together. Pour the mixture into a glass filled with ice and serve immediately.

# FILLED DOUGHS

FROM AROUND THE WORLD

To the home cook, recipes with a filling and folded dough may seem intimidating. It's a lot of busy work, or *patschke*, as they say in my family. Admittedly there are many steps to making filled dough pockets: prepping a filling; mixing, rolling, and portioning dough; assembling neat little packets; and baking, frying, or boiling—not to mention sometimes making a dipping sauce. Fear not. These are forgiving dishes that are delicious even if they aren't beautiful on the first try. There are at least three reasons you should get comfortable with these recipes: (1) The more often you make these recipes, the easier they get; (2) guests will be especially impressed when you serve these because they look difficult to make; and (3) making a meat-filled empanada is actually easier than prepping a "square meal"—protein, carbohydrate, and vegetable—since in one handheld bundle you can get all three.

This is a big chapter filled with exquisite little things: Pastellitos (empanadas Dominican-style, page 222, and Chilean, page 221) and Kreplach (page 206) destined for a bowl of my Bubie's Chicken Soup (page 204). There are Potato Knishes (page 209), Albanian Cheese Triangles (page 212), and Tibetan Momos (page 215). A veritable trip around the world in a handful of pages, these filled doughs and their accompaniments guarantee satisfaction and, I promise, not too much *patschke*.

*Potato knish with mushroom and broccoli filling (page 211)*

*PREVIOUS PAGES: Chilean Empanadas (page 221) and Pastellitos (page 222)*

## Tips for Filled Doughs

In addition to the tips below, you should review those on mixing doughs (page 15), dough on hands (page 15), and the role temperature plays in breads (page 17).

- Tender, flaky pastry dough, such as Empanada Dough (page 220), relies on integrating fat into flour. The goal is to create small pieces of fat coated with flour so that when you cook the dough the water in the fat turns to steam, creating flaky layers. The best and easiest way of doing this is to work quickly with cold fat. Cube the butter or lard and refrigerate it for a couple of hours before incorporating it into the flour. While some people prefer to use a pastry cutter or two table knives to cut the flour into the fat, I use my fingertips, crumbling the mixture between them as I work. Remember that the goal is to leave tiny bits of fat—not knead the dough and form gluten. If you're short on time or making a big batch of dough, use a food processor—just don't over-process the dough; short pulses work best.

- When rolling dough thinly—whether pastry dough for empanadas (pages 220 to 223) or a simpler dough like the one used for Tibetan Momos (page 215) or Kreplach (page 206), or even a good old pie crust—if the dough resists, cover it with a piece of plastic wrap, and let it rest for 5 minutes. Patience pays off here. Rested dough rolls more easily. The fight it's putting up? That's simply all the gluten trying to hold its shape. Letting the gluten rest will encourage it to relax.

- Before you seal the packet for filled doughs such as Kreplach (page 206), make sure to use your fingers to squeeze out any air that might be trapped between the layers of dough. This will help prevent fillings from escaping during cooking and will create prettier end results.

- Consider making a double or even triple batch of these recipes so you can put some in the freezer. To freeze filled doughs, fill, shape, and seal them. Line them up on a parchment-lined baking sheet and freeze them until they're solid, a couple of hours. Pop them off and store them in a sealed airtight bag or container—this way they don't stick to each other and are easy to cook. No need to thaw before cooking; just boil, fry, or bake them from their frozen state, adding a few extra minutes to the cooking time.

# BUBIE'S CHICKEN SOUP

SERVES 8

1 large (3- to 4-pound/1.4 to 1.8 kg) **WHOLE CHICKEN**, preferably kosher, cut into 8 pieces

1 pound/455 g **CHICKEN BACKS AND NECKS**, preferably kosher

1 head **GARLIC**

1 large **ONION**, peeled and left whole

2 **CARROTS**, peeled and cut into 3 large pieces each

1 **PARSNIP**, peeled and cut into 3 large pieces

2 teaspoons whole **BLACK PEPPERCORNS**

**KOSHER SALT**

2 large **CELERY STALKS**, cut into 3 large pieces each

½ head **CAULIFLOWER**, cut into large florets

½ **GREEN BELL PEPPER**, quartered

4 large sprigs **FRESH DILL**

3 sprigs **FRESH PARSLEY**

16 **KREPLACH** (optional; page 206), boiled

Chicken soup is like bread: Nearly every culture has its own version to which people are attached. I ate this heart-and-soul-warming chicken soup—affectionately dubbed "Jewish penicillin"—every week growing up. My grandmother has never written down her recipe, but she taught me how to make it. Her soup is like chicken essence—nearly a consommé uncontaminated by floating particles. She even uses white pepper so that there are no black flecks in the soup. I use whole black peppercorns because I think they have more flavor than white—but I strain them out after cooking. The secret is to make the soup with a kosher chicken, which is pre-salted, so it adds more flavor than a regular chicken. It is also important to degrease this soup by refrigerating it overnight, then removing the congealed fat.

Float cooked kreplach, matzo balls, or noodles in this soup. If you serve it Bubie's way—the broth accompanied by rounds of boiled carrots and parsnips, you'll have lots of moist boiled chicken left to make chicken salad or fill Potato Knishes (page 211). One pot of soup can feed my family for a week.

**1.** Put the chicken parts and chicken backs and necks in a pot with at least a 12-quart/11-liter capacity. Cut the top off the garlic head so that the cloves are exposed, but the head is still held together by the root end (discard the top) and add to the pot. Add the onion, carrots, parsnip, peppercorns, and 1 tablespoon salt. Cover everything with 4 quarts/3.75 liters cold water.

**2.** Bring the soup to a boil and let it boil vigorously for 5 minutes. Skim the surface and discard the foam or fat that bubbles to the surface. Reduce the heat and simmer the soup until the chicken is no longer pink on the outside, about 20 minutes. Add the celery and cauliflower and let them cook until they barely begin to soften, 5 to 10 minutes. Add the bell pepper and let the soup simmer until the vegetables are soft, about 45 minutes.

**3.** Using a piece of kitchen twine, tie the dill and parsley together and add the herbs to the soup. Simmer until the herbs smell fragrant, a final 10 minutes. Turn the heat off and allow everything to sit in the pot until it's cool enough to handle, about 2 hours.

**4.** Set up a colander over a very large bowl and use a slotted spoon to transfer the chicken and the vegetables to it. Press on the vegetables with a spoon to make sure all of their flavorful liquid is pressed out. Discard the herbs and vegetables except for the parsnip, carrot, and celery. Cut the parsnip and carrot pieces into small rounds and cut the celery into small pieces and set aside.

**5.** Shred the chicken meat into small pieces (discard the skin and bones).

**6.** Strain the cooking liquid through a fine-mesh sieve into a clean pot. Pour whatever liquid has accumulated in the bowl beneath the colander through the sieve into the pot, too. Bring the broth to a boil and taste it. It will likely need a generous amount of salt.

**7.** Degrease the soup by skimming off the liquid fat from the surface, or let the soup cool to room temperature and then refrigerate for at least 4 hours and remove the congealed fat with a spoon. Divide the reserved carrot, parsnip, and celery pieces evenly among 8 bowls. If you like, add some of the boiled chicken to each. If these vegetables and chicken have gotten cold while your broth reduced, simply warm them in a separate pot in a bit of warm broth.

**8.** Ladle the hot broth into the bowls and float 2 cooked kreplach on top of each, if desired. Serve hot.

# KREPLACH

MAKES 64 KREPLACH, OR 32 SERVINGS

2 cups/250 g **ALL-PURPOSE FLOUR**, plus more for shaping

**KOSHER SALT**

2 tablespoons **WARM WATER**

2 large **EGGS**

**MEAT FILLING** or **KASHA FILLING** (recipes follow)

**CANOLA OIL**

For two decades I made kreplach (the dumplings traditionally eaten in chicken soup; see page 204) with my grandmother and great-grandmother for Rosh Hashanah. My great-bubie kept a careful count by drying them in rows on kitchen towels—302 one year, 365 another. My favorite version is filled with meat, but during my vegan years, I developed a kasha recipe that's satisfying. Note the high yield of this recipe; the formed kreplach freeze well (see page 203)—a blessing since they are labor intensive.

**1.** Combine the flour, ½ teaspoon salt, the water, and eggs in a stand mixer fitted with a dough hook and mix on low until all of the ingredients are integrated, 2 minutes. Turn the speed up to medium and mix until a smooth dough forms, about 3 minutes. Transfer the dough to a board, cover loosely with plastic wrap, and let rest for at least 15 minutes.

**2.** Lightly dust a work surface with flour. Line a rimmed baking sheet with a clean kitchen towel. Unwrap the dough and dust it with flour on both sides. Cut it into 4 equal pieces (each weighing about 3½ ounces/100 g). Working with one piece of dough at a time (keep the rest covered lightly with plastic wrap), roll it into a 12-inch/30 cm square. If it resists rolling, let it rest for a few minutes before proceeding. Turn the dough as you roll it and flour the surface again if necessary. Trim into a rough square—save the trimmings and reroll. Cut the square into fourths one way and then into fourths the opposite way to make 16 (3-inch/ 7.5 cm) squares per piece of dough.

**3.** Fill a small bowl with water and set it on your work surface. Put a

heaping teaspoon of filling in the center of each square. Use your fingers to moisten the edges of the square with water and then fold the square in half to form a triangle with the filling snugly tucked into the center. Stretch the dough slightly as you do this. Pinch the edges to make sure the seam is sealed; be sure to press as you do this to make sure no air is trapped with the filling. With damp fingers, join the 2 short edges of the triangle in the front of the filling—it almost looks like someone with folded arms. A little water will help seal it. Put the finished kreplach on the cloth-lined baking sheet.

**4.** Continue rolling, filling, and forming the kreplach until you use up all of your dough and filling. You can cook the kreplach immediately or freeze them for future use. To freeze, let the kreplach dry on kitchen towels and then follow the freezing directions on page 203. The kreplach can be boiled straight from the freezer.

**5.** To cook the kreplach, bring a stockpot of water to a boil and salt it generously. Put half the kreplach in the pot. Once they float to the surface, reduce the heat to medium,

and cook, uncovered, until the kreplach are tender, 5 to 7 minutes. Use a slotted spoon or a handheld strainer to transfer the kreplach to a colander, then cook the second batch. Drizzle the cooked kreplach with a little canola oil to prevent them from sticking together. Serve immediately.

# MEAT FILLING FOR KREPLACH

**MAKES ENOUGH FOR 64 KREPLACH**

With chicken livers and beef, this filling also makes a hearty appetizer.

3 tablespoons **EXTRA-VIRGIN OLIVE OIL**

1 large **YELLOW ONION**, finely diced

**KOSHER SALT**

1 pound/455 g **CHUCK STEAK** or **STEWING BEEF**, cut into 1-inch/2.5 cm cubes

2 tablespoons **CHICKEN STOCK**, plus more if needed

¼ pound/115 g **CHICKEN LIVERS**, cleaned and roughly chopped

1 large **EGG**, beaten

Freshly ground **BLACK PEPPER**

Heat the olive oil in a large skillet over medium heat. Add the onion and season generously with salt. Cook, stirring now and then, until softened and just starting to brown, about 10 minutes.

Pat the beef dry with paper towels. Add the beef to the pan and cook, stirring now and then, until the meat is cooked through but not browned, about 10 minutes. If the onion or meat threatens to stick to the pan at any point, add a splash of chicken stock. Add the chicken livers and cook until they're opaque throughout (break a piece open with your spoon to check), about 5 minutes. Remove from the heat and let cool to room temperature.

Transfer the cooled mixture to a food processor and add the 2 tablespoons chicken stock and the egg. Pulse until finely chopped and spreadable, but not completely smooth, about 10 short pulses. The ultimate texture should be like that of chopped liver. Season the mixture with ½ teaspoon salt and plenty of pepper.

# KASHA FILLING FOR KREPLACH

**MAKES ENOUGH FOR 64 KREPLACH**

Kasha-filled kreplach floating in mushroom broth is a great start to a meal. You will not miss the meat.

1 cup/225 g **CHICKEN** or **VEGETABLE STOCK** or **WATER**

3 tablespoons **EXTRA-VIRGIN OLIVE OIL**

½ large **YELLOW ONION**, finely diced

1 small **CARROT**, peeled and finely diced

**KOSHER SALT**

½ cup/100 g **KASHA** (roasted buckwheat groats)

¼ teaspoon freshly ground **BLACK PEPPER**

1 tablespoon roughly chopped **FRESH DILL**

Bring the stock to a boil in a small saucepan. Reduce the heat and keep hot.

Meanwhile, heat the olive oil in a saucepan over medium heat. Add the onion and carrot and season generously with salt. Cook, stirring now and then, until softened and the onion is translucent, about 10 minutes. Add the kasha and cook, stirring, until it smells nutty and is slightly browned, about 5 minutes.

Add the hot stock, ½ teaspoon salt, and the pepper. Reduce the heat to low and simmer, uncovered, until all of the liquid is absorbed and the kasha is tender, 15 to 20 minutes. Be sure to stir the kasha now and then while it's cooking so it doesn't stick to the bottom of the pan.

Transfer the mixture to a food processor, add the dill, and pulse until the mixture is spreadable but not completely smooth, about 5 short pulses. The ultimate texture should be like that of chopped liver. Season the mixture with ½ teaspoon salt and plenty of pepper. Let cool before using.

# POTATO KNISHES

**MAKES 12 (2½-INCH/6 CM) KNISHES; SERVES 12 AS A SIDE DISH OR 6 AS A MAIN DISH**

2 tablespoons **SCHMALTZ** or **CANOLA OIL**, plus more for shaping and the pan

**KOSHER SALT**

2½ pounds/1.1 kg **RUSSET POTATOES**, peeled and cut into 2-inch/5 cm cubes

½ cup/50 g **MATZO MEAL** or **PANKO**

Freshly ground **BLACK PEPPER**

1 large **EGG**, beaten

**CHICKEN SOUP FILLING** or **MUSHROOM AND BROCCOLI FILLING** (recipes follow)

Knishes come in all shapes and sizes, but this Passover version—mashed potatoes wrapped around a filling—is my favorite. My father used to buy these at the butcher and serve them as a side dish with brisket. Just thinking about that feels heavy to me now, so these days I serve knishes as a main dish with a salad for a satisfying meal. I've offered two of my favorite fillings below, but almost anything can go inside of a knish—they're a great way to use up leftovers. Use cooked vegetables, kasha, or lentils with caramelized onions, leftover Chopped Liver (page 45), or even leftover Thanksgiving turkey mixed with a little gravy. Note that both formed and baked knishes freeze very well (see page 203). Either way, there's no need to thaw before baking; just note that your baking time will increase a little (more if they weren't already baked). If you do plan on freezing, you may want to double the recipe.

**1.** Preheat the oven to 400°F/205°C. Coat a rimmed baking sheet with canola oil.

**2.** Bring a large pot of water to a boil, season well with salt, and add the potatoes. Cook until the potatoes are tender when pierced with a knife, 15 to 20 minutes. Drain the potatoes well and return them to the dry pot. Mash them with a potato masher until they're quite smooth. Stir in the 2 table-spoons schmaltz and the matzo meal. Season to taste with salt and pepper and then stir in the egg. These will be pretty dry mashed potatoes, with a texture almost like that of Play-Doh.

**3.** Divide the potato mixture evenly into 12 pieces. With oiled hands, roll each piece into a ball and press down on each one to form into a 4-inch/10 cm patty. Working with one patty at a time, put 2 tablespoons of filling in the center. Using your hands, wrap the potato mixture around the filling so that it's enclosed. Use your palm to slightly flatten the knish into a 2½-inch/6 cm patty and then use your thumb to make a small indentation on top of the knish. Put the finished knish on the prepared baking sheet and continue forming knishes with the remaining potato mixture and filling. Evenly space the knishes apart on the pan.

**4.** Bake the knishes until they're golden brown, about 40 minutes. Serve hot.

# CHICKEN SOUP FILLING FOR KNISHES

**MAKES ENOUGH FOR 12 KNISHES**

I always serve Bubie's Chicken Soup (page 204) on Passover—but just the broth (with so much food coming, who needs chicken in the soup?)—and use some of the cooked chicken to fill these knishes. Of course, you don't have to make a pot of chicken soup to make knishes. This filling could easily be made with any leftover chicken or a rotisserie bird bought at the market.

1 small **COOKED CHICKEN BREAST**, skin and bones removed

2 tablespoons **EXTRA-VIRGIN OLIVE OIL**

½ small **YELLOW ONION**, finely diced

1 small **CARROT**, peeled and finely diced

1 small **CELERY STALK**, finely diced

**KOSHER SALT**

Shred the chicken with your hands into small pieces.

Heat the olive oil in a medium skillet over medium-high heat. Add the onion, carrot, celery, and a generous pinch of salt. Cook, stirring now and then, until the vegetables are soft and just barely beginning to brown, about 10 minutes. Stir in the chicken and season to taste with salt. Let the mixture cool to room temperature before filling the knishes.

# MUSHROOM AND BROCCOLI FILLING FOR KNISHES

**MAKES ENOUGH FOR 12 KNISHES**

I acknowledge that it is odd to have soy sauce in a knish. This isn't how they did it in the Old Country, but then they didn't have many vegetarians in the Old Country. The soy sauce adds umami to the mushrooms so you don't miss the meat filling.

2 tablespoons **EXTRA-VIRGIN OLIVE OIL**

½ small **YELLOW ONION**, finely diced

**KOSHER SALT**

Freshly ground **BLACK PEPPER**

½ pound/225 g **WHITE MUSHROOMS**, stemmed and roughly chopped

1 **GARLIC CLOVE**, minced

1½ cups/180 g finely chopped **BROCCOLI FLORETS**

1 tablespoon **WATER**

1 teaspoon **SOY SAUCE**

Heat the olive oil in a medium skillet over medium-high heat. Add the onion, a generous pinch of salt, and some pepper. Cook, stirring now and then, until the onion is soft and just barely beginning to brown, about 5 minutes. Add the mushrooms and continue to cook, stirring now and then, until the mushrooms begin to soften and brown in spots, another 5 to 10 minutes. Add the garlic, broccoli, water, and soy sauce and cook until the broccoli is bright green, about 2 minutes.

Transfer the mixture to a food processor and pulse until everything is finely chopped and well combined, but not at all pureed or smooth, just 3 or 4 pulses. Let the mixture cool to room temperature before filling the knishes.

# ALBANIAN CHEESE TRIANGLES

**MAKES 12 (3-INCH/7.5 CM) TRIANGLES; SERVES 12**

1¼ cups/160 g **ALL-PURPOSE FLOUR**, plus more for shaping

Pinch of **KOSHER SALT**

¼ cup plus 2 tablespoons/ 85 g **WARM WATER**

6 tablespoons/85 g **EXTRA-VIRGIN OLIVE OIL**

2 large **EGGS**

1½ cups/225 g crumbled **FETA CHEESE**

¼ cup/60 g **WHOLE MILK**

Ela, a native of Albania (see page 214), taught us how to make *byrek*, an Albanian filled pastry. It is made with several layers of a simple dough rolled thinly by hand and filled with a mixture of salty cheese, milk, and egg. Serve these warm or at room temperature with a chopped salad for lunch, or make bite-size ones for hors d'oeuvres. They're also a perfect picnic food. These freeze well: Follow the directions on page 203 and then bake them directly from the freezer.

**1.** Put the flour, salt, water, and 2 tablespoons/30 g of the olive oil in a large bowl and stir with a wooden spoon until a dough forms. Transfer the dough to a lightly floured work surface and knead until the dough is smooth, elastic, soft, and doesn't stick to your fingers, about 5 minutes. Return the dough to the bowl you mixed it in and let rest.

**2.** Meanwhile, crack 1 of the eggs into a small bowl and whisk lightly. Whisk in the feta, milk, and 1 tablespoon of the olive oil.

**3.** Preheat the oven to 350°F/180°C. Line a rimmed baking sheet with parchment paper.

**4.** Turn the dough out onto a lightly floured work surface. Divide the dough into 3 equal pieces (each weighing about 3¼ ounces/93 g). Working with one piece of dough at a time (keep the rest covered with plastic wrap), use a floured rolling pin to roll the dough into a thin 12-inch/30 cm square. If the dough resists as you're rolling it, let it rest for a few minutes before proceeding.

**5.** Drizzle the square with 1 tablespoon of the olive oil and use your fingers to spread it over the entire surface of the dough. Cut the dough into 4 even strips, each measuring about 3 inches/7.5 cm wide. Set a strip vertically with a short end facing you. Put 2 tablespoons of the feta filling at the top end of the strip, about 1 inch/2.5 cm down from the top and 1 inch/2.5 cm in from the right edge. Lift the upper-left-hand corner of the dough and fold it down and diagonally over the filling to meet the right edge of the dough and form a triangle. Now fold the triangle of covered filling down toward you, thus encasing the triangle in another layer of dough. Then fold that triangle over on the diagonal to line up with the left side of the dough strip. Continue with these two motions, like folding a flag, to encase the triangle in more layers of dough until you reach the end of the strip. Put the triangle, seam side down, onto the prepared baking sheet and repeat the entire process with the remaining dough, olive oil, and filling until you use everything up. You will have 12 triangles by the time you're done. Evenly space the triangles on the baking sheet.

6. Crack the remaining egg into a small bowl and beat lightly. Brush the triangles with the egg.

7. Bake the triangles, rotating the baking sheet front to back halfway through the baking time, until they're golden brown, 45 minutes. Let cool for at least 15 minutes before serving.

## LUELA OSMANAJ, BAKERY MANAGER, HOT BREAD KITCHEN

A native of Albania who emigrated to New York in 2011, Ela studied accounting in her home country, but left her education behind—not to mention her family and husband—when she was selected as part of an immigration lottery program. She's now in the process of bringing her husband to the United States. Ela supported herself in New York by working as a babysitter, mostly for Albanian families because she spoke little English. In 2013, Ela joined us as a trainee at Hot Bread Kitchen.

Ela is a natural and she learned how to bake like a pro before she knew kitchen English. Two things really helped with that. First, given her accounting background, she's incredibly good with numbers; Ela can look at the day's production and know it by heart going forward. The second thing is that she cares a lot about bread. Albania has a strong bread culture, so Ela came with the requisite eye for quality (don't miss the Albanian Cheese Triangles, page 212).

Ela advanced in our language classes and her English improved quickly. She says that she appreciates the community at Hot Bread Kitchen. "It was hard at first," Ela says about her time in New York, "but now I have a group of people to talk to and spend time with." The women at Hot Bread Kitchen are able to communicate skills and stories despite different languages and customs.

Ela graduated from the training program in the summer of 2014; we fast-tracked her through the training because she just "got" baking. Then we hired her as a bakery manager at Hot Bread Kitchen.

Looking forward, Ela plans to continue her education and return to accounting. She hopes to work at a bank one day and maintains that her experience at Hot Bread Kitchen has provided her with the ability to bake, but even more important, to communicate effectively with people from all over the world. Perhaps Ela will return as Hot Bread's CFO. Or maybe she'll get the job at Women's World Banking that I never did!

# TIBETAN MOMOS

**MAKES 48 DUMPLINGS; SERVES 6**

5 cups/625 g **ALL-PURPOSE FLOUR**, plus more for shaping

1½ cups plus 2 tablespoons/ 375 g **WATER**

2 tablespoons **EXTRA-VIRGIN OLIVE OIL**

1 large **WHITE ONION**, finely diced

½ fresh **RED CHILE**, seeded and thinly sliced

1 pound/455 g **VENISON** or **CHUCK STEAK**, excess fat trimmed, cut into ¼-inch/6 mm dice

**KOSHER SALT**

1 (1-inch/2.5 cm) piece **FRESH GINGER**, peeled and minced

1 cup/40 g finely chopped **FRESH CILANTRO LEAVES**

4 **SCALLIONS**, white part only, finely chopped

**CANOLA OIL**

**SEPEN** (recipe follows) or other **HOT SAUCE**

In the early days of Hot Bread Kitchen, Tashi, a baker from Tibet, revolutionized the way we made tortillas (page 92) based on the method her family used to make *momos*, meat-filled Tibetan dumplings. When we started making tortillas, we individually shaped the masa for each tortilla, painstakingly weighing them to make sure they were the same size. Tashi showed us how to roll the masa into a long snake. Then—quickly and precisely—divide the dough into evenly sized pieces. She saved us hours of labor. *Momos* are traditionally made with yak meat, but if you can't find yak, use beef or venison. These dumplings can be fried or served in soup, but the steamed version outlined here is the most popular, delicious with *sepen* hot sauce (see page 217). This is the simplest of doughs left a little thick for a hearty, toothsome dumpling.

**1.** Put the flour and water in the bowl of a stand mixer fitted with a dough hook and mix together until the dough comes together. Add a little more flour or water as needed so the dough not only pulls away from the sides of the bowl but also leaves the sides clean, about 4 minutes. Tent the dough loosely with plastic wrap and let it rest while you prepare the filling.

**2.** Heat the olive oil in a large skillet over medium-high heat. Add the onion and chile and cook, stirring now and then, until they're softened and just beginning to brown, about 10 minutes. Add the meat to the pan and sprinkle with a large pinch of salt. Cook, stirring, until it's browned and just cooked through, about 6 minutes. Transfer the mixture to a large bowl and add the ginger, cilantro, and scallions and stir to combine. Taste for seasoning. Set aside to cool.

**3.** Line a rimmed baking sheet with a piece of parchment paper.

**4.** Put the dough on a lightly floured surface and divide it into 4 equal pieces (each weighing about 9⅓ ounces/265 g). Roll each piece into a log that's 12 inches/30 cm long. Using a sharp knife, cut each one into 12 equal pieces (each weighing about ¾ ounce/22 g). Roll each piece of dough between the palms of your hands to make smooth balls. Keep the balls covered loosely with plastic wrap. Working with one ball at a time (keep the rest covered with plastic wrap), press the dough on a floured surface to make a small disk and then use a rolling pin to roll each disk into a 4-inch/10 cm round. Keep the rolled rounds covered loosely with plastic wrap.

**5.** Once all of the rounds are formed, working with one piece of dough at a time (keep the rest covered with plastic wrap), put 2 teaspoons of the meat filling in the center of the round.

*recipe continues*

**6.** Pinch and pleat the edges of the dough up over the filling so that they envelop the *momo* in overlapping layers (see photograph). Use a little water while you're forming them to guarantee that the pleats stay in place (the water will act as a glue). Alternatively, you can form the *momos* into half-moons with pleated edges by putting the filling in the center, folding the dough over to form a half-moon, and then pressing the edges with the tines of a fork. Transfer the formed *momos* to the parchment-lined baking sheet.

**7.** Once all of the *momos* have been formed, set up a bamboo or a metal steamer over a 1 inch/2.5 cm of boiling water and coat the surface of the steamer with canola oil. Add as many *momos* to the steamer as can fit in a single layer, cover the steamer, and cook until the dough is translucent and contracts slightly around the filling when you take the lid off the pot, about 10 minutes. Transfer the cooked *momos* to a warm serving platter and tent with foil while you repeat the steaming process to cook the remaining *momos*.

**8.** Serve the *momos* hot with plenty of *sepen*.

# SEPEN

MAKES ABOUT 1½ CUPS/360 ML

*Sepen* is a Tibetan hot sauce. You can substitute red chile flakes if you can't find whole peppers; as long as they bring heat, they'll do the job. Increase or decrease the garlic and ginger according to your taste.

1 cup/1 ounce/30 g dried whole **CHILES DE ÁRBOL** or other small **RED CHILES**, seeded

2 tablespoons **CANOLA OIL**

3 **GARLIC CLOVES**, roughly chopped

1 medium **RED ONION**, thinly sliced

1 **CELERY STALK**, thinly sliced

2 **PLUM TOMATOES**, roughly chopped

2 **SCALLIONS**, thinly sliced

Small handful of **FRESH CILANTRO LEAVES**, roughly chopped

½ tablespoon **KOSHER SALT**

Put the chiles in a bowl and cover with hot tap water. Let them sit while you prepare the rest of the ingredients.

Heat the oil in a large skillet over medium-high heat. Add the garlic and cook until it's fragrant, about a minute. Add the onion and celery and cook, stirring, until fragrant, another minute. Add the tomatoes, scallions, cilantro, and salt and stir everything together. Bring the mixture to a boil, reduce the heat, and simmer until the ingredients soften, about 10 minutes.

Drain the chiles (discard their soaking liquid) and transfer to a food processor or a blender. Add the tomato mixture and process until smooth. Once the sauce is cool, cover and store in the refrigerator in a jar for up to 1 week.

# SUMAC-SPINACH PIES

MAKES 10 INDIVIDUAL PIES

1 cup plus 2 tablespoons/140 g
**ALL-PURPOSE FLOUR**, plus more
for dusting

½ cup/65 g **WHOLE WHEAT FLOUR**

½ teaspoon **ACTIVE DRY YEAST**

⅔ cup/145 g **LUKEWARM WATER**

**KOSHER SALT**

6 tablespoons/80 g
**EXTRA-VIRGIN OLIVE OIL**, plus
more as needed

½ medium **ONION**, diced

Half of a (10-ounce/283 g) package
**FROZEN SPINACH**, thawed and
squeezed dry

1 teaspoon ground **SUMAC**

1½ teaspoons **FRESH LEMON JUICE**

Freshly ground **BLACK PEPPER**

1 large **EGG**, beaten

A talented chef from Palestine baked with us for a short time and inspired this recipe. These small pies are similar to Greek spanakopita, but instead of flavoring the spinach with feta, we use lemon and sumac, a tangy Middle Eastern spice. If you can't track down sumac (see page 291 for online sources), substitute the grated zest of 1 lemon plus ¼ teaspoon freshly ground black pepper. These make for a great vegan dish; brush them with olive oil instead of egg before baking them.

1. Combine the all-purpose flour, whole wheat flour, yeast, water, ½ teaspoon salt, and 3 tablespoons/40 g of the olive oil in the bowl of a stand mixer fitted with a dough hook. Mix on low speed until all of the ingredients are combined, about 2 minutes. Increase the speed to medium and mix until a soft, supple dough forms that leaves the sides of the bowl clean, about 10 minutes.

2. Oil the inside of a large bowl and using oiled hands, transfer the dough to the bowl. Cover the bowl with plastic wrap (or put the whole bowl in a large plastic bag) and let stand at room temperature until the dough is supple and soft, about 1 hour.

3. Meanwhile, heat the remaining 3 tablespoons/40 g olive oil in a large skillet over medium heat. Add the onion and cook, stirring now and then, until softened, about 10 minutes. Add the spinach, sumac, and lemon juice and stir to combine. Season to taste with salt and pepper and set the mixture aside to cool completely.

4. Preheat the oven to 450°F/235°C. Line 2 rimmed baking sheets with parchment paper.

5. Turn the dough out onto a lightly floured work surface. Divide the dough into 10 equal pieces (each weighing about 1½ ounces/40 g). Dust the pieces with flour, cover loosely with plastic wrap, and let them rest for 10 minutes.

6. Working with one piece of dough at a time (and keeping the rest covered), use a rolling pin to roll each piece of dough into a 5-inch/13 cm round. Put a heaping tablespoon of the spinach mixture toward one side of each round, leaving a ½-inch/1.5 cm border. Brush the exposed dough with water and fold the dough over to enclose the filling and form half-moons. Press the edges to seal and use a fork to crimp the edges. Repeat with the remaining dough and filling.

7. Transfer the spinach pies to the prepared baking sheets and brush the tops with the beaten egg. Bake the pies, rotating the pans between the racks and turning them front to back halfway through the baking, until golden, about 15 minutes.

8. Serve the spinach pies warm or at room temperature.

# EMPANADA DOUGH

**MAKES 2 POUNDS/905 G**

2 large **EGG YOLKS**

¾ cup/175 g **COLD WATER**

4 cups/500 g **ALL-PURPOSE FLOUR**

2 tablespoons **SUGAR**

2 teaspoons **KOSHER SALT**

2 tablespoons cold **UNSALTED BUTTER**, cubed

12 tablespoons/170 g **LARD** or **VEGETABLE SHORTENING**, chilled

Almost every country in Latin America has its own style of empanada. Sometimes people buy frozen empanada dough, already rolled and cut out—not unlike buying dumpling skins to make homemade wontons. Goya brand calls them *discos*. There's nothing wrong with that (I'm all for getting a good meal on the table, even if it takes a shortcut or two), but the dough that follows is easy to make and worth having in your repertoire. The bonus? It doubles as pie dough.

1. Whisk together the egg yolks and water in a small bowl.

2. Whisk together the flour, sugar, and salt in a large bowl. Add the butter and lard and, using a fork and your hands, work the fats into the flour mixture until it resembles very coarse sand. While stirring with the fork, drizzle in the egg yolk mixture and stir until the flour is thoroughly dampened (the dough will still be quite coarse). Use your hands to bring the dough together so it forms one mass, being careful not to overmix the dough. Wrap the dough in a large piece of plastic wrap and let rest in the refrigerator for at least 1 hour or overnight.

# CHILEAN EMPANADAS

**MAKES 12 EMPANADAS; SERVES 12**

2 tablespoons **EXTRA-VIRGIN OLIVE OIL**

2 large **YELLOW ONIONS**, finely diced

1 tablespoon chopped **FRESH OREGANO** or 1½ teaspoons dried

1 teaspoon ground **CUMIN**

¼ teaspoon **CAYENNE PEPPER**

1½ teaspoons **KOSHER SALT**

1 pound/455 g **CHUCK STEAK**, cut into ¼-inch/6 mm cubes

**ALL-PURPOSE FLOUR**

**EMPANADA DOUGH** (page 220)

3 hard-boiled **EGGS**, quartered lengthwise

¼ cup/25 g **RAISINS**

12 pitted **BLACK OLIVES**, halved

2 large **EGGS**, beaten

I spent a year studying abroad at the Universidad de Chile, a vegetarian in a meat-eaters' paradise and on a student's budget. Finding Fábrica de Empanadas around the corner from my house was a game changer. I ate their cheese and mushroom empanadas daily. Years later, when researching empanada recipes, I realized that what made the pastry so good and flaky was the copious amount of lard in the dough. So much for my vegetarian principles! I recommend making the filling and dough the day before and forming the empanadas with chilled filling.

**1.** Preheat the oven to 350°F/180°C.

**2.** Heat the oil in a large skillet over medium-high heat. Add the onions and cook, stirring now and then, until they're softened and just beginning to brown, about 10 minutes. Add the oregano, cumin, cayenne, and salt and cook, stirring, until the spices are fragrant, about 1 minute. Add the meat and cook, stirring, until browned, about 6 minutes. Transfer the mixture to a bowl and set it aside to cool.

**3.** Dust a work surface with flour and fill a small bowl with water. Line a rimmed baking sheet with parchment paper.

**4.** Divide the dough into 12 equal pieces (each weighing about 2½ ounces/75 g). Working with one piece at a time (keep the rest covered with plastic wrap), roll the dough until it's a thin round measuring 16 inches/40 cm in diameter. Use an 8-inch/20 cm round cutter (or use a plate as a template and trace with a paring knife) to cut 2 rounds out. Cut out all the rounds and then proceed to fill the empanadas.

**5.** Working with one round at a time (keep the rest lightly covered with plastic wrap), put 2 tablespoons of the meat filling in the center. Top with an egg quarter, 1 teaspoon raisins, and 2 olive halves. Use your fingers to moisten the exposed dough with water and fold it over to form a half-moon. Pinch the edges to make sure the seam is sealed—press from the inside as you do this to make sure no air is trapped in with the filling. Use a paring knife to trim the semicircle into a rectangle and then, using damp fingers, fold the edges over so that the exterior edges of the rectangle are raised (see photograph on page 200). Prick the top a few times with a fork. Transfer the empanada to the parchment-lined baking sheet. Continue rolling, filling, and forming the empanadas until you use up all of the dough and filling.

**6.** Evenly space the empanadas on the baking sheet. Brush the tops with the beaten egg. Bake until browned, about 30 minutes. Serve warm.

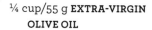

# PASTELLITOS

**MAKES 24 (6-INCH/15 CM) EMPANADAS; SERVES 12**

¼ cup/55 g **EXTRA-VIRGIN OLIVE OIL**

1 large **YELLOW ONION**, finely diced

1 large **FRESH TOMATO** or 2 canned **WHOLE PEELED TOMATOES**, diced

2 teaspoons minced **FRESH OREGANO** or 1 teaspoon dried

¼ teaspoon ground **CINNAMON**

¼ teaspoon ground **CUMIN**

**KOSHER SALT**

¾ pound/340 g **GROUND BEEF**

¼ cup/55 g **WATER**

2 tablespoons **TOMATO PASTE**

3 tablespoons **RAISINS**

¼ teaspoon freshly ground **BLACK PEPPER**

**ALL-PURPOSE FLOUR**

**EMPANADA DOUGH** (page 220)

**CANOLA OIL**, for frying

**VINEGAR-BASED HOT SAUCE**, such as Tabasco

These crispy empanadas filled with raisin-studded ground beef hail from the Dominican Republic, like many delicious things in New York City. They are enjoyed year-round and, in my family, are a must-have at Christmastime. Be sure not to overfill these or they will be difficult to handle and come apart when you fry them. The empanadas can be assembled ahead and frozen (see page 203). Don't thaw before frying; simply give them a few more minutes in the hot oil. The filling and the frying steal the show here, so a premade dough can be used.

**1.** Heat the olive oil in a large skillet over medium-high heat. Add the onion and tomato and cook, stirring now and then to break up the tomatoes with your spoon, until the vegetables are softened and beginning to brown and the liquid has evaporated, about 10 minutes. Stir in the oregano, cinnamon, cumin, and a large pinch of salt. Add the ground beef, season with salt, and increase the heat to high. Cook until the meat just begins to brown, about 10 minutes. Add the water, tomato paste, raisins, and pepper. Stir everything together and bring the mixture to a boil. Reduce the heat and simmer until the liquid is mostly evaporated and the raisins are plump, about 10 minutes. Season to taste with additional salt if needed and set the mixture aside to cool.

**2.** Dust a work surface with flour and fill a small bowl with water. Line a rimmed baking sheet with parchment paper.

**3.** Roll the dough into a log and cut it evenly into 24 pieces (each weighing about 1⅓ ounces/38 g); it's easiest to do this by cutting the log in half and then cutting each half into 12 pieces using a ruler as a guide). Using a rolling pin, roll each piece into a round measuring 6 inches/15 cm in diameter. Keep the rolled rounds covered loosely with plastic wrap while you roll out the rest.

**4.** Lay the rounds on the floured work surface and put ¼ cup/60 g of filling on each round slightly off-center. Use your fingers to moisten the exposed dough with water and fold it over to form a half-moon. With your rolling pin, lightly roll over the edges and then pinch the edges to make sure the seam is sealed. Use a fork to imprint the rounded edge with ridges (which will add extra insurance that the empanada is completely sealed). Transfer the empanada to the parchment-lined baking sheet and continue rolling, filling, and forming the empanadas until you use up all of the dough and filling.

**5.** Line a rimmed baking sheet with paper towels. Pour 3 inches/7.5 cm of canola oil into a large, heavy pot and heat over medium-high heat. Once the oil is hot (a pinch of dough will sizzle upon contact), add the empanadas, in batches as necessary so that they don't crowd the pot. Fry, turning once, until nicely browned on both sides, about 3 minutes per side. Use tongs or a slotted spoon to transfer the empanadas to the towel-lined baking sheet and sprinkle them with salt. Continue frying the rest of the empanadas.

**6.** Serve the empanadas immediately with hot sauce.

# TORTILLAS DE TIESTO

MAKES 12 (4½-INCH/11 CM) FILLED TORTILLAS; SERVES 12

3½ cups/455 g **WHOLE WHEAT FLOUR**

1¾ cups/225 g **ALL-PURPOSE FLOUR**

¼ cup plus 1 tablespoon/60 g **SUGAR**

1 teaspoon **ACTIVE DRY YEAST**

1 teaspoon **KOSHER SALT**

Scant 1½ cups/340 g **WHOLE MILK**

1 large **EGG**, beaten

16 tablespoons/225 g cold **UNSALTED BUTTER**, diced

1½ cups/225 g crumbled **QUESO FRESCO** or **FETA CHEESE**

A *tiesto* is a flat clay pot traditionally used in Ecuadoran cooking for many purposes, including these griddled *tortillas*—which should not be confused with Mexican corn tortillas or Spanish potato tortillas. Made with an ever-so-sweet whole wheat dough that's kept soft with plenty of butter and milk, the *tortillas* are filled with a bit of salty white cheese (feta works very well) and then griddled until charred in spots. The crunchy exterior yields immediately to the tender nutty interior. Often sold on the street as snacks, these *tortillas* go perfectly with a cup of Morocho (page 226).

1. Put the whole wheat flour, all-purpose flour, sugar, yeast, salt, milk, egg, and butter in the bowl of a stand mixer fitted with a dough hook. Mix on low speed until all of the ingredients come together, about 2 minutes. Increase the speed to medium and mix until the dough cleans the sides of the bowl, makes slapping noises against the sides of the bowl, is smooth, and doesn't stick to your fingers when you touch it, about 5 minutes.

2. Cover the bowl tightly with plastic wrap and let stand until slightly risen and soft and puffy, about 30 minutes.

3. Line a rimmed baking sheet with parchment paper.

4. Turn the dough out onto a lightly floured surface. Divide it into 12 equal pieces (each weighing about 4 ounces/115 g). Roll each piece into a ball. Keep the balls covered loosely with plastic wrap or a large plastic bag. Working with one piece of dough at a time (keep the rest covered with plastic wrap), use your hands to press and stretch the ball into a disk measuring 4 inches/10 cm in diameter. Keep the finished rounds covered loosely with plastic wrap as you prepare the remaining ones.

5. Put 2 tablespoons of feta in the center of a disk and then enclose the feta, pulling the dough around the cheese and pinching the seams together to make a ball with the cheese in the middle. Flatten the ball and roll it into a disk, this time measuring 4½ inches/11 cm in diameter. Transfer the cheese-filled *tortilla* to the prepared baking sheet and continue the process with the remaining dough and cheese.

6. Set a large cast iron skillet or griddle over medium heat and let it heat up. Working in batches as necessary to avoid crowding, add the *tortillas* to the hot pan and cook until they're browned on both sides, flipping them a few times as they cook, about 10 minutes total.

7. Eat the *tortillas* immediately while they're hot or enjoy them warm or even at room temperature. Leftovers can be stored in an airtight container in the fridge then reheated in a hot dry skillet.

# MOROCHO

**SERVES 12**

1 (16-ounce/455 g) bag **MAÍZ TRILLADO BLANCO, MAÍZ QUEBRADO,** or **MAÍZ PARTIDO**

1 quart/1 liter **WHOLE MILK**

3 **CINNAMON STICKS**

8 **STAR ANISE**

1 cup/200 g **SUGAR**

2 teaspoons **VANILLA EXTRACT**

Pinch of **KOSHER SALT**

¼ cup/30 g **CORNSTARCH**

½ cup/120 g **WATER**

The Ecuadoran rival to horchata, *morocho* is a sweet, warm, milky drink thickened with cracked white corn. Fanny scents her signature version with star anise and cinnamon. Often sold by street vendors, *morocho* can be enjoyed for breakfast or as an accompaniment to a little snack (come to think of it, *morocho* would be delicious alongside one of Margaret's Coconut Buns, page 238). The only difficult part of the recipe is finding the right type of dried cracked white corn. Look in Latin American grocery stores or see page 291 for online sources. Note that the corn needs to soak for at least 8 hours before you prepare this satisfying drink.

**1.** Put the corn kernels in a bowl and add enough water to cover by at least 2 inches/5 cm. Let soak overnight.

**2.** Drain the corn kernels and transfer them to a large pot. Cover with 3 quarts/2.8 liters cold water and bring to a boil over high heat. Reduce the heat and simmer, stirring now and then to make sure the corn isn't sticking to the bottom, until the corn is soft, about 45 minutes.

**3.** Increase the heat to high and add the milk, cinnamon sticks, star anise, sugar, vanilla, and salt. Cook until small bubbles appear around the edge of the pot, about 15 minutes. Reduce the heat to medium-low and cook, stirring, until the sugar is dissolved and the mixture is slightly reduced and thickened, about 15 minutes.

**4.** In a small bowl, whisk together the cornstarch and water. While stirring, slowly drizzle the cornstarch mixture into the *morocho* and cook until the *morocho* is as thick as a slightly melted milk shake, just a few minutes longer. Serve hot.

## FANNY PEREZ, OWNER AND CHEF, LAS DELICIAS DE FANNY,
### HBK INCUBATES MEMBER

When Fanny was growing up in Ecuador, her mother ran a restaurant out of the home. Food has been the driving force in Fanny's life for as long as she can remember. Fanny came to the United States in 1994. Because she lacked formal schooling and fluency in English, she worked for minimum wages at a variety of jobs. But she also ran an informal food business, Las Delicias de Fanny, out of her home to supplement her income. Her specialties included Ecuadoran ceviche, life-changing pernil (roast pork), and Ecuadoran baked goods.

Twenty years after moving to America, Fanny joined the bakery training program, improved her English, and learned how to bake professionally. She was an experienced home baker, making beautiful Guaguas de Pan (page 250) and Tortillas de Tiesto (page 225), but she had never worked in large-scale production. Fortunately, her experience paid off—she was a natural.

After she graduated from the Hot Bread Kitchen training program, Fanny applied to our food business incubator, HBK Incubates. Her goal was to grow Las Delicias de Fanny in a commercial kitchen, and that is exactly what Fanny has done—along with being inspected and licensed by the appropriate state and city agencies, Fanny notes that her experience at Hot Bread Kitchen taught her how to work with a sense of urgency and how to scale her recipes.

Fanny now caters parties and weddings, and is a favorite caterer for our staff events. Combining her traditional recipes with her new business know-how, Fanny supports her family with her growing company.

# EQUADORAN-STYLE SHRIMP CEVICHE

**SERVES 4 AS A MAIN COURSE OR 8 AS AN APPETIZER**

CANOLA OIL

1 (8-ounce/225 g) package **MAÍZ TOSTAR CARHUAY** (see Note)

KOSHER SALT

1 small **RED ONION,** halved and very thinly sliced into half-moons

4 **PLUM TOMATOES**

½ small **RED BELL PEPPER,** roughly chopped

½ small **YELLOW ONION,** roughly chopped

6 **GARLIC CLOVES,** smashed and peeled

Freshly ground **BLACK PEPPER**

Pinch of ground **CUMIN**

1 pound/905 g peeled and deveined medium **SHRIMP**

½ bunch **FRESH CILANTRO,** finely chopped

2 cups/350 g freshly cooked **WHITE RICE** (optional)

> **NOTE:** The secret ingredient that makes this ceviche memorable is the garnish: *maíz tostar Carhuay.* These large corn kernels are cooked in hot oil, which makes them turn caramel brown and take on a nutty flavor, like starchy versions of the not-popped kernels at the bottom of the popcorn bowl.

In addition to her recipe for Tortillas de Tiesto (page 225), we couldn't resist including Fanny's refreshing shrimp ceviche, made with fully cooked shrimp.

**1.** Line a rimmed baking sheet with a double layer of paper towels.

**2.** Heat 1 inch/2.5 cm of canola oil in a heavy pot over medium-high heat. Add the *maíz* and cook, stirring with a wooden spoon, until the kernels are evenly and deeply browned, about 15 minutes. Use a slotted spoon to transfer the kernels to the lined baking sheet and sprinkle generously with salt.

**3.** Put the red onion in a bowl of cold water and let soak.

**4.** Bring a large pot of water to a boil, add the tomatoes, and boil until their skins begin to peel off, about 1 minute. Scoop the tomatoes out of the water and into a colander. Measure out 1 cup/225 g of the cooking liquid, but leave the pot of water on the stove. Peel the tomatoes and transfer them to a blender.

**5.** Heat 2 tablespoons canola oil in a large skillet over medium-high heat. Add the bell pepper and yellow onion and cook, stirring, until the vegetables are barely softened, about 10 minutes. Transfer to the blender with the tomatoes and add the reserved tomato cooking liquid. Cover (and vent), then blend until smooth. Pass the mixture

through a fine-mesh sieve into a bowl, pressing down on the solids to extract their flavor (discard the solids). Chill the bowl over a bowl of ice and water.

**6.** Meanwhile, bring the pot of water used to cook the tomatoes back to a boil and add the garlic, a few grinds of black pepper, a large pinch of salt, and the cumin. Let the mixture boil for a few minutes. Reduce the heat and simmer, add the shrimp, and cook, stirring a few times, just until the shrimp turn opaque, 1 to 2 minutes. Use a slotted spoon to transfer the shrimp to a bowl and set them aside to cool. (Discard any garlic that was strained out with the shrimp.) Measure out 1 cup/225 g of the cooking liquid and discard the rest.

**7.** Drain the red onion and add to the tomato mixture along with the cilantro, 2 tablespoons canola oil, and the reserved shrimp cooking liquid. Whisk everything together. Add the cooked shrimp, season with salt and pepper, and let marinate for at least 20 minutes (keep the mixture chilled until serving) or refrigerate for up to 48 hours.

**8.** Serve the shrimp over cooked rice topped with fried corn kernels.

# MASA QUESADILLAS
## WITH WHITE CHEESE AND SQUASH BLOSSOMS

**MAKES 10 QUESADILLAS; SERVES 4 AS A LIGHT MEAL**

4 cups/1 pound/455 g **MASA FROM NIXTAMAL** (page 89) or **MASA FROM MASA HARINA** (page 90)

1¼ cups/150 g shredded **QUESO OAXACA, MOZZARELLA,** or mild cheese of your choice

10 **SQUASH BLOSSOMS,** stems discarded, torn into a few pieces

**CANOLA OIL**

Baker Nancy Mendez (page 91) makes these skillet-cooked quesadillas with fresh masa (pages 89 and 90) filled with Queso Oaxaca and served with salsa verde; the simple combination is a revelation. The outside is crisp, bits of cheese escape onto the griddle becoming crunchy and irresistible, the inside remains soft, and the whole thing tastes of freshly ground corn. If you are nixtamalizing corn for tortillas (page 92), consider making a bit extra for quesadillas.

**1.** Set a large cast iron skillet or a griddle over medium-high heat and let it heat while you prepare the quesadillas.

**2.** Press the masa into 10 (7-inch/ 18 cm) tortillas (see page 92).

**3.** Working with one tortilla at a time, put 2 tablespoons/15 g of the cheese on the tortilla slightly off-center. Top the cheese with a squash blossom. Fold the tortilla to form a half-moon and, using your fingers, press the edges of the tortilla together to seal and form a pouch. Repeat with the remaining tortillas, cheese, and squash blossoms.

**4.** Lightly brush the skillet with oil. Working in batches, cook the quesadillas, turning them once, until browned and crisp on the outside and the cheese is completely melted, about 2 minutes per side. Add more oil to the skillet as necessary as you cook the remaining quesadillas.

**5.** Serve the quesadillas immediately, while they're hot. To keep the cooked ones warm while you are making the rest, wrap them in a clean kitchen towel.

# SHORT AND SWEET

## QUICK BREADS AND HOLIDAY BREADS

The sweet breads in this far-reaching chapter fall into two categories. The first is quick breads, meaning that chemical leaveners like baking powder or baking soda help these breads rise. They don't require kneading or time to sit. These everyday breads are easy to make and are satisfying. Some, like Banana Bread (page 241), might be quite familiar to you, while others, like Coconut Buns (page 238), will introduce you to new flavors and quickly become favorites.

The second category is celebratory breads, loaves made for holidays and other special occasions in a variety of cultures. Some of these are a bit more complicated to make than the quick breads, but they're worth the effort, especially when they're made once a year for special occasions. We make some of these breads, like Stollen (page 244), which is full of almonds and dried fruit soaked in brandy, at the holidays. These are recipes passsed from generation to generation, often scribbled on note cards, from my family and from those of our bakers. The resulting collection is an eclectic mix, rooted in old traditions and sure to inspire new ones.

This chapter also includes my mother's granola recipe and several ways to enjoy it. While it's not a bread, it's a tradition in my family that is rooted so firmly in Hot Bread Kitchen's day-to-day production that I couldn't not include it here.

# Baking Tips for Quick Breads

This chapter includes recipes that use baking soda and baking powder as leavening agents, both of which work very quickly.

- Baking soda, also known as sodium bicarbonate, reacts with acid (such as lemon juice, buttermilk, or yogurt) to release carbon dioxide, which helps baked goods rise. To make sure your baking soda is active before adding it to your recipe, mix a little bit with vinegar. If it doesn't bubble, it's time for a new box.

- Baking powder is baking soda that's already been mixed with acid and either cornstarch or potato starch to absorb moisture. This keeps the alkaline and the acidic components in the baking powder dry and separate so that they don't react to each other before getting mixed with liquid. It also prolongs baking powder's shelf life and makes it easy to measure, since it doesn't clump.

- Most baking powder these days is labeled "double-acting," but there's also "fast-acting" and "slow-acting" kinds. Fast-acting baking powder means that the chemical reaction will occur at room temperature when the baking powder is combined with a liquid. Slow-acting baking powder's chemical reaction is heat-activated and happens in the oven. Double-acting, the kind you probably have in your cupboard, means a reaction happens first when the batter is mixed and then again in the oven. It is easier and more reliable than fast- or slow-acting baking powder, since you don't need to worry so much about how much time passes between mixing the dough and baking it.

- When mixing quick breads, it is important to remember not to overmix the dough; stir just until the ingredients come together and the flour disappears.

- When adding nuts, chocolate chips, and/or dried fruit to doughs and batters, a good way to keep them from sinking to the bottom is to toss them with a little bit of flour from the recipe, just enough to coat them, before stirring them into the dough. The light flour coating will act as a little buoy, helping to suspend the nut in the dough.

- Speaking of nuts and dried fruits, every recipe in this chapter that calls for either of these is an invitation for improvisation. Dislike candied lemon? Simply add an equal quantity of candied orange or dried apricots. Like pecans but adore hazelnuts? Swap them! It's easy to indulge your preferences with these kinds of one-for-one swaps.

# IRISH SODA BREAD

MAKES 1 (7-INCH/18 CM) ROUND LOAF; SERVES 6

1½ cups/190 g **ALL-PURPOSE FLOUR**

¾ cup plus 2 tablespoons/85 g **OLD-FASHIONED ROLLED OATS**

1 tablespoon **SUGAR**

1¼ teaspoons **BAKING POWDER**

1 teaspoon finely chopped **FRESH ROSEMARY**

1 teaspoon **KOSHER SALT**

½ teaspoon freshly ground **BLACK PEPPER**

⅓ cup/30 g coarsely grated **CHEDDAR CHEESE**

8 tablespoons/115 g cold **UNSALTED BUTTER**, diced

½ small **YELLOW ONION**, finely chopped

¼ cup/40 g pitted **KALAMATA OLIVES**, finely chopped

1 large **EGG**, beaten

5 tablespoons/75 g **WHOLE MILK**

To celebrate the Irish roots (shared by many New Yorkers) of my mother's mother, we make this bread for St. Patrick's Day. Our version is not typical. It contains olives, pepper, and cheddar cheese (you could use an Irish cheddar!), but it is as soft, crumbly, and satisfying as you would hope any Irish soda bread to be. As is the case with all quick breads, the most important thing to keep in mind when making this is not to overmix the dough or the bread will be tough; instead, stir just until the ingredients come together. Serve this hot out of the oven or sliced and toasted. Either way, be generous with the butter. The best way to enjoy Irish soda bread is alongside a hearty stew and a pint of Guinness. *Sláinte!*

1. Preheat the oven to 375°F/190°C. Line a rimmed baking sheet with parchment paper.

2. In a large bowl, stir together the flour, oats, sugar, baking powder, rosemary, salt, and pepper until blended. Add the cheddar and butter and crumble the ingredients between your fingers to form coarse crumbs. Add the onion and olives and stir until the pieces are separated and evenly distributed. In a small bowl, whisk the egg until frothy and then whisk in the milk. Add to the flour mixture and stir just until the dry ingredients are moistened. The dough will be quite shaggy.

3. With dampened hands, gather the dough into a ball and transfer it to the parchment-lined baking sheet. Pat the ball into a round loaf measuring 7 inches/18 cm in diameter. Use a serrated knife to slash a 1½-inch/4 cm cross about ½ inch/1.5 cm deep in the center of the loaf. Bake until lightly browned and a toothpick inserted into the center comes out clean, 40 to 45 minutes. Let the bread cool on a rack for at least 15 minutes before slicing and serving. Store any leftovers in an airtight plastic bag at room temperature for up to a couple of days.

# FRANCIS TRINIDAD, HOT BREAD KITCHEN GRADUATE, BAKER AT WHOLE FOODS

Francis has lived in New York for nearly a decade. She comes from the Dominican Republic and a family involved in health care: Her sister is a physician, her father is a hospital accountant, and her mother is a cardiologist's assistant. Upon her arrival in New York, Francis also became part of the caring community by working as a home health aide with the dream of becoming a nutritionist. One day, she happened to visit East Harlem's La Marqueta to purchase groceries for a patient living nearby. Francis saw a sign for Hot Bread Kitchen and, intrigued by the possibility of paid training, applied.

In our training program, Francis developed skills in scaling and mixing recipes, managing inventory, and maintaining quality control. She improved her English and earned a Food Handler's certificate. After a year with us, the training and hard work led Francis to Whole Foods, where she was hired in pastry production for the Upper West Side store here in New York City. She makes cookies, cakes, and icing and ensures that all catering orders are ready on time. She was recently named the Upper West Side store's Employee of the Quarter.

Following the health-care tradition of her family, Francis is working toward a degree in nutrition at Hostos Community College in the Bronx. After her eight-hour shifts at Whole Foods, she attends classes four nights a week. Her goal is to combine everything she's learning at school with everything she's accomplishing at work. "I see great opportunities at Whole Foods—there are nutritionists on staff who develop recipes for the stores and for demos that they do in stores," Francis told me recently. She also noted that the company is very supportive of its staff members and often promotes from within: "My boss started as a cashier."

Combining her family's commitment to promoting good health with her love and talent for baking, Francis's future looks sweet—even without too much sugar!

# TORTA: DOMINICAN CORN BREAD

**MAKES 1 (8-INCH/20 CM) ROUND LOAF; SERVES 8**

1 cup/125 g **ALL-PURPOSE FLOUR**

1 cup/150 g fine or extra fine **YELLOW CORNMEAL** (we use Goya brand)

1 cup/200 g **SUGAR**

2½ teaspoons **BAKING POWDER**

½ teaspoon **KOSHER SALT**

2 large **EGGS**

½ teaspoon **VANILLA EXTRACT**

1 cup minus 2 tablespoons/225 g **WHOLE MILK**

9 tablespoons/125 g **UNSALTED BUTTER**

One of the many benefits of being married to my husband, Eli, is having a whole new repertoire of family recipes from the Dominican Republic, including this *torta,* a quick bread made with ground corn. This particular recipe comes from my mother-in-law, Ydalia, and her version has been approved by the Dominican bakers who work at Hot Bread Kitchen. *Torta's* slight sweetness makes it welcome in the morning, especially when it's toasted and drizzled with a bit of honey, but it can also be served anytime and anywhere you might have corn bread, such as alongside a bowl of chili.

**1.** Preheat the oven to 350°F/180°C. Put an 8-inch/20 cm cast iron skillet in the oven to get hot.

**2.** Whisk together the flour, cornmeal, sugar, baking powder, and salt in a large bowl.

**3.** Whisk together the eggs and vanilla in a separate bowl.

**4.** Warm the milk and 8 tablespoons/115 g of the butter in a small saucepan over medium-high heat, stirring now and then, until the butter is completely melted. While whisking, slowly pour the butter and milk mixture into the flour mixture. Mix until smooth and uniform. Whisk in the egg mixture.

**5.** Take the skillet out of the oven and add the remaining 1 tablespoon butter. It should melt immediately. Tilt the skillet to spread the butter over its surface. Pour the batter into the skillet. Return the skillet to the oven and bake until the corn bread is barely golden brown and a toothpick inserted into the center comes out clean, about 30 minutes.

**6.** Let the *torta* cool completely before inverting out of the skillet and cutting into squares or wedges for serving. Store any leftovers in an airtight container at room temperature for up to a couple of days.

# COCONUT BUNS

**MAKES 12 BUNS**

4 cups/500 g **ALL-PURPOSE FLOUR**

½ cup/100 g **SUGAR**

2 teaspoons **BAKING POWDER**

½ teaspoon ground **CINNAMON**

¼ teaspoon **KOSHER SALT**

8 tablespoons/115 g **UNSALTED BUTTER**, at room temperature

3 large **EGGS**, beaten

1 teaspoon **VANILLA EXTRACT**

1 cup/50 g unsweetened **SHREDDED COCONUT**

¼ cup/35 g **RAISINS** (optional)

Scant ½ cup/110 g **COCONUT MILK**

**NOTE:** To make these with fresh coconut, crack open a coconut (the one with a brown shell—not a young/green coconut), using a hammer to help you. Smell the interior to ensure it isn't rancid, then strain the liquid into a food processor. Use a metal spoon to scrape the white coconut flesh away from the brown skin and put the white flesh into the food processor, too. Pulse the coconut until it is finely chopped. Measure out 1½ cups/160 g of this mixture and use it in the dough in place of both the shredded coconut and coconut milk.

Margaret (see page 240) bakes traditional easy-to-prepare Guyanese buns often for her kids for breakfast or as a snack after school. Easy to prepare, these buttery, crumbly buns are reminiscent of scones. They get a double dose of coconut, via both coconut milk and shredded coconut. To accompany the buns, Margaret recommends a mug of warm milk sweetened with sugar and flavored with a teaspoon of finely grated ginger.

1. Preheat the oven to 350°F/180°C. Line a rimmed baking sheet with parchment paper.

2. Put the flour, sugar, baking powder, cinnamon, and salt in the bowl of a stand mixer fitted with a dough hook. Mix on low speed to combine. Stop the mixer and add the butter, eggs, vanilla, shredded coconut, raisins (if using), and coconut milk. Increase the speed to medium and mix just until the ingredients come together to form a thick, sticky dough. Let the dough rest in the bowl for 5 minutes.

3. Using two spoons or lightly floured hands, divide the dough into 12 equal portions (each about 3 ounces/90 g), dropping them evenly spaced onto the parchment-lined baking sheet as you go (as if you were making cookies). Bake until the buns are golden brown and your kitchen smells like a toasted coconut, 30 to 35 minutes.

4. Transfer the buns to a wire rack to cool for at least 15 minutes before eating. Serve warm or at room temperature. Store any leftovers in an airtight plastic bag at room temperature for up to a couple of days.

# MARGARET RAYMOND, HOT BREAD KITCHEN GRADUATE, BAKER AT AMY'S BREAD

Hot Bread Kitchen found Margaret by essentially getting in her way. Before we moved into La Marqueta—the 1930s market building that we call home—people could walk through the building, a useful shortcut in a busy neighborhood. Once Hot Bread arrived, the shortcut got, well, cut. Margaret often shopped for groceries at La Marqueta and, one day, found her route interrupted. She decided to see what was going on and noticed that the building, which had been pretty motionless, was suddenly full of life and activity. She saw us baking and left with an application and an interest, as she puts it, in "meddling with flour."

Margaret backed up her

application with bread she had baked at home. Our Training Director tried it and told Margaret that her bread was good, if a little heavy. Margaret took the feedback with excitement: "I knew I had a lot to learn and I realized I was going to be able to find everything out through these doors."

Originally from Guyana, Margaret came to New York in 1987. Although she had significant secretarial experience, she had trouble finding a secretarial position in the United States. She worked in a home accessories packaging plant in Brooklyn. Other odd jobs followed, but Margaret longed for work that felt meaningful. She had no experience working in the food industry apart from a short stint preserving fruits for cakes in Guyana. Yet Hot Bread Kitchen provided exactly the kind of work and community she had been seeking: "I love working with all of the women here and learning more about where everyone is from and what they cook at home. It's so nice to feel like I know more people in the neighborhood and Hot Bread Kitchen gives us all good jobs."

Citing her mother as her culinary inspiration, Margaret couldn't help but find something beyond coincidence in the fact that the day we hired her was the same day that her beloved mother passed away. Margaret took it as a sign that at Hot Bread Kitchen she would find the next chapter of her life filled with new opportunities.

Margaret thrived in the training program. Over the course of a year, she went from the packing department to producing lavash and granola with Lutfunnessa and then learned to mix bread dough, shape it, and bake it. Margaret graduated to a job as a shaper at Amy's Bread, a large wholesale bakery located in Queens. When I met with Margaret recently she told me that she is quite happy with her new job, although she felt she had a lot to learn. The most valuable thing that she learned at Hot Bread Kitchen was accepting criticism and growing from it—an essential skill for professional improvement. The thing that she didn't learn here was the three-strand braid (we really focus on the one- and the two-strand), but she taught herself how to do it.

Entrepreneurial in spirit, Margaret has been dreaming about taking some of what she's learned at Hot Bread Kitchen back home to Guyana: "I will have everyone eating their curried chicken with challah!"

# BANANA BREAD

MAKES 1 (9 × 5-INCH/23 × 13 CM) LOAF; SERVES 6 TO 8

UNSALTED BUTTER

3 very ripe **BANANAS**

½ cup/100 g **GRANULATED SUGAR**

½ packed cup/110 g **DARK BROWN SUGAR**

2½ teaspoons **BAKING SODA**

½ teaspoon **KOSHER SALT**

2 large **EGGS**

¾ cup/180 g **BUTTERMILK** (see Notes)

¼ cup/55 g **CANOLA OIL**

2 cups/250 g **ALL-PURPOSE FLOUR**

½ cup/60 g chopped **WALNUTS** (optional)

**NOTES:** If you don't have buttermilk on hand (or don't want to buy a whole quart), you can substitute plain yogurt or stir 2 teaspoons white vinegar or lemon juice into ¾ cup/180 g whole milk. Let the mixture stand at room temperature for 5 minutes before adding to the batter.

This batter can also be made into 20 muffins that bake for about 1 hour.

Every month, we have open interviews to recruit new bakery trainees. We administer tests to measure speed, accuracy, and basic literacy, and we ask everyone what breads she knows how to bake. Some women name breads from their distant home countries; others are exploring recipes from the Food Network. But the bread they most commonly cite is banana bread. It fascinates me that women from every corner of the world seem to share the experience of having too many ripe bananas! This delicious version is baked low and slow and comes out dark and moist. For a sweeter version, substitute chocolate chips for the walnuts or go half-and-half nuts and chips. Another tasty tropical alternative is to substitute flaked coconut for the nuts.

1. Position a rack in the middle of the oven and preheat to 275°F/135°C. Butter a 9 × 5-inch/23 × 13 cm loaf pan, line the bottom with parchment paper, and then butter the parchment paper.

2. Puree the bananas in a food processor fitted with the steel blade until smooth. Add both of the sugars, the baking soda, and salt and process until combined. Add the eggs, buttermilk, and oil and process until combined. Transfer the mixture to a large bowl, add the flour, and mix just until all of the flour disappears and the batter is nearly smooth. Stir in the walnuts (if using).

3. Scrape the batter into the prepared loaf pan and bake until a toothpick inserted into the center comes out clean, 2 to 2½ hours. Let the bread cool for 5 minutes in the pan on a wire rack. Then turn it out of the pan onto the rack to cool completely. Store any leftovers wrapped tightly in plastic wrap at room temperature.

# MY GRANDMOTHER'S NUT ROLL

MAKES 4 (12-INCH/30 CM) LOAVES; SERVES 24

## FILLING

2 pounds/910 g ground **WALNUTS**

1½ cups/300 g **SUGAR**

1½ tablespoons **UNSALTED BUTTER**, melted

Grated zest of 1 **LEMON**

## DOUGH

1 tablespoon plus 1½ teaspoons **ACTIVE DRY YEAST** (2 envelopes)

½ cup/120 g **WHOLE MILK**, lukewarm

16 tablespoons/225 g **UNSALTED BUTTER**, melted and cooled, plus more for the bowl

1 cup/225 g **SOUR CREAM**

3 large **EGGS**, beaten

6 cups/750 g **ALL-PURPOSE FLOUR**, sifted, plus more for shaping

3 tablespoons **SUGAR**

1 teaspoon **KOSHER SALT**

**NOTE:** This recipe makes quite a bit: four whole loaves and each loaf provides a dozen generous slices, but it's so delicious that I suggest making the whole batch and giving away one or two loaves or freezing some to enjoy later.

My maternal grandmother, Rita Kozak, lived in Grand Rapids, Michigan—a seven-hour drive from Toronto, where I grew up. My family would visit several times a year, and the long journey was made barely tolerable by the knowledge that a hot slice of nut roll—a rich bread, spread thickly with butter—was waiting for us, along with the smiling faces of our grandparents. Interestingly, my Irish-American grandmother learned to make this bread from a Slovak cookbook given to her by her sister-in-law. This delicious yeasted dough, made with butter, eggs, and sour cream, is filled with a mixture of walnuts and sugar offset with a little bit of bright lemon zest.

**1.** To make the filling: Stir together the walnuts, sugar, melted butter, and lemon zest in a bowl.

**2.** To prepare the dough: Whisk together the yeast and warm milk in a medium bowl. Let stand until the surface appears foamy, about 5 minutes. Whisk in the melted butter, sour cream, and eggs.

**3.** Whisk together the flour, sugar, and salt in a large bowl. Add the milk mixture and stir until a uniform dough forms. Lightly grease the inside of a large bowl with butter and transfer the dough to it. Cover the bowl tightly with plastic wrap and let the dough rise for 1 hour; it won't double in size, but it will be softer and slightly puffy and much easier to work with.

**4.** Transfer the dough to a lightly floured work surface. Divide it into 4 equal pieces (each weighing about 13½ ounces/388 g). Working with one piece at a time (keep the rest covered with plastic wrap), use a floured rolling pin to roll the dough into a 12-inch/30 cm square. Evenly spread the surface with one-quarter of the nut mixture. Roll the dough up tightly so that you end up with a loaf measuring 12 inches/30 cm long and about 3 inches/7.5 cm both wide and high. Repeat the process with the remaining dough and filling mixture.

**5.** Line 2 rimmed baking sheets with parchment paper and transfer 2 nut rolls to each baking sheet, evenly spacing the rolls. Put the baking sheets in large plastic bags or loosely cover them with plastic wrap and set the pans in a warm spot in your kitchen to rise until they're soft, supple, and slightly larger, about 1 hour.

**6.** Meanwhile, preheat the oven to 350°F/180°C.

**7.** Uncover the nut rolls and bake them until they're golden brown, 40 to 45 minutes. Let them cool for 30 minutes on wire racks before slicing and serving. Serve warm or at room temperature. To freeze, wrap the whole thing tightly in plastic wrap and store in an airtight freezer bag. Bring to room temperature and reheat individual slices in a 300°F/150°C oven.

# STOLLEN

**MAKES 2 (12-INCH/30 CM) LOAVES**

## FRUIT

⅔ cup/80 g **RAISINS**

⅓ cup/40 g **DRIED CHERRIES**

2 tablespoons finely diced **CANDIED LEMON PEEL**

2 tablespoons finely diced **CANDIED ORANGE PEEL**

¼ cup/55 g **DARK RUM**

¼ cup/55 g **BRANDY**

½ teaspoon **VANILLA EXTRACT**

**HOT WATER**

½ cup/75 grams blanched **ALMONDS**

## FILLING

2½ tablespoons **ALMOND PASTE**

1 tablespoon fine plain dried **BREAD CRUMBS**, homemade (page 281) or store-bought

½ tablespoon **GRANULATED SUGAR**

½ tablespoon **UNSALTED BUTTER**, at room temperature

1½ teaspoons **WATER**

Stollen, a sweet bread filled with nuts and fruit and coated in sugar, is a German holiday tradition. It is now a Hot Bread Kitchen holiday tradition, too. Our customers love it so much that we ship it all over the world every December. A lot of love goes into our stollen: We use a huge amount of almond paste in the filling and stud the buttery dough with almonds and chopped dried fruit that we've soaked for days in plenty of booze. Stollen is the perfect holiday gift, and it has a long shelf life. Every February, someone on the Hot Bread Kitchen staff uncovers a leftover stollen in the bakery. Everyone is happy to see it and finds it more delicious than the day it was made. Note that this bread takes a bit of planning: The fruit soaks for three days! Use the photographs to help with the shaping.

1. To soak the fruit: Put the raisins, cherries, lemon peel, orange peel, rum, brandy, and vanilla in a large bowl and add enough hot water just to cover the mixture. Give everything a good stir, cover the bowl tightly with plastic wrap, and set it aside, at room temperature, to soak for 3 days. Before incorporating the fruit into the dough, drain the fruit well, being sure to press down on the fruit to get all of the liquid out. (Reserve the soaking liquid for another use such as spooning over ice cream or drinking over ice as a cocktail.)

2. Preheat the oven to 325°F/165°C.

3. Spread the almonds in an even layer on a small rimmed baking sheet and toast in the oven, stirring once or twice until they are lightly browned, 10 to 12 minutes. Set aside to cool and then cut each one in half with a paring knife.

4. To make the filling, put the almond paste, bread crumbs, and granulated sugar in a small bowl and pinch with your fingertips until the ingredients are blended into a crumbly paste. Cut the butter into pebble-size bits and work it into the paste with your fingertips. Add the water and stir until it is absorbed. Scrape the paste onto a sheet of plastic wrap and form into 2 equal balls. Wrap each ball in plastic and refrigerate until firm, at least 2 hours and up to 3 days.

### Booze-Free Stollen

For our Muslim staff who do not consume alcohol, we devised an alcohol-free version that hits the spot. Omit the rum and brandy and instead put 1 cup/240 ml water in a small saucepan, add 1 split and scraped vanilla bean and its seeds, and bring to a boil. Remove from the heat and let the water cool to room temperature. Discard the bean and use the vanilla water to soak the fruit.

*recipe continues*

## DOUGH

½ cup/120 g **WHOLE MILK**, lukewarm

2¼ teaspoons **ACTIVE DRY YEAST** (1 envelope)

2 cups/250 g **ALL-PURPOSE FLOUR**, plus more for shaping

2½ tablespoons **GRANULATED SUGAR**

½ teaspoon ground **CINNAMON**

¼ teaspoon ground **GINGER**

Pinch of ground **CARDAMOM**

Pinch of ground **CLOVES**

Pinch of ground **NUTMEG**

Pinch of **KOSHER SALT**

8 tablespoons/115 g **UNSALTED BUTTER**, at room temperature

## TOPPING

6 tablespoons/85 g **UNSALTED BUTTER**, melted

½ cup/100 g **GRANULATED SUGAR**

1½ cups/180 g **CONFECTIONERS' SUGAR**, plus more as needed

**5.** To prepare the dough: Pour the milk into the bowl of a stand mixer fitted with a dough hook. Sprinkle the yeast on top.

**6.** Add the flour, granulated sugar, cinnamon, ginger, cardamom, cloves, nutmeg, salt, and room-temperature butter to the bowl. On low speed, mix until the dough just comes together, about 3 minutes. It will be quite sticky at this point. Increase the speed to medium-high and mix until the dough is smooth, pulls away from the sides of the bowl (and leaves the sides clean), has a bit of shine, and makes a slapping noise against the sides of the bowl, about 4 minutes.

**7.** Add the toasted almonds and drained fruit to the dough and mix on low until integrated. Cover the bowl with plastic wrap and let the dough sit at room temperature until it's soft and supple, about 1 hour.

**8.** Transfer the dough to a lightly floured surface and divide the dough into 2 equal pieces. Lightly pat the dough into 2 rectangles and shape each into a loose log (see page 120) so that you have 2 (8-inch/20 cm) loaves. Cover the loaves loosely with plastic wrap or a large plastic bag and let them rise for 20 minutes.

**9.** Use your hands to press each rested loaf into a rectangle measuring 1 inch/2.5 cm thick. Press a dowel (or the handle of a long wooden spoon) that's at least 12 inches/30 cm long and about ½ inch/1.5 cm in diameter down the center of the dough to form a canal (see page 245). Roll the dowel back and forth a few times to create an indentation that's 2 inches/5 cm wide.

**10.** Retrieve the chilled filling and roll each portion into a snake that is as long as the loaf and will fill the indentation in the rectangle of dough. Working with one loaf at a time, and arranging it lengthwise in front of you, lay the filling in the indentation, positioning it toward the top of the indentation, and fold the top edge of the dough over it so that the dough covers the filling and touches the second edge of dough. Press your dowel down at the edge of the filling, about one-third of the way down from the top edge of the stollen. Push down so that the dough-covered filling gets pushed to the top third of the stollen and you create a distinct ridge of dough. The two edges of dough toward the bottom will naturally separate a little as you do this. Now take the dowel and push it into that separation, where the two folds of dough meet—roughly two-thirds of the way down from the top of the stollen—to create a second and third ridge. The final stollen should have 3 distinct ridges.

**11.** Transfer the stollens to 2 parchment-lined rimmed baking sheets. Put the baking sheets in large plastic bags or loosely cover them with plastic wrap and let them rise until they increase slightly in volume and feel light and puffy when touched, 45 to 60 minutes.

**12.** Preheat the oven to 350°F/180°C.

**13.** Bake the loaves, rotating the pans from front to back once, until they're browned (your kitchen will smell amazing), 25 to 30 minutes. Remove the loaves from the oven and let them cool for 10 minutes.

**14.** Brush the loaves on both sides with the melted butter—don't be shy, the loaves should be liberally coated. Whisk together the granulated sugar and ½ cup/60 g of the confectioners' sugar in a small bowl and dust each loaf heavily with the mixture. Let cool completely. Once they are cool, dust the stollen again, liberally, with 1 cup/120 g confectioners' sugar. The first layer of sugar will help the second layer to adhere.

**15.** Separately wrap each loaf tightly in plastic wrap and let sit for at least 1 day before serving. Stollen also freezes very well: Put each wrapped loaf into an airtight plastic bag and freeze for up to 1 month. Let the stollen thaw at room temperature and dust with additional confectioners' sugar before serving.

# PAN DE MUERTOS

MAKES 6 ROUNDS; SERVES 6

ALL-PURPOSE FLOUR

NAN-E QANDI DOUGH (page 69),
    prepared through step 2

1 large EGG, beaten

COLORED SUGAR (optional)

A traditional Mexican bread, *pan de muertos* is the centerpiece food of Día de los Muertos, the holiday that falls on November 1 and celebrates the lives of family members who have passed away. Nancy (see page 91), who hails from Puebla, Mexico, taught us how to form *pan de muertos* in the customary shape. We find that our Nan-e Qandi dough (page 69), which is buttery and rich, is a great substitute for the dough used in Mexico. Note that the *nan-e qandi* dough does have a long rising time—8 hours—so plan accordingly.

**1.** Turn the dough out onto a lightly floured work surface. Divide the dough into 12 pieces—6 larger pieces for the buns (3½ ounces/ 100 g each) and 6 smaller pieces for the bones (1¾ ounces/50 g each). Working with one piece of dough at a time (keep the rest covered with plastic wrap), shape the larger pieces of dough into rolls (see page 123). Put the rolls, seam side down, on the work surface and cover loosely with plastic wrap so that they don't dry out.

**2.** Next you'll shape the crossbones: To do this, cut one of the little portions of dough into 3 equal pieces. Using your fingers, roll 2 snakes, each about 2 inches/5 cm long, with bulges at the ends (like a leg bone). Use your palm to flatten each one slightly. The third piece should simply be rolled into a little ball, which you'll also flatten slightly. Repeat for the remaining pieces of dough, covering them with plastic wrap as you go.

**3.** Uncover one of the big buns and spray the top with a little water if it is dry. Put the first bone on the top of the bun, applying a little pressure so that it sticks. Arrange the second bone perpendicular to the first so you have a cross. Finally stick the little ball at the intersection of the two bones. Repeat the decoration steps above with the remaining 5 buns, arranging them on a parchment-lined rimmed baking sheet and covering loosely with plastic wrap.

**4.** Lightly brush each bun with the egg. If you choose to decorate them, sprinkle colored sugar on top of the buns. Let them rise at room temperature until they're softer than firm balloons, are supple, and hold indentations when pressed lightly, about 3 hours.

**5.** Meanwhile, preheat the oven to 350°F/180°C.

**6.** Bake the *panes de muertos* until they're golden brown, about 25 minutes. Cool slightly on a wire rack. Serve warm or at room temperature. Store any leftovers in a plastic bag for up to 4 days at room temperature. Reheat in a 350°F/180°C oven for a few minutes.

# GUAGUAS DE PAN

MAKES 2 (12-INCH/30 CM) BREADS

**BREAD FLOUR**

**TRADITIONAL CHALLAH DOUGH**
(page 175), prepared through
step 2

4 **RAISINS** (optional)

1 large **EGG**, beaten

Just as Pan de Muertos (page 249) is made for Día de los Muertos in Mexico, Ecuadorans celebrate Día de los Disfuntos (All Souls' Day), which falls on November 2, with *guaguas de pan*. All Souls' Day is a day of remembrance when people pray for those who have died, hoping the prayers release their loved ones from purgatory to enter heaven. *Guagua* means "baby" in the Quechua language, and the breads are shaped like small human figures, often ones that look very animated. The bottoms of the breads are placed in the ground in cemeteries to indicate where the dead have been buried and to serve as sustenance for the deceased.

Raúl Guzman, our production manager, who comes from a long line of Ecuadoran bakers, introduced the bread to Hot Bread Kitchen. He is a master dough decorator, even going so far as to shape the *guaguas de pan* so they look like they are wearing clothing and making all sorts of gestures. His general instructions follow, but feel free to improvise! These eye-catching edible dolls, which provide endless joy to children, are also delicious because they are made with our dense challah dough. We sell them in markets to mark Día de los Muertos, near Halloween. We recommend them for a spooky fall breakfast, served with butter, hazelnut spread, and a glass of Fanny's Morocho (page 226).

**1.** Line a rimmed baking sheet with parchment paper.

**2.** On a lightly floured work surface, divide the dough into 3 pieces: 2 weighing 14 ounces/400 g, the third weighing just 3½ ounces/ 100 g. Working with one large piece (keep the rest covered with plastic wrap), roll the dough into an oblong shape measuring about 8 inches/20 cm long. Pinch the dough 2 inches/5 cm from one of the ends and twist it so that it becomes a separate sphere, but remains attached to the larger section. This will be the head of the figurine. Use your palms to flatten the entire dough, both the head and the body, so that it is about ½ inch/1.5 cm thick. Repeat the process with the second large piece of dough.

**3.** Transfer the figures to the prepared baking sheet. Form the arms and legs: Use a knife or a bench scraper to make 2 diagonal cuts, each 2 inches/5 cm long, about 2 inches/5 cm below the heads and on either side of each piece of dough; this is for the arms. And make a single 2-inch/5 cm vertical cut at the bottom of both of the bodies; this is for the legs. Stretch the dough to form arms and legs in any size or shape you wish and feel free to use your imagination—make an arm wave or salute if you'd like. Use the bench scraper or scissors to make indentations to resemble fingers or feet.

**4.** Use the remaining small piece of dough to form little mouths, ears, clothes, shoes—whatever!—if you'd like. Press these bits of decorative dough into the dough figures. Use a couple of raisins or candies (if desired) to make eyes on each figure. Brush both of the *guaguas de pan* with the beaten egg and drape them loosely with plastic wrap. Set aside to rise until they're softer than firm balloons, are supple, and hold indentations when pressed lightly, about 45 minutes.

**5.** Preheat the oven to 350°F/180°C.

**6.** Bake the *guaguas* until they're browned, about 25 minutes. Transfer to a wire rack to cool completely. Store any leftovers in a sealed plastic bag at room temperature.

# ROSCA DE REYES

MAKES 1 (12-INCH/30 CM) ROUND LOAF; SERVES 8 TO 10

## DOUGH

2¼ teaspoons **ACTIVE DRY YEAST** (1 envelope)

¼ cup/60 g **LUKEWARM WATER**

¼ cup/60 g **WHOLE MILK**

¼ cup/50 g **GRANULATED SUGAR**

4 tablespoons/60 g **UNSALTED BUTTER**

1 teaspoon **VANILLA EXTRACT**

½ teaspoon ground **CINNAMON**

1 teaspoon **KOSHER SALT**

3½ to 4 cups/435 to 500 g **ALL-PURPOSE FLOUR**, plus more for shaping

1 tablespoon finely grated **LEMON ZEST**

2 large **EGGS**, beaten

## TOPPING

1 cup plus 3 tablespoons/150 g **BREAD FLOUR**

¼ teaspoon **BAKING POWDER**

¼ teaspoon **KOSHER SALT**

7 tablespoons/100 g **UNSALTED BUTTER**, at room temperature

¾ cup plus 1 tablespoon/100 g **CONFECTIONERS' SUGAR**

¾ teaspoon **VANILLA EXTRACT**

This sweet Mexican holiday bread, the "Kings' Ring," is made to celebrate Three Kings Day on January 6. It's customary to insert a plastic figurine of the Baby Jesus in the bread, and whoever finds it is blessed. If you can't track down a figurine, a coin wrapped in foil can be substituted; just make sure guests know it's somewhere in the bread. Because of liability issues at the bakery, we sell the plastic baby with the cake and instruct customers on how to insert it.

1. To make the dough: Stir together the yeast and water in the bowl of a stand mixer fitted with a dough hook.

2. Combine the milk, granulated sugar, butter, vanilla, cinnamon, and salt in a small saucepan. Cook over medium heat, stirring now and then, until the butter is melted and the sugar is dissolved, about 5 minutes. Set aside to cool.

3. Add 3½ cups/435 g of the all-purpose flour to the bowl with the yeast mixture along with the milk mixture, lemon zest, and eggs. Mix on low just until the flour is integrated, and then turn the speed to medium-high and mix until the dough just begins to pull away from the edges of the bowl and is smooth and elastic, a few minutes. If the dough is a bit too wet, add up to ½ cup/65 g flour until a soft dough forms.

4. Lightly dust the surface of the dough with flour. Cover with plastic wrap (or put the entire bowl in a large plastic bag) and let stand at room temperature until the dough is softer than a firm balloon, is supple, and holds an

indentation when pressed lightly, about 1 hour.

5. To make the topping: Whisk together the flour, baking powder, and salt in a bowl. Put the butter and confectioners' sugar in the bowl of a stand mixer fitted with a whisk attachment and beat on medium speed until creamy, about 4 minutes. Beat in the vanilla extract. Add the flour mixture, reduce the speed to low, and beat until just combined. The mixture should be the texture of cookie dough.

6. Transfer the topping to a work surface. Flatten it with your hands and put it between two large rectangles of parchment paper. Roll out the mixture into a long rectangle that is about ½ inch/1.5 cm thick. Remove the top parchment and, using a sharp knife, cut the topping into 8 strips. Cover with plastic and set aside.

7. Turn the dough back out onto the floured surface and roll it into a rope 24 inches/60 cm long. Transfer the dough to the baking sheet, joining the ends of the rope to form a ring, and pinching the

## DECORATION

1 large **EGG**

8 **CANDIED CHERRIES**

4 **CANDIED ORANGE PEELS**

4 **CANDIED LEMON PEELS**

ends together to seal. Insert a little plastic or ceramic baby figurine into the bread from the bottom if you'd like.

**8.** Preheat the oven to 350°F/180°C. Line a rimmed baking sheet with parchment paper.

**9.** To decorate: In a small bowl, beat the egg with 1 tablespoon water and brush the top and sides of the bread with it. Decorate the ring by firmly

arranging strips of topping and candied cherries and citrus peels across the ring to create rows. Let the bread rest, covered, for another 20 minutes.

**10.** Bake the bread until golden, 35 to 40 minutes. Transfer the *rosca de reyes* to a wire rack to cool completely. Serve by the wedge. Any leftovers can be wrapped in plastic and stored at room temperature for up to 3 days.

# HOT CROSS BUNS

MAKES 12 INDIVIDUAL BUNS

## BUNS

1 teaspoon **ACTIVE DRY YEAST**

¾ cup/180 g **WHOLE MILK**

3 cups plus 2 tablespoons/405 g **BREAD FLOUR**, plus more for shaping

¼ cup/50 g **GRANULATED SUGAR**

1 teaspoon **KOSHER SALT**

½ teaspoon ground **CARDAMOM**

4 tablespoons/60 g **UNSALTED BUTTER**, at room temperature

2 large **EGGS**

½ cup/65 g **RAISINS**

½ cup/65 g **DRIED CURRANTS**

**CANOLA OIL**

## ICING

½ cup/65 g **CONFECTIONERS' SUGAR**

2 teaspoons **WHOLE MILK**

½ teaspoon **VANILLA EXTRACT**

Pinch of ground **CARDAMOM**

These sweet, delicious rolls celebrate Easter and mark spring at Hot Bread Kitchen, but they're great any time of year. To make them, we scent a simple yeasted, buttery dough with cardamom, stud it with raisins and currants, and form it into small rolls, which we bake close together so that they stay soft—similar to how the Parker House Rolls (page 181) are baked. Once cooled, each bun gets topped with a cross of cardamom-spiked icing.

**1.** To make the buns: Stir together the yeast and milk in the bowl and of a stand mixer fitted with a dough hook. Add the bread flour, granulated sugar, salt, cardamom, butter, and 1 of the eggs. Mix on low speed until the dry ingredients are combined. Add a little water if this hasn't happened in 3 minutes. Increase the speed to medium-high and mix the dough for an additional 4 minutes to develop the gluten. Do the windowpane test (page 16) to ensure the gluten is fully developed. Once the dough is ready, you'll also hear a slapping sound on the sides of the mixer and it will be quite shiny.

**2.** Add the raisins and currants and mix on low speed until just combined, 1 to 2 minutes.

**3.** Coat the inside of a large bowl with oil and transfer the dough to it. Cover loosely with plastic wrap or put the whole bowl in a large plastic bag, and let stand at room temperature until the dough is softer than a firm balloon, is supple, and holds an indentation when pressed lightly, about 1 hour.

**4.** Line a rimmed baking sheet with parchment paper. Turn the dough

out onto a lightly floured work surface. Divide into 12 equal pieces (each weighing 2½ ounces/75 g). Form each piece into a small bun (see page 123) and transfer to the baking sheet as you work, setting the buns seam side down and arranging them in a 3 × 4 grid so that their edges touch each other. Put the entire baking sheet in a large plastic bag or cover the buns loosely with plastic wrap and let rise until they're softer than firm balloons, are supple, and hold indentations when pressed lightly, about 1 hour.

**5.** Meanwhile, preheat the oven to 350°F/180°C.

**6.** Lightly beat the remaining egg, uncover the buns, and brush them with the egg. Bake the buns until they're beautifully browned and quite firm to the touch, about 30 minutes. Separate the rolls with a thin knife to ensure that they are baked through—not gummy. Transfer the buns to a wire rack to cool completely.

**7.** To make the icing: Whisk together the confectioners' sugar, milk, vanilla, and cardamom in a bowl. Gradually add more milk

or more sugar to achieve the right consistency. Transfer the mixture to a piping bag or a plastic bag with the small tip of a corner cut off.

8. Pipe a straight line down the middle of each row of buns. Give the buns a quarter turn and then pipe a line down the middle to create a cross on the top of each bun. Serve at room temperature. Store any leftovers in an airtight container at room temperature for up to 3 days.

# CHOCOLATE CHERRY ROLLS

**MAKES 12 ROLLS**

½ cup plus 1 tablespoon/75 g
**DRIED CHERRIES**

1 ounce/30 g **BITTERSWEET
CHOCOLATE** (60% to 70% cacao),
melted, plus 5 ounces/
140 g additional bittersweet
chocolate, cut into ⅜-inch/
1 cm chunks

1 cup minus 1 tablespoon/210 g
**WARM WATER**

2⅓ cups/295 g **BREAD FLOUR**

¼ cup/20 g **UNSWEETENED COCOA
POWDER**

2¼ teaspoons **KOSHER SALT**

Scant ¼ teaspoon **ACTIVE DRY
YEAST**

⅓ cup/80 g (risen and deflated)
**PÂTE FERMENTÉE** (page 126),
cut into walnut-size pieces

**CANOLA OIL**

**NOTE:** This recipe calls for
chocolate three ways: chunks,
melted, and cocoa. The dough
requires extra time to rise, but
the results are rolls that are
dark and dense.

We developed this delicious bread for Valentine's Day to reinvigorate slow February sales. The balance of the tart sourdough with rich dark chocolate and sweet cherries places this bread firmly in the wonderful space between brunch, dessert, and cheese plates. A fun way to use these is to put them in individual bowls, scoop out some of the top of each roll (eat or save for another use), and fill the hollowed-out rolls with scoops of ice cream and douse them with hot espresso—affogato bowls! Leftover rolls can be torn into pieces and used to make bread pudding (page 272).

**1.** Cover the cherries with hot water and set aside to soak.

**2.** Put the melted chocolate in the bowl of a stand mixer fitted with a dough hook, and let cool until warm (about 100°F/38°C). Gradually whisk in the warm water (if you add water too quickly or if the water is too cold, the chocolate will break up). Add the flour, cocoa powder, salt, yeast, and *pâte fermentée*. Mix on low speed until all of the ingredients are combined, 1 to 2 minutes. Increase the speed to medium-high and mix until the dough is smooth, pulls away from the sides of the bowl (and leaves the sides clean), has a bit of shine, and makes a slapping noise against the sides of the bowl, 5 to 6 minutes. You will know the dough is ready when you lightly tug a piece of the dough and it doesn't pull right off—it snaps back.

**3.** Drain the cherries and add them to the dough along with the chocolate chunks and mix on low speed until just combined, about 2 minutes. The dough may feel slightly soft and sticky, but it will firm up nicely during the long rising time.

**4.** Coat the inside of a medium bowl with oil and transfer the dough to it. Cover the bowl with plastic wrap and let stand at room temperature until it has risen, 2½ to 3 hours. Alternatively (for slower fermentation), let rise at room temperature for 45 minutes until you start to see the dough getting softer and rising slightly. Fold the dough in half and cover tightly with plastic wrap and refrigerate for a minimum of 4 hours and a maximum of 12. Allow the dough to come to room temperature before proceeding.

**5.** Line a rimmed baking sheet with parchment paper. Turn the dough out onto a lightly floured work surface. Gently divide the dough into 12 equal pieces (each weighing around 2½ ounces/70 g). Working with one piece at a time (keep the rest covered with plastic wrap), shape each into a roll (see page 123). If chocolate chunks or cherries break through the surface, push them back into the dough with a finger and pinch the hole to seal it. Transfer the rolls to the baking sheet, seam side down, arranging them so that they're

*recipe continues*

nearly touching each other but aren't too tightly packed. Loosely cover the rolls with plastic wrap and let stand until they almost fill the pan, 2½ to 3 hours.

**6.** Meanwhile, preheat the oven to 400°F/205°C. Put a baking dish on the bottom of the oven.

**7.** Score each roll with an "X." Put the baking sheet in the oven and put 10 ice cubes in the baking dish. Bake until the rolls are even darker brown, the tops feel crusty, and when you gently separate the rolls with a thin knife, the interior dough is fully cooked, not gummy, 15 to 20 minutes.

**8.** Transfer to a wire rack to cool completely. Store rolls in a plastic bag for up to 4 days.

I have a friend who runs a nonprofit and has children older than my own. She told me that when she had her first son, she realized she could leave her impressive career and be a mother, or continue in both capacities—and be a maniac. Being a maniac, she said, sounded like a whole lot more fun.

If I had a surefire method to balance parenthood with running a business, I would likely be writing that book. The truth is that I have embraced my inner maniac, like my friend. I have also developed a few strategies along the way that have made this balancing act a little easier.

My family lives in Harlem, a seven-minute walk from Hot Bread Kitchen. Given what we do, I think that it is important for me to live in the community, but it also means that I can run home to check on a baby with a sniffle and sneak in for a kiss before naptime. It's also really easy for my kids to come to activities and events at the bakery. Dahlia spent so much time at Hot Bread in her first year of life that her first word was *pan* ("bread" in Spanish). Whenever the kids are in the bakery, they have thirty loving aunties who are watching them grow up.

I am lucky to have a great partner in my husband, Eli, and support from our extended family. Many days, it feels like Eli and I pass off the baton in a relay race of parenthood, but knowing that Eli is always there to keep running has allowed me to grow Hot Bread Kitchen and impact the lives of the women we serve. My mother-in-law, Ydalia, who lives on Long Island, has been a regular caregiver for both kids, a tender and hands-on *abuela*. My mom lives in Toronto, but she's frequently in New York to lend a hand. We have dubbed her the Flying Bubie because she spends fifty percent of her time shuttling between me and my brother—also an entrepreneur with young kids—who lives in California. It takes a village.

Interestingly and wonderfully, I have found that in many ways being a mother makes me a better CEO and being a CEO makes me a better mother. When Dahlia was born in 2011, I had to step away from controlling every detail at Hot Bread Kitchen for the first time. Pulling away made me a better manager because it meant I had to delegate more work and trust my staff to execute it well. I took a bit more time off when Emile was born in 2013. Hot Bread Kitchen had grown, yet I was able to be away savoring those early months of my son's life. My kids—and my staff— were thriving.

Becoming a parent also made my job more sustainable. I don't know if I could have continued working flat out as I did before I had kids. By taking weekends off or going home before dinnertime (things I never did before I had children), I have gained more balance. But one of the most valuable by-products of motherhood is that it has helped me to create an organization that respects and values parenthood. In 2013, Hot Bread Kitchen staffers and incubator members had nine babies. I am happy and proud to run a business—and work in one—where we're making beautiful bread and beautiful kids and figuring it all out together.

# MY MOM'S NUTTY GRANOLA

MAKES 8 CUPS/ABOUT 1 KG

½ cup/60 g raw **ALMONDS**

½ cup/55 g **UNSALTED PEANUTS**

½ cup/60 g raw **WALNUT HALVES**

½ cup/70 g raw **PUMPKIN SEEDS**

½ cup/70 g raw **SUNFLOWER SEEDS**

3 cups/300 g **ROLLED OATS**

¼ cup/15 g **WHEAT GERM**

¾ cup/255 g **HONEY**

½ cup/110 g **VEGETABLE OIL**

1 tablespoon **BOILING WATER**

1 teaspoon **KOSHER SALT**

½ cup/65 g **RAISINS**

## Nut-Free Granola

Leave out the nuts and double the amount of raisins—or do half raisins and half dried cherries, or any other combination of dried fruit.

When I was a kid, my mother used to make fresh granola—and this was in the '70s before you could find packaged granola in every supermarket. There was always a fresh batch in a glass jar on the kitchen counter. We now sell My Mom's Nutty Granola at Hot Bread Kitchen. (My mother jokingly likes to call it "Nutty Mom's Granola.") It's not too sweet, the flavor is rich from long-roasting the nuts, and the texture is almost muesli-like. At the bakery we leave out the walnuts, but at home I add them; the choice is yours.

**1.** Position a rack in the middle of the oven and preheat to 325°F/165°C.

**2.** Put the almonds, peanuts, walnuts, pumpkin seeds, and sunflower seeds on a rimmed baking sheet in a single layer. Roast the nuts and seeds, stirring now and then, until they smell nutty and are lightly browned, about 15 minutes. Transfer to a large bowl. Stir in the oats and wheat germ.

**3.** In a small bowl, whisk together the honey, oil, boiling water, and salt. Use a rubber spatula to scrape the mixture into the oat mixture and stir thoroughly to combine. Transfer the mixture back to the baking sheet.

**4.** Bake the granola, stirring every 10 minutes, until nearly dry, about 40 minutes. It should be dark brown.

**5.** Turn the oven off and open the door. Let the granola cool in the oven as the oven itself cools down, being sure to stir it now and then to make sure the granola is cooling evenly. It will crisp as it cools. Once it is cooled, stir in the raisins. Store in a sealed glass jar up to 2 weeks.

# NUTTY GRANOLA WAFFLES

**MAKES 8 (4-INCH/10 CM) OR 2 (8-INCH/20 CM) WAFFLES**

1¾ cups/220 g **ALL-PURPOSE FLOUR**

¼ cup/15 g **WHEAT GERM**

2 tablespoons **SUGAR**

2 teaspoons **BAKING POWDER**

½ teaspoon **KOSHER SALT**

2 large **EGGS**

1½ cups/360 g **WHOLE MILK**

4 tablespoons/60 g **UNSALTED BUTTER**, melted, plus more for the iron

½ teaspoon **VANILLA EXTRACT**

1 cup/170 g **MY MOM'S NUTTY GRANOLA** (page 261)

**FRESH BERRIES**

**WARM MAPLE SYRUP**

I had an amazing breakthrough one morning when I sprinkled our granola into waffle batter while it was still on the waffle iron. It adds texture and great oaty flavor—just the kind of easy-but-unexpected touch that makes a weekend breakfast extra special. To make the waffles themselves even healthier, and to echo the flavors in the granola, I add a little wheat germ to the batter. Feel free to leave it out if you wish—just use 2 full cups/250 g of flour instead.

**1.** Preheat the oven to 200°F/95°C.

**2.** Whisk together the flour, wheat germ, sugar, baking powder, and salt in a large bowl. Whisk together the eggs, milk, butter, and vanilla in a small bowl. Stir the egg mixture into the flour mixture to fully incorporate all of the ingredients, but do not overmix.

**3.** Heat a waffle iron according to the manufacturer's instructions. Once it's hot, coat both sides of the iron with butter and ladle the batter into the iron. Sprinkle the batter evenly with a little bit of the granola—the amount will depend on how big your iron is. Close the iron and cook the waffle according to the manufacturer's instructions. Put the waffle on a baking sheet and transfer to the oven to keep warm while you continue making waffles. If the waffles stick to the iron, use more butter.

**4.** Serve the waffles warm, topped with berries and drizzled with maple syrup.

# BREAKFAST OF CHAMPIONS

**SERVES 4**

1½ cups/340 g **FRESH RICOTTA CHEESE**

2 cups/275 g **CHERRIES** (see Note), pitted and halved

2 cups/340 g **MY MOM'S NUTTY GRANOLA** (page 261)

1 cup/240 g **WHOLE MILK**

Mornings at Hot Bread Kitchen are especially busy, since that's when we mix our doughs. The morning shift requires good, long-lasting fuel. This combination of fresh ricotta cheese with cherries and granola is not only packed with protein and healthy carbohydrates, it also takes about a minute to make and can be eaten out of a bowl or a cup on the go. Try making this in a small paper cup and giving it to your kids to enjoy on the way to school on those mornings when there just isn't enough time to sit and enjoy breakfast at home. For an easy, Black Forest cake–inspired dessert, simply serve this topped with lots of shaved dark chocolate.

Divide the ricotta among 4 shallow bowls. Top with the cherries, granola, and milk. Serve immediately.

**NOTE:** Any fresh fruit, such as berries or sliced peaches or apples, works very nicely here in place of the cherries if they're not in season.

# ROASTED APPLES
## WITH GRANOLA AND CRÈME FRAÎCHE

**SERVES 4**

4 large firm, **TART APPLES**, such as Honeycrisp (largest you can find)

4 tablespoons/60 g **UNSALTED BUTTER**, at room temperature

½ packed cup/110 g **DARK BROWN SUGAR**

1 teaspoon ground **CINNAMON**

Pinch of **KOSHER SALT**

1 cup/170 g **MY MOM'S NUTTY GRANOLA** (page 261)

½ cup/120 g **CRÈME FRAÎCHE**

This is as easy as dessert gets. By roasting the apples with brown sugar and cinnamon, you get the flavor of apple pie without the hassle of a making a crust. The granola adds nutty flavor and a welcome crunch. Leftover roasted apples are great for breakfast with more granola and plain yogurt; in fact, it's worth doubling the batch just so you have leftovers.

**1.** Preheat the oven to 350°F/180°C. Line a rimmed baking sheet with parchment paper.

**2.** Cut a little thin slice off of the bottom and top of each apple and then, using an apple corer or a small spoon, remove the seeds and core, but leave ½ inch/1.5 cm of flesh at the bottom of the apples. You are creating a vessel out of your apples. Put the apples on the prepared baking sheet. The small slice at the bottoms of the apples will help them sit upright.

**3.** Mix together the butter, brown sugar, cinnamon, and salt. Evenly spread the mixture over the exposed tops of the apples. Bake the apples until they're tender when pierced with a paring knife and browned, about 30 minutes.

**4.** Transfer the apples to serving dishes. Scatter each serving with granola and then dollop crème fraîche on top. Serve immediately while the apples are still warm.

# WASTE NOT

## WHAT TO DO WITH LEFTOVER BREAD

Commercial bakers, like home cooks, are always creating new ways to use up leftovers. Some of our breads, like Traditional Onion Bialys (page 159) and Stollen (page 244), use bread crumbs as part of their fillings. Old bread becomes new bread, over and over. Some of the most delectable and satisfying dishes (Chilaquiles, page 287; Saltie's Ribollita, page 284) use leftover bread as their jumping-off point. This is, of course, a time-honored baking tradition. Many artisinal bread doughs utilize old dough to extend the fermentation process and add flavor complexity.

Many of our staff meals start with the following question: *What should we do with yesterday's bread?* Enter a wealth of creative solutions, like Winter Panzanella (page 279) and Summertime Tomato and Tuna Bread Salad (page 280), Grilled Cheese French Toast with Caramelized Peaches (page 271), and memorable desserts like Tres Leches Bread Pudding with Mexican Chocolate Sauce (page 272).

When we really can't craft a recipe, we donate hundreds of loaves of day-old bread every week to City Harvest and New York Common Pantry, which work to combat hunger in New York City. In addition we drop our prices to "pay what you can" at Hot Bread Almacen, our small retail bakery, at 2 p.m. every day. These efforts minimize waste and ensure our breads feed as many people as possible, no matter their income level.

## Recipe for an Entrepreneur

This recipe is definitely tongue-in-cheek, but it highlights an important aspect of what we bake up at Hot Bread Kitchen. We are in the business of identifying individuals with high potential for success in the food economy. We then provide technical training and space to grow so that they can build businesses and create better lives for their families. To riff on a classic proverb, we teach women to fish. But we also show them how to fillet their catch, batter and fry it, and then sell their fish with an appropriate markup.

3 parts **RESILIENCE**
2 parts **CLEAR VISION**
2 parts **SCRAPPY NATURE** (can substitute **WILLINGNESS TO BEND THE RULES**)
2 parts **COMPETITIVE SPIRIT**
1 part **TIRELESS PROMOTER**
Pinch of a **THICK SKIN**

## The Food Entrepreneur

Take the above attributes and mix in:

1 part **PHYSICAL STAMINA REQUIRED FOR LONG SHIFTS IN THE KITCHEN**
1 part **MANIACAL COMMITMENT TO QUALITY CONTROL**
1 part **TECHNICAL KNOW-HOW**

## The Social Entrepreneur

Take all the above attributes and mix in:

2 parts **DESIRE TO LEAVE THE WORLD A BETTER PLACE**
1 part **PASSION FOR PEOPLE**

# GRILLED CHEESE FRENCH TOAST
## WITH CARAMELIZED PEACHES

**SERVES 4**

7 tablespoons/100 g **UNSALTED BUTTER**

2 **NOT-TOO-RIPE PEACHES**, thinly sliced

2 tablespoons **SUGAR**

2 tablespoons **LEMON JUICE**

8 large **EGGS**

½ cup/120 g **WHOLE MILK**

½ teaspoon **KOSHER SALT**

¼ teaspoon ground **CINNAMON**

8 (¾-inch/2 cm) slices day-old **CHALLAH**, homemade (page 175 or 188) or store-bought

1 cup/95 g coarsely grated **EXTRA-SHARP CHEDDAR CHEESE**

My dad loved to cook. He made a mean version of his mother's chicken soup (page 204), including the bird's scaly feet when he could find them at the butcher. He made delicious chicken schnitzel (page 282) and even deep fried chicken in the backyard. But this breakfast-lunch-sweet-savory hybrid stands out from the many delicious things he made when I was growing up. I have no idea how or why he started making it, but it is the most satisfying comfort food you can imagine. When peaches aren't in season, apples are especially good in their place.

1. Melt 3 tablespoons/45 g of the butter in a large skillet over medium-high heat. Add the peaches in as even a layer as possible and sprinkle with 1 tablespoon of the sugar. Cook the peaches, flipping them once, until they're browned on both sides, just a minute or so per side. Remove from the heat and drizzle the lemon juice over the top.

2. In a large baking dish, whisk together the eggs, milk, salt, cinnamon, and the remaining 1 tablespoon sugar. Add the challah, making sure each slice gets evenly coated, and let it sit to fully absorb all of the mixture.

3. Melt 2 tablespoons/30 g of the butter in a large skillet or griddle over medium-high heat. Put 4 slices of the soaked challah in a single layer on the skillet and cook until the undersides are just barely browned, about 1 minute. Carefully turn 2 of the slices over and divide ½ cup/50 g of the cheddar cheese between them. Lift the remaining 2 slices of challah and put on top of the cheese so the barely browned side touches the cheese. Press down on each sandwich with your spatula and then cover the pan (or tent the griddle with foil) and let the sandwiches cook until the undersides are very nicely browned, about 2 minutes. Uncover the pan, flip the sandwiches, and cook until the second side is well browned and the cheese is melted, just another minute. Transfer the sandwiches to a serving platter. Repeat the process with the remaining butter, soaked bread, and cheese.

4. Top the sandwiches with the peaches and drizzle whatever liquid is left in the peach skillet on top of the sandwiches. Serve immediately while everything is warm.

# TRES LECHES BREAD PUDDING
## WITH MEXICAN CHOCOLATE SAUCE

SERVES 8 TO 10

6 large **EGGS**

1 (14-ounce/396 g) can **SWEETENED CONDENSED MILK**

1 (12-ounce/354 ml) can **EVAPORATED MILK**

2 cups/480 g **WHOLE MILK**

3 teaspoons **VANILLA EXTRACT**

1 teaspoon ground **CINNAMON**

1 teaspoon **KOSHER SALT**

1 (1-pound/455 g) loaf day-old **CHALLAH**, homemade (page 175) or store-bought, torn into 1-inch/2.5 cm pieces

½ cup/55 g sliced **ALMONDS**

½ cup/65 g **RAISINS**

1 tablespoon **UNSALTED BUTTER**, at room temperature

1 cup/240 g cold **HEAVY CREAM**

2 tablespoons **SUGAR**

**MEXICAN CHOCOLATE SAUCE** (recipe follows)

When I make bread pudding, I throw together whatever bits of dairy I have, including, but not limited to, milk, cream, sour cream, eggs, and butter. I add some sugar, toss in a handful or two of raisins, add torn stale challah, bake it, and call it a pudding. There's nothing wrong with that impromptu bread pudding, but this *tres leches* version is a showstopper. Topped with whipped cream and a rich cinnamon-infused chocolate sauce, it's a memorable ending to a dinner party. The staler the bread, the better; dry bread absorbs more of the decadent milk mixture.

**1.** Preheat the oven to 350°F/180°C.

**2.** Whisk together the eggs, all three milks, 2 teaspoons of the vanilla, the cinnamon, and salt in a large bowl. Add the bread, almonds, and raisins and use your hands to mix everything together. Let everything sit for 5 minutes to let the bread absorb the mixture.

**3.** Coat a 2½-quart/2.3-liter baking dish with the butter. Transfer the bread mixture to the dish. Bake the bread pudding until the top is browned and the pudding is set, 45 minutes to 1 hour.

**4.** Let the bread pudding cool for at least 10 minutes before serving.

**5.** While it's cooling, combine the cream and remaining 1 teaspoon vanilla in the bowl of a stand mixer fitted with a whisk attachment. Whisk on high speed until soft peaks form. Whisk in the sugar.

**6.** Serve the bread pudding warm topped with the whipped cream and chocolate sauce.

# MEXICAN CHOCOLATE SAUCE

**MAKES 1⅓ CUPS/350 G**

This sauce takes bread pudding or even a plain bowl of vanilla ice cream to another level. Mexican chocolate has sugar and cinnamon, which adds the characteristic spice (see page 291 for sources). If you can't track it down, feel free to substitute an equal amount of chopped dark chocolate and add a hefty pinch of ground cinnamon.

7 ounces/200 g **MEXICAN CHOCOLATE**, finely chopped

1 ounce/30 g **BITTERSWEET CHOCOLATE**

½ cup/120 g **HEAVY CREAM**

Bring a small saucepan of water to a boil and then reduce to a simmer. Put the two chocolates and the cream in a heatproof bowl and put it on top of the saucepan. Make sure the water isn't directly touching the bowl (if it is, simply pour a bit out). Heat the mixture, stirring, until the chocolates are completely melted and the sauce is smooth. Serve immediately. If you would like to make the sauce ahead, let it cool to room temperature, cover with plastic wrap, and store in the refrigerator for up to 1 week. Reheat in the double boiler.

# ARUGULA SALAD WITH SEPHARDIC CHALLAH CROUTONS AND LEMON VINAIGRETTE

**SERVES 4**

½ cup plus 3 tablespoons/155 g **EXTRA-VIRGIN OLIVE OIL**

3 tablespoons fresh **LEMON JUICE**

1 small **GARLIC CLOVE**, minced

**KOSHER SALT**

6 loosely packed cups/200 g **BABY ARUGULA**

½ loaf day-old **SEPHARDIC CHALLAH** (page 190) or other bread, cut into ½-inch/1.5 cm cubes (4 cups/400 g)

Freshly ground **BLACK PEPPER**

Because of the spices in Sephardic Challah (page 190), leftovers make delicious croutons. You can, of course, substitute any day-old bread. While we're discussing substitutions, any bitter green can be used in place of arugula including, but not limited to, chopped radicchio, dandelion greens, or escarole.

**1.** Whisk together ½ cup/110 g of the olive oil, the lemon juice, garlic, and a large pinch of salt in a large bowl. Put the arugula in the bowl, but don't stir it in quite yet.

**2.** Heat the remaining 3 tablespoons/45 g olive oil in a large skillet over medium heat. Stir in the bread cubes and sprinkle with a healthy pinch of salt. Cook, stirring now and then, until they're browned all over and crisp, about 5 minutes. Transfer the croutons to the bowl with the arugula and stir everything to combine. The warm croutons will wilt the arugula a little bit. Season to taste with salt and pepper. Serve immediately.

# WINTER PANZANELLA

⅔ pound/300 g day-old **BATARD** or **CIABATTA**, homemade (page 128 or 141) or store-bought, torn into 1-inch/2.5 cm pieces (about 2 medium loaves)

1 pound/455 g **BUTTERNUT SQUASH**, peeled, seeded, and cut into 1½-inch/4 cm cubes

1 pound/455 g **BRUSSELS SPROUTS**, trimmed and halved

½ cup plus 3 tablespoons/155 g **EXTRA-VIRGIN OLIVE OIL**

**KOSHER SALT**

2 teaspoons **DIJON MUSTARD**

2 teaspoons **MAPLE SYRUP**

3 tablespoons **APPLE CIDER VINEGAR**

Freshly ground **BLACK PEPPER**

½ bunch **TUSCAN KALE**, ribs discarded, thinly sliced (about 3 cups/200 g)

½ small **RED ONION**, finely diced

½ cup/50 g shaved or grated **PARMESAN CHEESE**

I think of summer when I think of bread salads (see Summertime Tomato and Tuna Bread Salad, page 280), but a crisp piece of bread is just as good at soaking up all the delicious flavor from roasted winter vegetables and a mustardy dressing. This hearty salad is perfect for lunch on a cold day.

**1.** Preheat the oven to 400°F/205°C.

**2.** Put the bread cubes on a baking sheet and bake, stopping to stir now and then, until browned and crisp on all sides, about 15 minutes. Transfer the bread to a plate or bowl.

**3.** Put the squash and sprouts on the baking sheet and toss together with 3 tablespoons/45 g of the olive oil and ½ teaspoon of the salt. Roast the vegetables, stirring now and then, until they're browned and tender, 35 to 40 minutes. Remove from the oven and let them cool slightly while you prepare the dressing. (This salad is quite nice with the warm vegetables, but if you prefer to roast them ahead, it works well with them at room temperature, too.)

**4.** Whisk together the mustard, maple syrup, and vinegar in a large bowl. While whisking, drizzle in the remaining ½ cup/110 g olive oil. Season the dressing to taste with salt and plenty of pepper.

**5.** Add the toasted bread, roasted vegetables, kale, onion, and half of the Parmesan and stir to combine. Season to taste with more salt and pepper. Transfer the panzanella to a serving bowl, scatter the remaining Parmesan on top, and serve immediately.

# SUMMERTIME TOMATO AND TUNA BREAD SALAD

**SERVES 4**

¾ pound/340 g day-old **BATARD** or **CIABATTA**, homemade (page 128 or 141) or store-bought, thickly sliced (about 2 medium loaves)

1 large **GARLIC CLOVE**, peeled

2 tablespoons **BALSAMIC VINEGAR**

¼ cup plus 2 tablespoons/85 g **EXTRA-VIRGIN OLIVE OIL**

¼ cup/55 g **COLD WATER**

**KOSHER SALT**

½ small **SPANISH ONION**, finely diced

1 large **TOMATO**, cut into ½-inch/1.5 cm dice

1 tablespoon brined **CAPERS**, drained

¼ cup/40 g **KALAMATA OLIVES**, pitted and halved

1 (7-ounce/200 g) jar **OLIVE OIL–PACKED TUNA**

1 tablespoon fresh **LEMON JUICE**

¼ packed cup/10 g **FLAT-LEAF PARSLEY LEAVES**, roughly chopped

Freshly ground **BLACK PEPPER**

This satisfying bread salad speaks to my love of everything that is flavorful in the salt department; it's got an abundance of capers, olives, tuna, and vinegar, which is just what you need on a hot summer evening. It's okay if this sits for a while before serving. In fact, it gets better over time.

**1.** Preheat the oven to 400°F/205°C.

**2.** Put the bread on a rimmed baking sheet in a single layer and bake, turning once, until browned and crisp on both sides, 15 minutes total.

**3.** Rub one side of each piece of toast aggressively with the garlic. Tear the bread into 1-inch/2.5 cm pieces and leave them on the baking sheet.

**4.** Whisk together the balsamic vinegar, ¼ cup/60 ml of the olive oil, the water, and a pinch of salt in a small bowl. Pour the mixture over the bread and toss the bread to make sure each piece gets some of the liquid. Let the bread sit for at least 15 minutes so it softens and absorbs the oil and vinegar.

**5.** Put the onion in a large bowl and sprinkle with a large pinch of salt. Use your hands to stir the salt into the onion and then let sit for a couple of minutes.

**6.** Add the tomato, capers, and olives to the onion. Use a fork to lift the tuna out of the jar and add it to the mixture. Add the lemon juice and the remaining 2 tablespoons/30 ml olive oil. Stir everything together and season to taste with salt and pepper.

**7.** Stir the bread into the tomato mixture and let sit for at least 15 more minutes to let all of the flavors come together. Gently stir in the parsley and season to taste with additional salt and plenty of freshly ground black pepper before serving.

# SEASONED BREAD CRUMBS

**MAKES 2 CUPS/460 G**

1 loaf day-old **BREAD**, cut or torn
    into 1-inch/2.5 cm cubes
    (8 cups/455 g)

1 teaspoon **KOSHER SALT**

1 teaspoon **DRIED PARSLEY**

½ teaspoon **GARLIC POWDER**

½ teaspoon freshly ground **BLACK
    PEPPER**

Pinch of ground **CUMIN**

### Plain Bread Crumbs

Simply omit the dried
parsley, garlic powder, black
pepper, and cumin.

Homemade bread crumbs are simple to make and are superior to store-bought. Simply keep a large resealable plastic bag in your freezer to house the ends of your baguettes or the slices of ciabatta that you never quite got to. Once you have a couple of cups' worth, whiz up a batch of bread crumbs to keep your supply going. These will keep 2 weeks in an airtight bag at room temperature or up to a month in the freezer.

**1.** Preheat the oven to 400°F/205°C.

**2.** Put the bread in a single layer on a baking sheet and bake until the bread is browned, dry, and crisp, stirring now and then, about 15 minutes altogether. Set aside to cool.

**3.** Working in batches as necessary, pulse the dried bread in the food processor until you have fine crumbs. Add the salt, dried parsley, garlic powder, pepper, and cumin to the bread crumbs and give it all a couple of final pulses to make sure all the spices are well distributed.

# CRISPY CHICKEN SCHNITZEL
## WITH LEMON PICKLED RED ONIONS

**SERVES 6**

2 pounds/905 g boneless, skinless **CHICKEN THIGHS** (about 8 pieces), trimmed

¾ cup/85 g **ALL-PURPOSE FLOUR**

**KOSHER SALT**

1 teaspoon **GARLIC POWDER**

4 large **EGGS**

2 tablespoons **WATER**

3 cups/690 g seasoned dried **BREAD CRUMBS**, preferably homemade (page 281)

**CANOLA OIL**, for frying

**LEMON PICKLED RED ONIONS** (recipe follows)

This is another recipe from my dad. While it works with chicken breasts, I much prefer it made with boneless, skinless chicken thighs, which have much more flavor and stay moist. Best of all, this schnitzel is a vehicle for the lemony pickled onions, which could not be easier to make or more delicious to eat. Be patient and let the schnitzel fry up nice and dark.

**1.** Pat the chicken dry with paper towels. Put one of the chicken thighs between two large pieces of parchment paper and use a meat pounder or a small heavy pot to pound the chicken to a thickness of ¼ inch/6 mm. Repeat for the rest of the chicken.

**2.** Put the flour in a shallow dish and whisk it together with 1 teaspoon salt and the garlic powder. Whisk together the eggs and water in a small bowl. Pour the egg mixture into a second shallow baking dish or plate. Put the bread crumbs on a third shallow dish.

**3.** Dredge each piece of chicken first in the flour, tapping off any excess. Then dip the floured chicken into the egg and, finally, coat it evenly with the bread crumbs. Put the coated chicken on a baking sheet.

**4.** Line a baking sheet with two or three layers of paper towels. Pour 1 inch/2.5 cm of oil into a large skillet and heat over medium-high heat until a pinch of bread crumbs sizzles upon contact.

**5.** Working in batches as necessary to avoid crowding in the pan, and adding more oil as needed, fry the chicken until it's browned and crisp on both sides, 5 to 7 minutes per side. Transfer the browned chicken to the towel-lined baking sheet and sprinkle with salt.

**6.** Serve hot with plenty of lemon pickled red onions.

# LEMON PICKLED RED ONIONS

**MAKES ABOUT 1 CUP/225 G**

This might be the simplest recipe in the book and is certainly one of the most versatile. These onions provide a bright, snappy bite that offsets the fat and crunch of the schnitzel.

1 medium **RED ONION**, thinly sliced into rings

½ teaspoon **KOSHER SALT**

Juice of 1 **LEMON**

Put the onion in a small bowl and sprinkle with the salt and toss with your hands. Add the lemon juice and let the onion sit until softened, at least 15 minutes at room temperature or up to 1 or 2 days covered in the refrigerator.

# SALTIE'S RIBOLLITA

**SERVES 8 TO 10**

1 pound/455 g **DRIED CRANBERRY** or **CANNELLINI BEANS**

1 small bunch **FRESH THYME** (about 24 sprigs)

1 small bunch **FRESH SAGE** (about 12 sprigs)

6 dried **BAY LEAVES**

20 **GARLIC CLOVES**, peeled; 12 of them halved lengthwise, the remaining 8 thinly sliced

¾ cup/170 g **EXTRA-VIRGIN OLIVE OIL**, plus more for drizzling

**KOSHER SALT**

2 medium **SPANISH ONIONS**, finely diced

2 large **CARROTS**, peeled and finely diced

4 **CELERY STALKS**, finely diced

1 bunch **FLAT-LEAF PARSLEY**, tough stems discarded, roughly chopped

2 (28-ounce/795 g) cans **WHOLE PEELED TOMATOES**, crushed with your hands, juice reserved

¼ small head **SAVOY CABBAGE**, cored and thinly sliced

6 large leaves **TUSCAN** or **LACINATO KALE**, thinly sliced

6 cups/300 g **STALE CRUSTY BREAD CUBES**

Saltie is a small sandwich shop in Williamsburg, Brooklyn. The owner, Caroline Fidanza, was one of the first wholesale buyers of Hot Bread Kitchen bread, long before she opened her shop. I was nervous and excited when Caroline called to set up a lavash tasting for the restaurant she managed; she soon became a great advocate. This recipe for ribollita, an Italian bean and vegetable soup thickened with bread, is adapted from her cookbook, *Saltie*. It's one of my favorite ways to use leftover bread, especially focaccia or ciabatta. *Ribollita* means "reboiled," and the soup is traditionally made one day and then heated up and eaten the next day. The bread is added to thicken it upon reheating.

1. Pick over the beans and discard any small stones. Put them in a bowl and add enough water to cover them by at least 2 inches/5 cm. Let soak overnight.

2. Drain the beans and put in a pot with at least a 12-quart/11-liter capacity. Add 3 quarts/2.8 liters cold water and bring the beans to a boil over high heat. Skim any foam that rises to the surface, then reduce to a simmer. Tie the thyme and sage together with a piece of kitchen twine and add the herbs to the pot along with the bay leaves, the 12 halved garlic cloves, and ¼ cup/60 ml of the olive oil. Simmer the beans until they're really tender, anywhere from 45 minutes to 2 hours, depending on the age of the beans. Add a bit more water as you go along if the beans need it. They should always be covered with liquid.

3. Once the beans are tender, but not mushy, season them to taste with salt and remove and discard the herb bundle and bay leaves. The beans can be cooled and stored in their liquid in an airtight container in the refrigerator for up to 3 days.

4. Meanwhile, heat the remaining ½ cup/120 ml olive oil in a large soup pot over medium-high heat. Add the onions, the 8 sliced garlic cloves, and a large pinch of salt and cook, stirring now and then, until the onions just begin to soften, about 5 minutes. Add the carrots and celery and another large pinch of salt and reduce the heat to medium. Cook the vegetables, stirring now and then, until they're softened and almost jammy, about 20 minutes.

5. Add the parsley and the crushed tomatoes and their juice. Increase the heat to high and bring to a boil. Immediately reduce the heat to low and season to taste with salt. Simmer the soup until all of the flavors are well combined, about 30 minutes.

**NOTE:** If you are making the soup ahead, remove from the heat before adding the bread, let the soup cool to room temperature, and store it covered in the refrigerator for up to a week. Incorporate the bread when you reheat the soup.

**6.** Add the cabbage and kale to the pot along with 1 quart/1 liter fresh water. Bring to a boil again, then reduce to a simmer, season with salt, and cook just until the cabbage is wilted, about 10 minutes.

**7.** Drain the beans (discard their cooking liquid or reserve it for another use—it will add too much starch here) and add them to the pot along with another 1 quart/ 1 liter water. Bring to a boil, season lightly with salt, then reduce the heat as low as it can go, and put a lid on slightly ajar. Simmer ever so gently until everything is meltingly tender and the flavors are deep and well developed, a solid 2 hours.

Give it a stir now and then to make sure the beans aren't sticking to the bottom and add a splash of water now and then if things are looking like they're dry. The vegetables will surrender their color and crispness—this is a good thing. As the Saltie women say, when the soup looks like rust, you know it's done.

**8.** Season the soup with salt to taste one final time—don't be shy, it will require quite a bit. Stir in the bread cubes and cook the soup for a final 5 minutes until they absorb lots of liquid and begin to fall apart. Ladle the soup into bowls and serve each portion drizzled with olive oil and sprinkled with a bit of salt.

# CHILAQUILES

**SERVES 4**

**CANOLA OIL**, for frying

12 (6-inch/15 cm) **CORN TORTILLAS**, homemade (page 92) or store-bought, cut into sixths

**KOSHER SALT**

3 cups/780 g **SALSA VERDE** (page 108)

¼ cup/60 g **SOUR CREAM**

2 tablespoons **WHOLE MILK**

½ cup/50 g grated **COTIJA** or crumbled **FETA CHEESE**

Small handful of roughly chopped **CILANTRO LEAVES**

Chilaquiles, fried tortillas simmered in salsa verde, provide the best way to use leftover tortillas. We often have a lot of leftover tortillas at the bakery, so this comforting dish makes a favorite meal. I also love serving this at brunch with fried eggs on top.

**1.** Line a baking sheet with paper towels. Pour 1 inch/2.5 cm of oil into a large skillet and heat over medium-high heat. Working in batches, add a large handful of tortillas and cook, turning them each once, until crisp and golden brown, about a minute per side. Use tongs or a slotted spoon to transfer the chips to the lined baking sheet and season with salt. Continue cooking, adding more oil to the pan as necessary and letting it heat up, until you've fried all of the tortillas.

**2.** Pour off and discard the oil from the skillet, add the salsa verde, and bring to a boil. Reduce to a simmer and add the tortilla chips. Cook, stirring now and then, until the chips have softened and absorbed some of the salsa, about 5 minutes.

**3.** Meanwhile, whisk together the sour cream and milk in a small bowl and season to taste with salt.

**4.** To serve, drizzle the sour cream mixture over the chilaquiles, scatter the cheese and cilantro on top, and serve hot.

# PASSOVER BUTTERCRUNCH BRITTLE

**MAKES 1½ POUNDS/680 G**

4 tablespoons/60 g **UNSALTED BUTTER**

½ cup/170 g **HONEY**

½ cup/100 g **SUGAR**

3 cups/240 g **MATZO FARFEL** or **MATZO,** homemade (page 42) or store-bought, broken into (½-inch/1.5 cm) pieces

½ cup/60 g sliced **ALMONDS**

½ cup/60 g **PECAN HALVES**

I know that leftover matzo is not a major concern for most people, but if you were to find yourself with boxes and boxes of it, I know just what to do with it. This sweet, taken directly from my mother's three-ring recipe binder, is an awesome dessert that has become a Passover ritual in my family. If you don't have a microwave, you can make this brittle on the stovetop in a pot over medium-high heat. Just follow all of the same cues. Serve these with tea or coffee or crush into really small pieces and serve as a topping for ice cream.

**1.** Line a rimmed baking sheet with parchment paper.

**2.** Combine the butter, honey, and sugar in a medium microwave-safe bowl and microwave on high until boiling and golden, 5 to 6 minutes depending on your microwave. Be sure to stop the oven and stir the mixture once or twice during cooking.

**3.** Stir in the matzo pieces, almonds, and pecans, and return to the microwave. Microwave on high until everything is golden brown, 4 to 5 minutes longer (stop after 2 minutes to give the mixture a stir). To test if it's ready, drop a small amount of the mixture into a cup of cold water—it will turn crisp. If it doesn't, keep microwaving until a test sample does.

**4.** Transfer the mixture to the prepared baking sheet and let it cool for a few minutes. With wet hands, press down firmly to flatten the mixture. Let it stand until firm, about 1 hour. Break the brittle into small pieces and serve. Any remaining brittle can be stored in an airtight container for a few days.

# Sources

**amigofoods.com** for toasted corn kernels (search for *maíz tostar*) for Fanny's Ecuadoran-Style Shrimp Ceviche (page 228) and the cracked corn kernels (search for *maíz partido*) for Morocho (page 226). These are both available from the Goya brand on **amazon.com,** too.

**bobsredmill.com** for rice flour, teff flour, semolina flour, masa harina, cornmeal, rolled oats, dark rye flour, millet, flaxseeds, cracked wheat, rye berries, wheat bran, wheat germ, kasha, and dried cranberry beans and dried cannellini beans.

**cafedumonde.com** for chicory coffee for Iced Vietnamese Coffee (page 199) or **trung-nguyen -online.com** for chicory coffee and Vietnamese-style coffee percolators.

**canningsupply.com** for calcium hydroxide (lime) for making tortillas.

**food52.com/shop,** where you can get all sorts of beautiful objects and tools for baking and also copies of *The Baker's Appendix*, an incredibly handy little book filled with all sorts of measurements, ratios, and tips for home bakers.

**indusorganics.com** for black cumin seeds.

**Kalustyan's** (located at 123 Lexington Avenue in New York City and online at **kalustyans.com**) has ghee; candied fruits, including candied orange and lemon peels and whole candied cherries; all sorts of nuts and nut pastes, including almond paste; and all spices, including ones that can be a bit difficult to find in grocery stores, such as za'atar, nigella seeds, ground cardamom, Mexican oregano, sumac, and berbere spice.

**kingarthurflour.com** for bread flour, all-purpose flour, whole wheat flour, medium rye flour, semolina flour, rolled oats, and cocoa powder. King Arthur also has an incredible selection of equipment and tools, including pizza stones and peels (they have a folding one that is easy to store), storage containers, rolling pins, bench scrapers, scales, measuring utensils, parchment paper, and more.

**kitchenaid.com** for stand mixers and grain mill attachment.

**lehmans.com** or **ebay.com** for corn grinders for making homemade tortillas from scratch. Corona is a good brand to look out for.

**manischewitz.com** for matzo farfel and matzo meal.

**mexgrocer.com** for most things that you need for the "Masa y Mas" recipes (pages 83 to 115) and more, including corn mills for grinding corn, tortilla presses, *comals*, tamale steamers, corn husks for tamales, Cotija cheese, queso de Oaxaca, *crema*, Mexican oregano, and Mexican chocolate.

**negacasa.org** or **breadtopia.com** for dent corn for making homemade masa from *nixtamal*. Or we can help you from Hot Bread Kitchen! Check out **hotbreadkitchen.org** for more information.

**shop.khanapakana.com** for black cumin seeds and *panch puran* spice mix.

**theteaspot.com** for Chinese gunpowder green tea for Fresh Mint Tea (page 33).

**webstaurantstore.com** for baking sheets. Investing in restaurant-grade stainless steel half-sheet pans (which are typically heavier than most sold for at-home use) will result in better browning on your baked goods.

# Acknowledgments

To the team at Clarkson Potter/Publishers who made this beautiful book possible: Rica Allannic, the most talented and reasonable editor in the business; Marysarah Quinn; Christine Tanigawa; Kim Tyner; Erica Gelbard; Kevin Sweeting; Sara Katz; Doris Cooper; and Aaron Wehner.

To Julia Turshen, who made an impossibly intimidating process seem doable and who brought wit and levity to every situation.

To Cait Hoyt, Jeff Jacobs, and the team at CAA, thank you for finding me and then guiding me through book writing.

Jen May, Erin McDowell, Evan Sung, Barbara Turk, for making our breads and our staff look jaw-droppingly gorgeous.

To Steven Schmidt and Mitchell Woo for meticulous testing. And to our other careful testers: Janet and Jeremy Bloom, Geraldine Bowman, Jessica Edwards, Felice Waldman, Barb Ward, and Dave Ward.

The following members from the Hot Bread family contributed glorious recipes: Mark Fiorentino, Hiyaw Gebreyohannes, Raúl Guzman, Lutfunnessa Islam, Olga Luna, Nancy Mendez, Luela Osmenaj, Thuy Nguyen, Fanny Perez, Elidia Ramos, Bourchra Rashibi, Margaret Raymond, and Tashi.

In addition to the Hot Bread Kitchen bakers, my family contributed recipes: Thank you to Mini Starkman via Masha and Leora Ami, Rita Kozak via Patty Sugar (I know you both would have loved to see the nut roll in full color), Bubie Ruth Perlmutter, Dennis Waldman (I hope this book would have made you proud), Ydalia Rodriguez, and Eli Rodriguez.

And another recipe contributor, Caroline Fidanza, one of my first wholesale clients and an inspiring entrepreneur.

Aileen Sementz, Peter Endriss, and Karen Bornarth: Your careful suggestions, testing, and baking insights were invaluable. Karen, thank you for knowing exactly how to teach complicated concepts. Adrianna Campbell, thank you for answering so many questions! Mark Fiorentino, mentor, friend, and baker, thank you for all that you have contributed.

The recipes and DNA of Hot Bread Kitchen's head bakers are baked into this book. Over the years, these individuals have developed beautiful breads and talented bakers who now work citywide. In chronological order,

I thank Lauren Peterson, Peter Endriss, Sandy Kim, Ben Hershberger, and Aileen Sementz. All have left an indelible mark on Hot Bread Kitchen and the women they trained.

A committed board of directors is essential to growing a nonprofit organization. I want to acknowledge each director's contributions to Hot Bread Kitchen and this book. Of course, this kind of board couldn't be possible without a game-changing board chair like Joanne Wilson—thank you for all that you do. In order of tenure, thank you to Antonia Bowring for your friendship and advocacy for the women and businesses we serve; Ben Leventhal for always bringing the perfect business insight at the right moment; Emily Susskind who has supported us in innumerable ways and is a tireless promoter; Christina Tosi whose skill and insight as a chef, author, accountant, operations guru, and bakery owner are unmatched and always spot-on; Gail Simmons for your ongoing advocacy and for being a trusted adviser somehow finding the time to support us between travel, photo shoots, and motherhood (it is also important to always have another Canadian on-board); Dana Cowin for inspiring greatness, being a role model, and supporting me through the book-writing process; Jordan Levy for laser-focused financial insight; Kay Blackwell for supporting the whole team and providing pragmatic insight when we need it most; Ivy Grant for bringing intellectual rigor and a sense of humor to the driest of topics; Giuseppe Scalamogna for being a baker and backyard tomato farmer; and thank you to Joe Gold and Mary McCaffrey who have recently joined this extraordinary group. To my founding board, without whose patience and perseverance we may never have reached this point, Agathe Blanchon-Ehrsam, Jessica Edwards, Mark Fiorentino, and Michelle Chasin, thank you for being early adopters and ongoing supporters.

The staff at Hot Bread Kitchen have supported and endured a lot to get this out the door. To the Cabinet—Shimme, who keeps us ticking and laughing, and Jasmyn Farris, who manages with grace and finesse—thank you for all that you do. Kobla, Linda, Grace, Bryan, Yeneri, Debbie, Natalie, Fabiola, Marie, Ilyssa, Sandra, Molly, Beatriz, Rachael, Katrina, Elidia, Robin and everyone who has worked at Hot Bread Kitchen since launch in 2008 . . . Too many to list, but this book is a collaboration of all of our hard work.

Eli Rodriguez, I dedicated this book to you, but I also want to acknowledge your contributions to this growing social enterprise. You have been my emotional ballast, my partner in all of it, an eternal optimist, and you have the most refined bread palate of anyone I know. I love you and thank you. Dahlia and Emile, you elevate my spirits even on the most PERFECT days.

To the "Junior Editor," my always supportive cheerleader, the person who taught me to love being in the kitchen and how to write books, Nell Waldman, my mom. From proposal to final proofread, this book would not have gotten done if it weren't for your contributions to the narrative, your careful edits, and your moral support. And to the "Senior Editor" who has also been a tireless cheerleader and literary guru, my stepfather, Lorne Rubenstein.

My family: Jaron, Martha, Myer, Dennis, Ydalia, Juan, Bubie Ruth, Barb, Bob, Steve, Felice, Sarah, Mark, Dan, Anne, Martin, Juan, Desire, Isobel, and dear cousins who share my love of food and whose love and support enables this work.

Jessica Edwards, you fit into so many categories here—recipe tester, board alum, aesthetic adviser, and deep emotional support—thank you. Thank you, too, to Gary and Hazel Hustwit.

Erica Kopyto and Lucky Budd, dearest friends and insightful readers.

To the team at Bank Street Family Center who care every day for Dahlia and Emile with love and creativity.

Peter and Janet Bloom, you saw a glimmer early on and your friendship and support have meant the world to me and Hot Bread Kitchen.

Christina Minardi (and your team at Whole Foods), you have been a tireless advocate and have opened countless game-changing doors. Thank you to Ellen Galinsky and Tracey Zabar for early advice in this process. To Mimi

Sheraton and Peter Madonia, two people who have, over the years, perhaps unbeknownst to them, provided inspiration, insight, and support.

NYC City Council and the NYCEDC teams who brought us to La Marqueta. Kathy Wylde, Maria Gotsch, and the team at the New York City Investment Fund. Ken Knuckles and Hope Knight at the Upper Manhattan Empowerment Zone for your capital and moral support and for being advocates for innovative economic development in Harlem.

GrowNYC, Michael Hurwitz, and the Greenmarket staff for providing the ideal platform to bring our mission to life and for being one of our earliest advocates.

Philanthropic support makes it possible for Hot Bread Kitchen to do our life-changing work. I want to thank Anthony Berger, Eileen Fisher, Echoing Green, Freygish Foundation, Jaron and Martha Waldman, and the New York Women's Foundation for being the first to invest in a crazy vision. Thank you to the Robin Hood Foundation for its support of our business development team. Citi Community Development and Capital One for their continuing support of low-income food entrepreneurs in HBK Incubates. Barclays for its support of young women in both programs. Only the Brave Foundation for its support in helping expand our reach to the African immigrant community. Goldman Sachs for providing support to take our programs to scale. The Rockefeller Foundation for supporting replication. And to the many charitable family foundations, including the Patrina Foundation, the Price Family Foundation, and the Leslie and Daniel Ziff Foundation, for providing critical general operating support and scholarships for our bakery trainees.

# Index

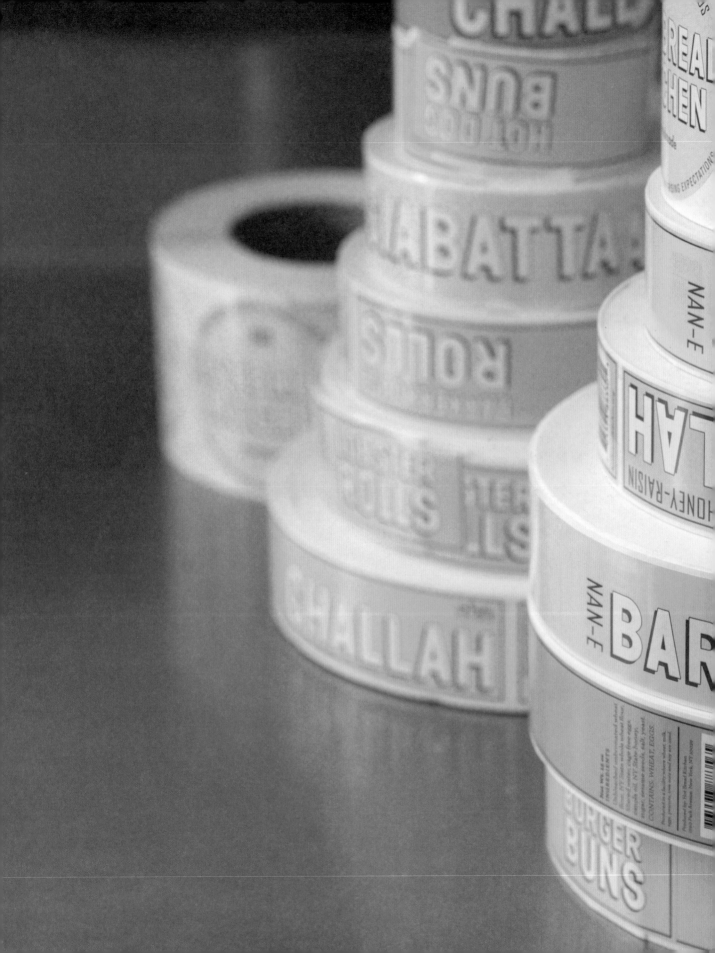